DAUGHTERS of NAZARETH

Trisha Hughes

FOREWORD

Writing this full version of my memoir *Daughters of Nazareth* has been my own personal challenge. It's been difficult because it cuts deep into my being.

An early version of my story was told twenty years ago and published by Pan MacMillan Australia. It went on to become a best-seller in Australia at the time but it left quite a lot out. There was a huge gap in the middle that I wasn't quite ready to reveal to the world. Not yet. I thought it showed weakness and vulnerability, both of which I believed I'd overcome. Twenty years later, I feel I've healed enough to finish my story and share the full version with you. I've grown enough to learn that creativity is born of chaos and grief in the dark muddy places of our hearts and minds.

I'm not a good judge of anyone's writing. I know what I like and I respect and admire anyone who attempts to write their life on the cliff of a computer screen and then opens their heart to share it with the world.

I have poured what I've learned about life and being human into writing this story and I pray it helps others who have experienced similar trials in their life. I want them to know they are not alone in their grief and pain.

PRAISE FOR DAUGHTERS OF NAZARETH

A book of triumph over adversity; incredible forgiveness; and more real life twists than could ever be convincingly made up. The best memoir I have ever read.

Paul Aubert

A compelling, moving memoir.

The Daily News

Trisha Hughes has given the world a stellar story.

E. Lewis

DEDICATION

For my father, Ernest Joseph Gourgaud
I'll never stop missing you

COPYRIGHT

The right of Trisha Hughes to be identified as the author of this work has been asserted by her in accordance with the Copyright, Design and Patents Act 1988.

All rights reserved. No part of this publication may be reproduced, transmitted, or stored in a retrieval system, in any form or by any means, without permission in writing from the publisher, nor be otherwise circulated in any form of binding or cover other than that in which it is published and without a similar condition being imposed on the subsequent purchaser.

Copyright © 2019 Trisha Hughes

ISBN

Cover Illustration by DC Cover Design

ALSO BY TRISHA HUGHES

Historical Fiction Trilogy

Book 1

Vikings to Virgin - England's story from

The Vikings to The Virgin Queen

Book 2

Virgin to Victoria - England's story from

The Virgin Queen to Queen Victoria

Book 3

Victoria to Vikings - England's story from

Queen Victoria to The Vikings

The Circle of Blood

The Tartan Kings - A Powerful & Rich Story of Scotland

Mystery / Crime

Dragonfly

Chameleon

CONTACT THE AUTHOR

Contact the author at trisha.hughes.books@gmail.com

For updates and discounts on new releases,
join Trisha Hughes mailing list

Find out more about Trisha's books here!

CONJURING UP THE IMAGES

There are moments which mark your life. Moments when you know nothing will ever be the same again and time is divided into two parts: before this and after this. Sometimes you can see these moments coming but sometimes not, and as with me, they hit you when you least expect them.

My moment was February 27th, 1997.

At forty-one, I was a single mum holding down a full-time job and raising two teenage boys, a big enough job on its own, while maintaining a house and the chores that go with it. It was only days until autumn arrived and it was unseasonably hot so I'd taken advantage of Thursday's 'late night shopping' where I could at least be in air-conditioning. The shops were packed with customers and the aisles were jammed with trolleys. I pushed mine around impatiently, dodging the slower shoppers like a racing car driver, eager to get home.

My whole day had been a rush from 5am when I'd risen for work through to my brief arrival home at 4.30 pm. I hurriedly put dirty clothes in the washing machine and prepared dinner for my two boys and myself before rushing out to do the grocery shopping.

With the boot of my car full of food, I pulled into the driveway, stepped out and ran my fingers through my shoulder-length blonde hair as I glanced at the long grass and the garden full of weeds.

Autumn was a sad time of year for my garden. The gardenias, wattle and agapanthus had already bloomed and the dead flowers hung forlornly on the end of straggly stalks. I enjoyed the solitude of gardening but there just never seemed to be enough time to get around to it, what with school meetings, basketball games and personal crises for each of my two boys. Something always came up that was more important, and all too often it became difficult juggling my work-free time between the both of them, without even thinking about how much time I needed to put the garden into some semblance of order.

When I look back on the day my life changed forever, it still surprises me the things I remember. I remember thousands of tiny sand flies hovering around the outside light like a grey cloud. I remember a few tiny drops of rain falling onto the leaves of the Leopard tree that I kept promising myself to trim back before it took over the yard. I heard the leaves rustling. The sorrowful barking of a dog. A baby crying in the distance. The buzzing of mosquitoes. The memories are all so clear.

That year, it seemed that Queensland let go of its grip on summer reluctantly. What never ceased to amaze me were the magnificent blue skies and the endless starry nights. This day, however, had been only a series of sun breaks. Now, under the heavy sky, the afternoon had moved into night and I saw lightning flicker through the neighbour's fig tree. I could see a patch of pansies I'd planted glowing like droplets of fire in the night as a gust of wind rippled across the grass, rolling through it like the muscles of an animal might ripple. It's as if everything is engraved in my memory. I remember it all.

I opened the boot of my car and took out two bags of groceries, leaving the rest for the boys to bring in, before walking towards the front door. Asleep on the mat, as usual, was my seal-point Persian cat, Oscar. I manoeuvred both bags into one hand as I unlocked the front door with the other hand and stepped over him, muttering, "Don't get up, Oscar. I know you must be exhausted. Please don't disturb yourself."

He recognised my voice and twitched an ear but still lay comatose on the doorstep.

I stepped into the foyer, grateful for the soft illumination of a corner lamp the boys had turned on for me and tossed my keys into a ceramic bowl on the sideboard to my left. Resting on top was an opened Valentine's Day card and clearly visible were the words, *'With all my love forever, David.'* I smiled and blew a kiss to the card, then placed a shopping bag in each hand before continuing on to the kitchen.

Lazing in the lounge room, one on each couch, were my two teenage boys. Their eyes and their smiles gave me a moment's attention, but I knew their brains were still absorbed by the sit-com on the television.

They were good friends despite the differences in age, although there were certainly times when both of them fought like a couple of stray cats. Mark, the eldest, was seventeen and Tony was fourteen and even though they had the inevitable squabbles, they remained loyal and protective of each other.

Through my tiredness, a feeling of pride surfaced as I watched them. The unselfconscious happiness I was witnessing was what I'd been working for during the past ten years. It had been a long struggle after my divorce, but I had been determined that I would make our new life work for us.

I've often thought that by now I'd have my life in good shape. I'd be a wife, a mother and a businesswoman. I'd serve my customers in my coffee shop by day, help my children to study at night, find time for the basketball games and snuggle up to a loving husband at the end of each day. I'd have plenty time for all the fun things in life as well as the not-so-fun things, like gardening and housework. In fact, the only part of my life I was happy with was the children. *That*, I assured myself, was a huge success story. There was no way I would let their lives be affected by the break-up of my marriage the way mine had been affected when my own parent's relationship had disintegrated. Their break-up, when I was seven years old, had been the beginning of an uncertain, insecure life full of pain that I would never allow my children to endure.

As I walked into the kitchen, I called out a bright hello to the boys and asked them to bring in the rest of the shopping for me from the car. Ten minutes later I was placing the last of the grocery items haphazardly in the pantry, thanking God the day was nearly over.

Tiredness washed over me again as I walked to the bathroom to splash cool water on my face. As I glanced in the mirror, I noticed that dark circles were etched in the soft skin under the muddy green eyes that gazed back at me and my hair could do with a trim and a freshening of colour. I tucked the loose strands behind my ears and made a mental note to call the hairdressers in the morning.

I had always tried to take care of myself. I exercised regularly, never smoked, rarely drank and I watched what I ate. Now I couldn't remember ever feeling more tired.

In my weariness, having started thinking of my history, I didn't have the resistance to stop my mind from conjuring up the images of the past. When my mind remembers those events, it's like I'm teetering on the lip of a chasm, breathless and struggling to steady myself, so as not to tip over the edge.

The memories of those early days are disjointed, but in the end horrifying to me.

PEG DOLLS AND STRING BAGS

*H*appiness for me at five years old was skipping the three kilometres to the local swimming pool on a hot summer's day with a towel around my neck and one shilling in my pocket. I was alone and oblivious to any peril as I skipped happily back again at dusk, more often than not to an empty flat.

When I look back on my childhood, it amazes me that I didn't become a statistic, a small child abducted, raped or worse still, left for dead by the side of a quiet road. There certainly were a few characters that looked capable of doing such a thing.

We lived in Spring Hill, Fortitude Valley, which is in the heart of Brisbane yet on the fringe of the central business district. In those days, people came to live there with little or no income. They could exist on a pension, pay affordable rent and survive on a shoestring budget. What was typical of these low-income areas was the large number of bars and pubs dotted around where everyone gravitated as their only means of entertainment and escape. Even though money was inevitably in short supply, spare cash could always be found for a round or two of drinks with friends at the pub. It was a place where both men and women retreated to keep warm in winter and to cool down in the summer.

In Brisbane, winter brought clear blue skies and bitterly cold westerly winds that howled relentlessly through the cracks of walls and cut through every layer of clothing like a knife while summer brought beautiful hot, humid days and the inevitable afternoon thunderstorm. This rainy season seemed to shorten the days, making the early evenings just plain murky, with the flickering streetlights doing very little to brighten the dismal streets.

Although Fortitude Valley had its occasional beauty, it also had a forlorn feeling about it, and a hint of hopelessness. It never occurred to me to be astonished that so many riches could exist in the city centre only three streets from the abject poverty of this neighbourhood I loved so much.

It's said that the most important years of a person's life are the ones before the age of five because these early experiences build character and shape personality. For me, they made me self-reliant and independent far beyond my years, although I sometimes wonder what other people would have made of me at that age and what possible future they would have predicted.

My mother, Merle Rose Mooney, carried inside her all the legends and superstitions of the Irish, a part of her that I have inherited, much to the consternation and amusement of my friends. She was a pretty dark-haired woman whose ancestors were born in Cookstown, Ireland, before immigrating to New York in the early 1800's like many other Irish. Times were very hard and again like so many, they came to Australia, 'the land of opportunity', where jobs were supposed to be plentiful and the streets were said to be paved in gold. They all had a sad shock coming when they realised they had moved from one impossible situation to yet another one.

Memories of my mother from this time are very fragmented due to the fact she was absent a lot of the time. When I try to picture her, I see her at the hairdressing salon, obviously a big occasion for her, while I sit on the doorstep with a Matchbox car in my hand. Other times, I see us walking hand in hand on our way to and from my school, with cars zipping past us along busy St Pauls Terrace, or every Sunday, walking to St Stephens Cathedral to Mass. You couldn't call us devout Catholics, but

I guess you could say we tried. When I was young, I didn't appreciate all the pomp and ceremony. I just liked the bobbing up and down.

I do remember one day towards the end of my first year of school, when I wore a party hat home that I had just won in a game of 'Simon Says'. I practically slept in it, until eventually it broke causing torrents of tears. This must have pulled at my mother's heartstrings because I remember her desperately trying to fix it, even though by then, it was destined for the bin.

I spent most afternoons after school playing outdoors for hours, only running inside at sunset and coming to a startled halt at the sight of my mother, hands on hips, legs slightly apart, looking down at me. Inevitably, her heart-shaped face would be creased in a frown, her lips pressed tightly together and her eyes luminous and flashing with annoyance.

On many occasions, I remember looking up at her and noticing her dark hair always permed and set in place, her dress always clean. She had a full figure, green eyes and a fair complexion, sometimes sallow from too many hours spent indoors, and I remember her once saying to me, *"Just look at yourself!"* At five years old, I took this statement literally and I glanced over to the full-length mirror on the wardrobe door. I saw myself, a tiny child, still with that little-girl chubbiness, no front teeth and my fine hair hanging untidily in my eyes. My overlarge dress was filthy from hours spent on the dusty footpaths while cars drove past belching smoke from their exhausts and dust from their tyres. I looked down at my shoeless feet and saw tiny toes that resembled black jellybeans. I must have scraped my shin at some time during the day because a small trail of blood had run down one of my bandy legs and dried in the shape of a dead worm. At the time, I had no idea what she was talking about. I looked no different than I did most days.

Another memory that stands out in my mind is my mother's warning, *"Beware of strangers. Some of them are devils in disguise."* Up until then, I'd had no fear of strangers as I wandered the streets, but from that point on, before I spoke to a person, I always looked for a tail sticking out behind them first.

Although memories of my mother are few, I do know that I didn't choose to forget things about her – she just wasn't around enough for me to remember much about her.

My father, Ernest Joseph Gourgaud, on the other hand, is forever turning up in so many memories and was the one constant in my life. He was a handsome Frenchman with almost black hair and large deep-set cornflower-blue eyes that seemed to shine when he smiled. He appeared very tall to me as I looked up at him. A giant almost. His voice was a quiet rumble that could have been the result of too many cigarettes and his nicotine stained fingers always seemed to have a cigarette lodged in them.

He could trace his ancestors back to General Gaspar Gourgaud, Napoleon Bonaparte's private physician and one of the people with Napoleon on the island of St Helena at the time of his death. General Gourgaud was subsequently the prime suspect in the poisoning since he was the doctor. Obviously, the fall of France led to a slight decline in fortunes for the Gourgaud family as well.

My father was an uneducated man and this, without doubt, led to a tough life, which eventually saw him enlisting to fight in the Second World War at the age of twenty-two in the famous 9th Division of the Australian Army. He served as one of the 'Rats of Tobruk' in the trenches of North Africa and later helped repel the Japanese advance in New Guinea.

To some, the 9th Division heralded fame in battle, but to others it spelt death or disablement. Dad saw it all as an orderly with the medical corps, collecting the dead and injured near the front lines and bringing them back for care, or identification and burial. It was during his time in the military that he contracted Tuberculosis (TB) and was shipped back home where he subsequently had his left lung removed. The loss of his lung gave him a slightly lop-sided appearance, with the concave area of his back quite obvious through the jacket of his suit. His condition saw him in and out of hospital regularly, as the remaining lung had been damaged considerably as well. His heavy smoking couldn't have helped.

Many times I would accompany him, patiently waiting in the X-Ray Department of Greenslopes Repatriation Hospital (at that time a repatriation hospital for ex-service men and women and their families) for our names to be called. Even though I never felt unwell, it was always both of us who had our chests X-rayed, standing in long green gowns with our chests pressed firmly against the cold metal plate, tickling me into giggles, while the technician told us to *"Breath in. Hold it. Okay. Breath out."* This seemed to happen every few months for no reason whatsoever and Dad always made a game of it, treating it like an adventurous outing.

When I think back now, I realise that I always associated Dad with colours. When he was around, my life was a golden colour, like a glorious sun breaking out from behind a dark cloud, but when he was in hospital, it was the dull grey of a dismal, rainy day. I remember sitting on the grassy slopes outside Ward 12/13 of Greenslopes playing with the toads that were in abundance, (the very thought sends shivers down my spine now), oblivious to the incapacity my father lived with, while my mother sat inside talking softly to him.

He was a kind and gentle man who never so much as raised his voice to me as far as I can recall, although like any child I probably deserved it at some time or other. He had other ways of chastisement that left more of an impression than any physical punishment.

There was one time when on my way to the swimming pool, the sight of a beautiful doll in a shop window caused me to forget all about my planned swim. I ran back home to ask if I could have the doll, as any five-year-old would do. A handful of wooden clothes pegs that I'd drawn smiling faces on were the closest thing I had to dolls, and this doll dressed in a flowing wedding dress, had all the physical attributes my peg family didn't have. I instantly and desperately wanted it.

Finding no one at home, but seeing Mum's purse in the kitchen, I searched through it to find the ten-shilling note that matched the price tag I had seen. Not even thinking about how I would pass this new addition off at home later on, I raced back to the shop only to find that someone else had bought the doll in the meantime.

Too dejected to continue on to the swimming pool, and fully intending to return the money to my mother's purse, I arrived home only to find Dad in the kitchen fully aware of the missing money. The disappointment in his eyes sent a knife through my heart. As he knelt down to look straight at me, he asked quietly, *"Why did you do it?"*

This question was all the punishment I needed. I realised that I hadn't measured up to his ideal of me and that taking the money was something he hadn't expected of me. I knew I'd let him down and no spanking was required as I silently vowed never to do anything like that again. I realise now just how much money was involved in this act of petty larceny. It must have been divine providence that the doll had already been sold, so that I never had the opportunity to spend what must have been a large part of their week's income on something so trivial.

I also discovered that Dad had a subtle sense of humour. One day while walking home from the Alliance Hotel, we saw a woman with flaming red hair, and I commented on how beautiful it was. In reply to my asking what colour it was, Dad told me that it was 'strawberry blonde'.

"What's mine?" I asked.

"Honey blonde," was the reply.

I looked up at him as he smiled back down at me and asked what colour his hair was.

"Mine is chocolate blonde," he said with a wink. I remember laughing so hard, I had hiccups for hours.

Later I would learn that my parent's relationship was doomed from the start due to the fact that my father was already married with three children when he met my mother. His wife was a Catholic, so any suggestion of a divorce was out of the question, which left my parents no other alternative than to 'live in sin'. I'm sure this would have triggered my mother's insecurity, especially knowing that her situation would result in a certain amount of disgrace. After emotional outbursts, she would disappear for indefinite lengths of time, perhaps looking for that security she craved. But despite all the separations, she always came back to Dad.

The combination of my wonderfully French father with his carefree passion and humour, together with my fiery Gaelic mother, was the perfect recipe for a life, if not harmonious and smooth, then certainly interesting and unpredictable. Each of them had Celtic ancestors and were therefore dramatic, as well as romantic, people. Celts have often been dreamers who looked beyond the daily cycle of drudgery to a world of infinite possibilities. The outward expression of this resilient optimism is a love of beautiful things, as well as music and stories in which men were strong and brave but were enthralled by women whose passions defied convention.

I can see that with such a heritage, my parents may have been drawn to each other with passion forsaking reason and while caught up in a relationship that they couldn't live without, they would also have found it increasingly difficult to live with. I never thought to ask myself if they loved each other. Did I even know what love was at that age? Love was simply something the nuns at school told me about.

As I write this account of my life, I remember in my later teens having a compulsion to make my parents live in front of my eyes again, to bring them out of the shadows and have them play their parts for me once more. I wanted to see where things went wrong, where the threads of our lives started to unravel. I wanted them both to be as clear to me as two photographs might be. Of course, that never happened.

I suppose my parents needed each other and that could be called a love of sorts. I can only surmise that like so many people, both then and now, in defiance of their families and finding themselves in a socially frowned-upon relationship, they gravitated to the city in search of some degree of anonymity.

***

HOME FOR US IN 'THE VALLEY' was a small flat consisting of two rooms, the largest being a bedroom with an unused brick fireplace at one end concealed by two wooden doors that opened from the centre outwards. This old fireplace served as a storage cupboard for us and housed our summer clothes in winter and our winter clothes in summer. My parents' bed and mine were on opposite sides of a narrow walkway that led away from the fireplace, with a small wardrobe that held our meagre selection of clothes at the base of my bed, and a bench seat that was our lounge, at the foot of theirs. There was no radio, no drapes and no carpet on the cold linoleum floor, just a thin grey blanket on my bed. On the other side of a curtain that separated the two rooms was a ramshackle kitchen containing a table, three chairs and an old icebox. I would crouch out of sight behind this curtain once a week, watching a huge man with a bald head and black curly hair on his back and shoulders, fill our doorway while carrying a large block of ice in a pair of vicious looking callipers, placing it with ease in the top of our icebox. He had seemed like someone out of a Brothers Grimm story, full of witches and trolls and hulking woodsmen. Another curtain partitioned off a tiny alcove that contained a toilet and a bath and I remember sitting in the bath at night asking why our soap had no smell and why it was 'scratchy'.

Visitors were rare at our home. A few of the other tenants in our block sometimes showed up smelling of stale beer, sweat and cigarettes. On one occasion, an old, gnarled man with a gappy smile, a scrawny neck and unkempt grey hair that stood out like a halo around his head, tried to have me sit on his lap. He was probably no more than fifty, but his five o'clock shadow, red eyes and haggard appearance made him look a lot older. When he whispered that I should take my knickers off first, my father unceremoniously threw him out. Although the reason for the old man's request was never fully explained to me at the time, I put it down to the fact that I had been playing outside in the dirt and my knickers must have been so dirty that he didn't want his own clothes dirty as well.

Sadly, this was the sort of request I was to hear too many times in later years.

Our occasional visitors were the same men who would sit on the wooden bench in our courtyard, surrounded on three sides by flats, looking through the clothes hanging on the clothesline at other residents walking by. It wasn't unusual to see them sitting on their doorsteps in the shade on hot, sticky summer days with temperatures up in the thirties, wearing only their underpants in an attempt to keep cool, a glass of beer in one hand and a newspaper in the other brushing flies away from their faces. The smell of trash, piled high in unemptied bins, lingered strongly in the humid air and ensured there were plenty of flies to keep them busy.

A regular visitor to the flat was our fat landlord, Mr Conlon, always dressed in a black suit and tie like an undertaker with his thinning hair greased over his balding head. Compared with our neighbours and the way they dressed, he seemed akin to an actor in costume. Every week he would show up and pat me on the head while waiting for the rent money.

After he left, my mother would say, *"He's such a snob. Nobody wears full suits anymore."* The first time I heard her say this, I hunched my shoulders and covered my mouth with my hand, trying to stifle my uncontrollable giggles. Not knowing what I was laughing at, my mother and father both looked at me with raised eyebrows and quizzical looks. I was actually imagining fat Mr Conlon collecting the rent in his underpants, minus his suit, and looking just like all the other old men who were our neighbours.

Always an occasion to look forward to was a visit from Pop, Dad's father. This statuesque white-haired man, invariably well dressed and wearing a hat would cross his legs and sit me in the hollow of his upturned foot, bouncing me up and down while holding onto both of my hands. Other times, he would walk around the room with both my feet on top of his, my hands caught in his hands, while I giggled delightedly. He could make coins disappear magically from his hands and make them reappear from behind my ears. My mother never smiled much when he was around, and she would always make an excuse to go somewhere else soon after he arrived.

I thought my life was pretty normal, not having any comparison even though the dominant emotion of my early years was of being alone. With Mum working at nights and Dad visiting the hospital, the horse races and the pub on weekends, I had a lot of spare time that I spent alone. What an amazingly undisciplined world existed for me as I walked around the neighbourhood finding my own fun and entertaining myself, making friends with anyone who would talk to me, as long as there was no tail poking out of their coats. My favourite pastime was to sit outside our flat in the gutter with my basket of wooden clothes pegs, playing 'families' with them, imagining them to be the brothers and sisters I didn't have.

To anyone reading, it may sound like a lonely existence, but to me, my life was wild and exciting, and I was unbelievably happy. Happier than any other place in the next fifteen years. I can remember the utter bliss as I sat in the gutters with my peg family wearing a pair of scruffy oversized pants bought from the local second-hand shop while other little girls walked past me in their pretty pink dresses with their stiff underpants showing. I can still hear the scratchy sounds every time they moved, and I can only imagine how the starched ruffles scratched the tops of their legs.

More scored in my memory is the image of them bending over in public, flashing their frilly bottoms. Thankfully for me, performing underpants were not an option because my parents couldn't afford such a luxury.

I loved walking barefoot in these same gutters on rainy nights when I had been sent to the local shop for bread and milk. I would splash and kick my legs through the flooding water, coming back totally drenched, with the milk (glass bottles in those days) carried in an old string bag, and sometimes minus the change that had fallen out of my pockets while I skipped back home.

As a five-year-old, going to the corner shop was a challenge in itself when one of the streets to be crossed was St Paul's Terrace, a busy street even by today's standards. There were no traffic lights, so waiting for a break between cars was the only means of crossing to the other side of the road.

Once I had successfully crossed a few times, bringing the change home was the next obstacle to overcome. The loose change was sorely needed in our home and after the first few losses, methods had to be taken to ensure its safe arrival. I couldn't be trusted to simply walk now that I had learnt how to skip, so my mother would lay out one of my father's large handkerchiefs on the table, place the money in the centre, collect all four corners together and tie them in a knot. This process was repeated by the shopkeeper with the change, and the handkerchief was placed in the bag with the milk for me to take home.

Foolproof – or so everyone thought.

My newfound success in returning with the change obviously went to my head and these trips to the shop became an anticipated outing. My exuberance was expressed by a gradual increase in skipping, jumping and swinging of arms now that the change was 'unloseable'.

Unfortunately, on one fateful night, I started swinging the bag and its contents of milk bottles in high circles, angled from ground level to above my head and back again so it turned like a Ferris wheel.

I soon discovered the law of physics through practical application. A misplaced skip in the middle of my swinging ended the game abruptly when the inevitable happened: both bottles smashed together above my head, saturating me with milk.

This couldn't have happened in a worse place than outside the local electrical store where people were crowded around the front window watching the flickering blue lights of the televisions that were still a novelty in 1960, and a totally unaffordable luxury for all our neighbours. I'm sure that most adults with children have seen something similar in their own children's lives and as such would have regarded me with amusement and understanding. However, to me it felt like the whole world was witnessing my embarrassment as I stood dripping on the footpath, dreading the reception I knew would be waiting for me at home.

On my return, I sheepishly presented the bag full of broken glass to my mother, only to be given a bath in stony silence after an exasperated look. I was then dispatched straight back to the shop again for a final attempt at bringing two bottles of milk back to the house intact. This incident was never repeated; the look on my mother's face as she held the bag of broken glass in her hand was enough to curdle the milk. But, at least, I'd brought the change back!

The old string bag I used to carry milk served more than one use for me. At this time, my hair was an unruly mess, cut fairly short because of its straightness and fineness, and always on my face and in my eyes. But I yearned for long hair that I could tie back in a ponytail. Regularly, I would secure the plastic handles of the bag on top of my head with bobby pins while the crisscrossed strings fell down my back in a blue cascade as I imagined I had my longed-for tresses. The sight of me sitting in the gutter, laughing and talking to my handful of pegs with this blue string bag on top of my head, never failed to bring smiles to the faces of passers-by.

If I wasn't playing in the gutters, I was wandering the streets alone and barefooted sometimes poking my head into the shops, smiling and waving, saying, "*Hello.*" It was a sparkling world, full of adventure and promise.

On our street, next to the electrical store was a newsagent where I would stand and flick through the pages of comics on display before the shop owner waved me away saying, "*Off with you, then. Go on, off with you.*" Next, there was a post office where pictures of beautiful stamps covered the walls. There were always people coming and going so I never lingered long. After that, there was a bakery where the lovely smell of fresh bread wafted out at me as I smiled and waved. Sometimes the shop owner would call me in and give me the broken legs or arms from the gingerbread men before shooing me away gently as if I were a stray hen.

I was well known to most of the shop owners by the time I was six years old and most of them would reply to my greeting with a, *"Hello Trish,"* as I made my way up the road to the 'Alliance Hotel' where I knew Dad would be.

The sour smell of beer wafting out to me will forever be etched in my memory when I remember standing outside the pub on the footpath, waving happily to him. After seeing me, he would smile widely and wave me in, then produce a handkerchief and spit in it to make it moist enough to wipe some of the dirt off my face and hands before buying me a drink. This hotel where my father would sit and talk to his friend Larry was the meeting place for most of our neighbours and was situated on the opposite side of the road from the corner shop.

Larry, a timid, quiet man with an almost submissive manner, had a large disfiguring strawberry birthmark on his face that started at the hairline above his left eye and extended downward over his cheek, ending just above his chin. Although he always lowered his eyes and stared at his beer glass whenever anyone passed by, he was happy to sit and talk quietly to my father for hours. While they both consumed glass after glass of beer, I swung my feet on a high stool, eating chips, pickled onions and drinking 'double sarsaparillas', made from a mixture of sarsaparilla cordial and sarsaparilla fizzy drink, absorbed in my peg family. Although I cannot recall Larry so much as saying a word to me, Dad would often look over at me, wink and smile, and then continue with his conversation, leaning forward slightly to hear Larry's quiet voice. I adored my father with his clear blue eyes and wished that mine were like his instead of the muddy green ones like my mother's.

The hotel was only a couple of streets away from our flat and it was only a short walk to Nana Mooney's house as well. Nana Mooney was my mother's mother and seemed to be a tyrannical woman with small piercing eyes, like stabbing blocks of ice, staring at me from a scowling, wrinkled face. They would travel up and down my tiny frame and she would frown, a small tutting noise slipping through her pursed mouth. She seemed to reserve what emotion she had for me and my father, giving both of us withering looks, no doubt to emphasise her disapproval of the situation Dad had put her daughter in. Displeasure was very evident in her every gesture. Visiting Nana Mooney would lead to endless visits to the bathroom to wash my hands, almost unheard of for me, just to smell her 'Cashmere Bouquet' soap.

Nana Mooney lived in a small cottage in Rose Street with an abundance of fish-bone ferns growing in front of her white picket fence. The street was barely wide enough for one car to drive through, much less two-way traffic, so the few cars owned by the residents were parked on the footpaths close to the fences. I often wished Mum and Dad had a garden full of flowers and plants growing along the fence like Nana Mooney did instead of the endless bundles of trash resting against the side of our apartment block.

She was not very prominent in my life, choosing to ignore me, perhaps in the hope that I would just go away. I rarely saw her, and I can't remember her ever visiting us at our flat. The last time I remember seeing her was when I was four years old. My father and I were standing hand in hand on her front doorstep as she turned away, shaking her head in a definite 'no' before closing the door on us. Dad looked down at me, crossed his eyes and screwed his face up as he pocked his tongue out, making me giggle, before we turned and left. This preceded my first visit to Nazareth House, a home for neglected and abandoned children, as my father was once again admitted to Greenslopes Hospital for treatment. At the time, I had no idea where my mother was.

Being only four, my memory of this visit to Nazareth House is scant to say the least. All I know is that a few months later, I was back home again in time to start Grade I at St Stephens School.

On the several occasions that my father was admitted to the hospital, my mother's social life seemed to increase greatly. My mother worked part-time as an usherette in our local cinema and somewhere deep in my subconscious, I have this distant memory of whispered words spoken to me late at night. These memories are too vivid to be dreams. Too intense to be from the imagination of a small child.

When thinking about her now, I can imagine her settling into a worn, soiled plush seat in the back row of our theatre with the soles of her cheap shoes resting quietly on the sticky rubbish on the floor. The audience is scattered, mostly solitary individuals, and she's confident that she can sit quietly to the end of the movie and no one will know who she is and where she lives. Nor do they guess at the tragic circumstances of her life. They have no idea that she sits there in the dark, her head forced back by the angle of the screen before her as she gives herself up to her dreams. Like reflections in water, the movie light ripples across her face and she is lost in awe. She is no longer in the first bloom of her youthful beauty but when she is in this other world, sitting enthralled in the cinema, she is radiant and beautiful and in another world. And she is happy.

Working nights at the local cinema obviously brought her into contact with a large group of people and she would often come home late either drunk or with a gentleman, but mostly both. You see pubs were her real weakness.

I suppose there is a good side to drinking in pubs. A pub has regulars. People who drink away their lives with other people who drink away their lives. No one demands anything of you in a pub and no one is judgmental. I could see how Mum was attracted to that sort of life.

I would sometimes wake up in the middle of the night to hear strange grunting noises from the other bed. I knew instinctively that I had to be quiet and go back to sleep but not before I had a quick peek through the hole in my old grey blanket. This resulted in no enlightenment for a five-year-old. It only gave rise to the unspoken question, *"What's that man doing to Mummy?"*

When she went to work, I was supposed to stay inside. *"I'll be back at twelve. You be asleep by then,"* she would say. I soon learnt to guess the time that she was due home and always made sure I was 'asleep' in bed when she arrived. But not before I'd made myself a bread and tomato sauce sandwich, skipped across busy Boundary Street to the electrical store with the televisions piled high on top of each other, and sat on the footpath cross-legged watching program after program. I only went home when I either felt tired or I thought Mum would arrive home soon.

One Christmas Eve, the last one I remember spending at home, the electrical store owner arranged for a man to dress as Santa Claus and be in the store waiting for all the neighbourhood children who had been invited.

I arrived wearing all my Christmas presents: a beautiful pink party dress, black patent leather shoes and a pink bow in my hair, tidy for once. I felt like a princess and at the age of six I was deliriously happy. I had everything I could possibly want.

All the children stood around with eyes agog, looking at a huge table decorated with tinsel and laden with chips, cakes and sweets, while in a far corner a real Christmas tree stood dressed in baubles and flickering coloured lights. After sitting on Santa's lap and each receiving a small present, we were let loose on the table in what seemed like a feeding frenzy. We gorged ourselves and at the end of the night we went home feeling sick but happy.

It was the best Christmas I'd ever had.

* * *

IN THE MIDDLE of my second year at school, one week after my first communion and three days before my birthday in May, I awoke to the sound of silence at home.

There was no noise of rattling plates coming from the kitchen or any smell of tea and toast wafting through to me. I don't remember feeling upset or worried in any way so I think waking up with no one there must have been a regular occurrence. I had no idea of what time it was, but I did know it was a school day. I vaguely remember that the day before had been sports day, Wednesday.

I knew that if I didn't go to school without a good reason, I would get the cane, like I had the day before for whistling. And the year before, when I had been in Grade 1, I regularly hid underneath the four steps leading up to our front door that overlooked the main road, knowing that no one could see me. The result was that I missed the school bus and I stayed there all day pretending to be at school. I had my lunch and my pegs, what else did I need? But I knew I couldn't do that this time – I could almost feel the cane on my hand from the day before.

I jumped out of bed and made my way to the kitchen, passing the pile of dirty clothes in the corner. I had to wear the clothes I'd worn the day before but that hadn't bothered me. I'd only worn them for half the day; I'd worn my sports clothes all afternoon.

I put my homework in my bag, made a jam sandwich for lunch and sat on the end of my bed eating another one for breakfast while I looked out of the window and waited for the electrical store to open. That meant it was 8.30am and there was a half hour to go before school started.

With bag in hand, I crossed the busy main road and started walking to school since there was no money for the bus, feeling very proud that I'd done it all by myself.

It was that afternoon, after lunch, that I found myself in the back of a police car on the way back to Nazareth House, minus my party dress and peg family, and with only the clothes I was standing up in.

I never saw my mother again.

BLACK DOGS

I arrived at the orphanage with my hair askew and the melted ice cream I'd been given by the policemen liberally spread over the back seat of the police car and myself. I felt very pleased with myself for having missed most of the afternoon at school but I was unsure why two policemen had collected me when I could easily have walked home. Pretty soon, I realised that home wasn't where I was going.

It seemed like an endless journey until I heard one of the policemen say, "Here we are," as we turned and drove through iron gates and on to a vast driveway. Beneath an iron archway the words 'Nazareth House' loomed high above me in large letters.

And there, perched on top of a hill, high above Wynnum, overlooking the other old convict station of St Helena in Moreton Bay, stood Nazareth House and somewhere in the back of my mind, a feeling flickered that I'd been there before, although as hard as I tried to remember, the memory retreated back in the recesses of my mind, out of reach.

This Catholic nunnery and care house for the aged and poor was built in 1922. It was run by the Sisters of Nazareth, an order that had been founded in London in 1854 and in 1926, the work for children commenced when twenty-five girls from various Nazareth Houses in England and Ireland arrived to be cared for by the Sisters. Over the ensuing years, thousands of girls were fostered and adopted after a short stay at the home.

As we drove, I looked around at the green paddocks on either side of us. On this day, there was a storm brewing and shafts of afternoon sun filtered through the clouds, highlighting Nazareth House as if a spotlight were shining on it. The glittering towers and arches were starting to catch the orange rays and through the dark storm clouds, I could see fierce-looking gargoyles crouching menacingly around the parapets and steeples rising into the clouds staring down at me. The building looked eerie and gloomy sitting high on the hill as lightning flashed in the distance.

We were met at the entrance by the 'Virgin Mary', a large white stone statue with her hands pressed together in prayer, sitting at the base of the stairs leading up to the double front doors. I couldn't believe how much bigger this building was compared with my school in the Valley. I can close my eyes now and see myself as I must have looked then: a tiny awkward, dishevelled creature clutching the remains of a dripping ice cream in my sticky hands, my mouth opened in fright, as I gazed up at the monsters and devils with sharp teeth looking down at me from the top of the imposing building.

I was by now quite used to the sight of nuns, so when one met us in the foyer, my fear subsided a little. I was, however, still unsure of why I was at Nazareth House at all.

Led by the hand, I was taken to a stark office and told to sit and wait till someone came for me. I remember wondering as I sat and looked around, how Mum and Dad were going to find me in this huge place. As I sat swinging my feet, I noticed a picture on the opposite wall of Jesus with his heart exposed and a crown of thorns around his head. While I waited in silence, I moved my body from side to side and his eyes followed me. I made a mental note to stay seated as I'd been told because no matter what I did, it seemed I would be watched.

The lady in the office continued working but glanced up often to smile at me until a different nun entered carrying a bundle of clothes in her arms. Taking me firmly by the hand, she glanced down at me and said, "Your face could do with a scrub." Then with a "Come child", we headed off down a long marble corridor, her habit swishing on the marble floor as my feet pitter-pattered beside her. Layered on top of the clatter and clanging of kitchen utensils in the scullery was the sound of children and that's when I started to get scared. I remembered that noise and I was beginning to remember the last time I had visited the orphanage.

Even though I was used to raucous kids at school, this noise seemed to be everywhere all at once. It echoed off the walls and the cold marble floor and seemed to increase in volume all around me, overwhelming me, as the sound of my feet echoed on the floor.

In my uncertainty, I'd begun to drag my feet and pull back, so my hand was clutched more firmly as I was hauled along the corridor. We made our way to the very end of the long hallway then turned right, passing a set of stairs on our left leading upwards, before entering a massive room with shiny wooden floors that looked like it held fifty beds or more. They lined the walls on either side of a walkway, the bed ends facing each other on either side.

Standing at the entrance to this vast room, the nun said, "Count four beds along the left side Patricia, and that one is yours."

We turned right and entered another room. Lockers were lined up on the left side, along the outside wall of the dormitory.

"Count four again Patricia, and this locker is yours. Make sure you remember that."

The bundle of clothes and shoes were put in the locker, my hand was gripped and off we went again.

We made our way steadily towards the source of the noise, passing another large room on the right that could only have been the bathroom. Glancing in as we passed, I saw four baths. Four baths in one room! On the opposite wall from the baths were cubicles that contained toilets and along the walls were basins. I couldn't believe the size of this room!

Then we were through the double doors and outside to the noise.

"This is the play area, Patricia."

The nun clapped her hands with a sharp snap and called out loudly to a girl in a group tossing a ball to each other.

"Monica! Come here, please, child."

The nun turned to me. "Monica will look after you," she announced. She then turned back to Monica. "You are to look after Patricia. She is your ward now so be mindful of her."

Without another word to either Monica or me, she turned around and disappeared back through the doors, her habit billowing and flapping behind her, leaving me standing on the concrete surrounded by girls my own age, some older.

Monica had tortoiseshell glasses with lenses that looked like the bottom of Coke bottles and she blinked at me myopically. She had thick wavy brown hair that she kept pushing behind her ears.

As I sat down on a nearby bench, I turned to Monica self-consciously. "You go and play. I want to wait here for my Mum and Dad to come and get me."

She looked at me sadly. "Your parents aren't coming, you know." She pushed her glasses back up to the bridge of her nose. "We all thought that at first, but no one ever comes."

"Mine will," I confidently replied. *If they can find me,* I thought a little less confidently.

She shrugged and ran off to the group of girls, leaving me to sit and look around at my new surroundings.

Leaning back against the wall of what appeared to be the dining room, I looked over at a concrete area about the size of two basketball courts filled with girls aged between five and twelve. Everyone seemed happy enough, bouncing balls against a wall or jumping rope – just like at school. I sat quietly, my nervous hands clutched together in my lap, and watched for what seemed like hours until a nun appeared with a bell and began ringing it, breaking the reverie.

Monica ran over to me. "Come on, it's dinner time. You sit next to me."

We made our way into a room with five tables on both sides of a walkway. There were eight chairs around each table and except for two or three, every chair was filled with a noisy girl, everyone speaking at the same time.

Then, in walked a nun dressed totally in black except for a white wimple.

The chatter in the room quickly quietened down to a shuffle of feet until there was total silence.

Monica leant sideways, her eyes glued to the figure at the front of the room, and whispered in my ear, "That's Sister Philomena."

I was to find out that Hell hath no fury like a 160-pound Irish Catholic nun. Sister Philomena's formidable presence was as powerful as a physical blow. Her hands were hidden inside her overlarge sleeves and her black rosary beads jangled around her waist and fell against the skirt of her voluminous black habit. The only skin visible was that on her face. Her ample bosom rose and fell as her eyes roamed around the room and when she pursed her mouth, I noticed fine dark hair on her upper lip. With her back ramrod straight and her head held high, her piercing eyes had the power to silence the whole room in an imperious manner that would have done Caesar proud.

Not a word was spoken by her or by us. The only sound in the silent room was the meal trolley rattling up the corridor outside. Two women in pink dresses and white aprons appeared and the smell of cooked food filled the room. In silence, they served plates of food to a girl at the end of each table and she in turn passed it along until everyone had a plate in front of her.

My first night's dinner was pale mince in watery gravy, mashed potatoes and peas with bread and butter, all eaten in relative silence, and I remember greedily gobbling everything on my plate. The meal tasted wonderful as my last few at home had been self-made with whatever was available in the cupboard to put on a slice of bread, nearly always tomato sauce or jam.

After dinner, we were mainly left to our own devices, with some girls reading and some playing in the recreation room. With my tummy full of food, I resumed my vigil in the playground, feeling more uneasy and scared as time went by.

Soon it was time for bed and we were all told it was time for a bath. While the other girls rummaged under pillows for their pyjamas, I remembered the nun depositing some clothes in an outside locker for me. I made my way to the corridor outside the dormitory and turned left as before, counting four along as the nun had told me. On opening the door, I discovered that I had magically been given three outfits, two pairs of shoes and socks, a set of pyjamas and three pairs of undies; my complete wardrobe.

I took out the pyjamas and returned to join the single line of girls heading off to the bathroom. With pyjamas in one hand and picking up a towel at the bathroom entrance with the other, we formed four rows leading to the four baths, slowly making our way towards the baths.

It seemed the older girls were responsible for taking turns to wash the younger ones and as I stood in the queue watching, I soon grasped the procedure. When you were at the front, you took your clothes off, ready to step into the bath as soon as it was free, you were washed, you stepped out, dried off, picked up your clothes, deposited your towel in a basket near the door and you went back to your bed.

As I stripped off and stepped into the bath, an older girl soaped up a washer and scrubbed my face, ears, back, feet and hands. I was out again before I knew what had happened and the next girl in the queue was ready to step in for her turn.

It soon became obvious that it paid to be one of the first in line to have a bath because the baths were only filled once, at the beginning, so the hot, clear water rapidly turned cold and grey.

Dried and dressed, I followed everyone else to the lockers to put our day clothes away again before heading back to our beds. Just a couple of beds away, Monica smiled and wiggled her fingers at me in a wave as everyone knelt by their bed to say prayers as a nun walked around watching us closely. Minutes later, mosquito nets were pulled down from above the bed-heads and were tucked expertly in place around the base of the bed. Never having done this before, I struggled a little with the netting and clumsily tucked mine in before hurriedly climbing into bed. The sheets felt deliciously clean and crisp and I snuggled down deep as the lights were turned out and the nun's shadowy figure stalked around with a torch, shining it on everyone to make sure they were all in bed.

Outside, thunderclouds swirled in the night sky allowing very little light into the darkened dormitory and as I lay in bed, the mosquito net shimmered eerily, casting unfamiliar shadows on the polished floors. Somewhere in the distance, I heard a dog howl and in fright, I pulled the covers up high around my chin as a jumble of thoughts ran through my head.

Holy Dooley was I ever going to be in trouble! Mum told me never to go outside and to be in bed when she got home. She'll be home and I won't be! What'll I say when she eventually finds me? If I tell Dad that the police brought me here, he won't believe me because he always said policemen were nice and that if I ever got lost, to ask one for directions and he would take me home. But I wasn't lost, I didn't ask and I'm not home!

I imagined the policemen who brought me there looking everywhere for me once they realised their mistake, starting with the office where they'd left me. Suddenly determined to remedy the situation, I pushed back the covers and jumped out of bed as quietly as I could. Tip-toeing out of the dormitory I came to the corridor, disorientated. I turned right, stepping into a corridor that was at the top end of a "T". To my right was a long room that ran parallel to my dormitory and to my left, through a doorway, was a classroom with two rows of desks leading away from a blackboard.

Wrong way, I thought. *Getting lost around here could be very easy - no one else will ever be able to find me.*

I turned around and made my way back to the corridor and headed towards a dim light in the distance where the faint outline of a doorway lured me. Desperately, I hoped it would lead me to the outside and to the driveway that snaked through the trees to the front gate. Totally forgetting that I was still in my pyjamas, I passed another dormitory, the dining room and an office. I was nearly free, nearly to the foyer, out into the night, and on my way home. Away from staring eyes that constantly watched me. Away from the endless noise and chatter. Away from the many horned creatures hovering menacingly on the roof staring down at me. The thought of my peaceful home in the Valley loomed tantalisingly in my mind as I tiptoed towards the front door.

Suddenly, cutting through the silence, a voice spoke my name.

"Patricia!"

I spun around, my heart hammering in my chest, to see Sister Philomena standing behind me in the hallway, her hands tucked away inside her habit.

Almost in slow motion, her right hand appeared and I was summoned wordlessly, her finger pointing to the ground in front of her. Meekly I obeyed and walked forward.

"Where do you think you're going?" she asked in a broad Irish brogue.

"Home," I whispered.

"This is your home now," she replied, looking down at me.

I had heard that statement too many times that afternoon and I'd had enough.

I stamped my foot. "It is not! I hate you and I hate it here. I want to go home!"

I must have looked like a defiant creature with both hands planted on my small hips and my eyes sparkling with anger as I glared up at her.

My defiance did not even make her blink. The dim light made her eyes sparkle as she stared down at me in silence. There was no softness hidden behind those penetrating eyes or pursed lips. No kindness or tenderness. No indecision.

Finally, she replied, speaking the words slowly. "Patricia, it's about time you realised which side your bread is buttered on."

I looked at her blankly. *What did bread and butter have to do with anything and what did it matter what side of the bread you put the butter on?*

While I blinked at her uncertainly, she reached down and gripped my hand firmly then led the way down the dim corridor, past the numerous doorways and stairwells. Thank goodness she didn't just say, *"Go back to bed."* I would never have found it. Instead she led me all the way back to my bed.

Her eyes glittered in the soft light as she pulled the covers up over me.

"Did you see the creatures on top of the building when you arrived this afternoon?" she asked as she smoothed the blanket over my body with her pale hands.

I nodded, remembering the many horned gargoyles with clawed feet and wings crouching and watching me as I arrived.

"Those creatures come alive at night and turn into black dogs with long sharp teeth and evil eyes," she said. "These dogs are really devils that love to eat little children and they know if you're awake or asleep. They walk around looking for hands that are hanging over the beds and they eat them. Every night, you must place your arms on your chest in the shape of the cross and the Lord will look after you and protect you and the devils will pass you by. Do you understand Patricia?"

I nodded, terrified, remembering the howl I had heard just a short time ago.

"Good night then, Patricia. Stay in bed."

My eyes must have been as large as dinner plates as I watched the shadowy shape of Sister Philomena as she floated towards the door, her habit softly billowing behind her. Too scared to move, I kept my arms firmly crossed over my chest in terror.

She wouldn't lie, would she? Not a nun!

I lay in bed that night, petrified and corpselike, barely breathing, listening for the sound of dogs' claws on the wooden floors and imagining moving shadows in every corner. I closed my eyes tightly willing sleep to come so I couldn't see the glowing red eyes of the devils as they prowled the corridors, their tails sticking out behind them, looking for little girls who were not yet asleep. I remember wondering if this was my punishment for something I'd done.

The storm had finally arrived and I could see flashes of lightning through my closed lids. At every clap of thunder, I jumped in fright.

When people say they slept like a baby, they mean that they slept well. But to me, sleeping like a baby means waking up every half hour crying. And that was how I ended my first day, listening to the water gushing down the drainpipes outside the locker room, thinking home wasn't 'home' anymore.

Sister Philomena's words were remembered many times over the next twenty years or so and the sight of a black dog would cause my heart to skip a beat every time.

MR PINKY

I came face to face with the reality that I would never return home the same way a runaway car comes face to face with a brick wall.

After that first day in the home, weeks turned into months with very little change in routine, punctuated only by special events, holidays and treats for good behaviour. Unfortunately for me, Monica's prophecy had turned out to be correct. My parents never arrived to collect me and take me back to the only happiness I had ever known. This 'home' could have been straight out of a Charles Dickens novel not the tiny flat with its broken blinds and bare floors that I loved so much and where the peg family I so longed for waited patiently for my return.

Over the first few days, Monica took me on a guided tour of Nazareth. She took me up the stairs to the old people's quarters where we tiptoed arm in arm and whispered, watching bent figures in dressing gowns shuffling around the corridors, never lifting their feet off the floor. Then we went down a set of stairs to an area below the main floor which was the play area for the pre-schoolers. The kitchen, smelling like boiled cabbage, was next to this playroom and had an amazing contraption hidden in the wall, Monica called a dumb waiter, which sent food upstairs to our scullery and on further to the old people on the top floor.

Tucked away out back of the main building past the playground was the laundry, which continually droned with the endless washing and drying that had to be done for all the children and the elderly people. Further still down the slope past the laundry and the swings, was the nuns' cemetery.

Settling into this new way of life wasn't easy and it took me a little while to adjust. I was forever in trouble. Forever being punished. Most of the time I couldn't even understand why. I wasn't doing anything different to what I'd done at home. Why should I be punished now?

In those early weeks, however innocent, I was probably seen as the organiser of any devilry that began to happen in the home. I guess I tilted at their windmills a little. My problem was I had come from absolute freedom to strict routine and discipline and the transition was difficult. Life was now structured and regimented where once it had been spontaneous with no restrictions or rules.

Initially I rebelled, but not for long. Stamping feet and pouting lips meant nothing to the nuns. I had started my life at Nazareth by trying to resist but my independence was soon noticed and kept under strict control, giving me no choice but to accept this new way of life where we were expected to be docile. My fire, spirit, emotion and opinions, were not acceptable and defiance was an attitude from my past life only. It was hard, but I finally adjusted.

Eventually I became used to the home and everything that went with it. I had a bed to sleep in, the company of other children and three meals a day – most of which I had never experienced before. I was learning to co-exist and I slowly became part of Nazareth House, learning more and more about the place they called a 'home' but which in reality bore no resemblance to the one I loved and craved.

My life had become so very different from anything I had experienced before. So much so that when I remembered things from before I went to Nazareth House, the memories came only in bursts and flashes. Where once my life had been spontaneous, it had become so regimented, I could recite exactly and precisely what happened day in, day out at the orphanage, because there was no change or variation in the routine. The memories of home hurt so much, the only way I could survive from one day to the next was to try and forget what I knew about living.

I was to find that routine was the basis of life at Nazareth House, with everything ruled by the clock. Each period of our day had a precise starting time and duration. Like getting up at 5am every morning to go to Mass.

In winter, the bitter wind howled around us and the white vapour of our breaths hovered about our heads like opaque clouds. In the early dawn light, the shuffling queue of girls heading to the chapel must have looked like tiny ghosts. My knees turned red from kneeling in the cold chapel and most mornings I breathed out frosty breath as I shuffled along with the rest of the girls. I remember noticing Sister Philomena's head bent reverently and I often wondered how she could be so harsh with us all and yet so reverent in church.

Every day held the same routine. Before church, as soon as we were up, we made our beds and dressed. I found that each item in the small array of clothes given to us was designed for a specific purpose. One dress was for visitors' days (once a month), one was for playtime, and the last, a dress in a black and white checked pattern, was an everyday school uniform. This small selection of clothes hadn't bothered me at all. I'd never had a big variety anyway.

But when it came to underwear, a girl's personal items were just that – personal. Now, every second day we changed our day clothes and on alternate days, first thing in the morning, we were lined up to have our underwear inspected. I was never terribly fussy as a child, forever dirty or untidy, but this took personal hygiene to a new level that caused my mouth to gape in amazement. This inspection must have been a fun job for the duty nun, as an obviously pre-calibrated nose was placed close enough to our undies to assess the damage of the previous day. If our undies were clean, we got to turn them inside out and wear them for another day. If they were soiled in any way, we visited Sister Philomena. Her hand would grow magically out of one sleeve and reach into the pocket of her skirt to produce a pink hairbrush.

I was to find out what everyone else already knew, that this brush had a name. Mr Pinky.

Anyone who had ever lived at Nazareth House had felt the back of Mr Pinky on the palms of their hands at some time or other. Sister Philomena and Mr Pinky were inseparable. Her favourite room for punishment was the bathroom, and from wherever a misdeed was done, an earlobe would be held tightly as we were led to the bathroom to receive due punishment. From my personal experience at school in St Stephens, teachers preferred the cane. But for all of us at Nazareth, discipline lay buried in the left-hand pocket of Sister Philomena's habit while her rosary beads jangled noisily in the other one. I sometimes think a more appropriate statue at the front door would have been The Virgin Mary with Beads and Hairbrush.

With the inspection completed, the older girls would dress themselves, and then walk quickly down the endless corridor to the stairs leading down to the nursery to help Sister Rose dress the smaller children. The older children, including myself after a stay of one year and at not quite eight years old, were each assigned to help look after one or two smaller children depending on how many were at the home at the time.

As Sister Rose, plump, round-faced and always happy, changed nappies and fussed and cooed to the babies in the nursery, she would call out instructions to us. Her plait, as thick and hard as rope, hung down to her waist and lay hidden inside her habit. Every now, the bulk of it could be seen under her habit, resting down the middle of her back like a thick snake. She would occasionally smile and let us all feel her plait before shooing us away. In the dim light, we hurriedly made the beds assigned to us then headed back upstairs, with the hand of a small child in ours, to stand in the queue in the dark corridor for the daily Mass. Mass completed, we wound our way, hand in hand and double file, to the dining room for breakfast, where the older girls fed the smaller ones their porridge before heading off to school for two hours of religious instruction.

Morning tea consisted of warm milk and jam sandwiches, dry now from being left in the sun, served in the playground. We chattered quietly as we ate our food before a nun clapped her hands together loudly; ready to return us to the classroom for lessons until lunchtime. School resumed at 1pm after lunch but finished at 2pm when we would walk to the chapel once more for Stations of the Cross and rosaries. After changing out of our school uniforms into play clothes, afternoon tea was served, again in the playground, before leaving us to our own devices until dinnertime.

Mealtimes rapidly became unexciting to me after that first much-needed meal. I realise now that most institutions have a strict budget and that basic fare is the easiest and cheapest to prepare. Nazareth House's catering was no exception.

Providing food for up to a hundred growing children could not have been easy, and variety was not a vital part of the routine. Still, an active imagination was obviously in play, with mince, the favoured meat, disguised in stews, rissoles and other assorted meals, indicating some deviousness of mind. Other dishes included haddock, (a bitter orange fish), sausages or saveloys and, on Fridays, fish fingers. The culinary specialty that led to the most colourful responses and trips to the bathroom was tripe. Desserts, always a highlight of dinner for children, were sago, tapioca, rice pudding or jelly served with custard. They were filling and sweet, and my dream.

After our baths, all clothes were returned to our lockers, prayers were said on our knees by our beds, and the lights were turned out. My favourite, Sister Magdalene, always did our bed check and she seemed to float instead of walking. Her face shone as she smiled and I imagined that this was what an angel looked like: beautiful and serene. In all the years that I spent at the home, she was the only one who ever remembered my birthday with gifts of talcum powder, boxed soap or a prayer card and they became my treasures. When you had nothing else to call your own, everything was special.

And that was how our days were filled between Monday and Friday.

Because there were only a few nuns assigned to the children, I understand now that this routine was possibly the best, and only, way the nuns could keep so many children in line. And I'm sure that was what my nemesis, Sister Philomena thought. She was a very strong disciplinarian, ruling with an iron hand and a wooden brush. She had our days organised, planned as precisely as a military exercise leaving no time for idleness. Her motto was, *"Idle hands are the devil's tools"*, and if we weren't cleaning or praying, we were sitting quietly knitting beanies and scarves for the cold winter months ahead.

She knew everyone's name and whereabouts at any time of the day – nothing escaped her. I was terrified of her and froze whenever she entered the room, my knees trembling when she called out my name. On any given weekend, she could be found marching like a General down the corridor with children following behind her resembling a straggly army, on some work detail or other.

One such detail, organised regularly during the summer months, was the weeding of the nuns' cemetery. A group of girls would be taken to pull the weeds and rake up the leaves.

Weeds flourished in the dry ground around the gravesites, and on one occasion, finding these weeds to be very uncooperative, we were told that it was because *'the devil was hanging on to them'*. I was always an inquisitive child, asking questions when I should have just accepted what I was told like everyone else, but this statement surprised me.

"Why is the devil down there with the nuns? Haven't they been good enough to go to heaven? Why is the devil hanging on to the weeds?" I asked, my questions spoken in rapid succession.

Many times in the future, as on this occasion when a difficult question was asked, the answer was always the same. "Sit down and be quiet, Patricia!" During religious instruction, when the story of how Adam and Eve had been made by God, of how they'd had children and then those children had children, my question was, "But who did they marry?" Again, I was told, "Sit down Patricia." The same answer was given when I questioned the story told of Noah and the Ark. "Did they marry their sisters and brothers since everyone else was dead?" I asked innocently.

"Be quiet, Patricia. Why must you always rock the boat?"

The look from Sister Philomena had been frightening as she dismissed my question with a wave of one hand as the other hand reached warningly to the bulge in her left pocket where I knew Mr Pinky sat waiting. I could imagine her saying, *"Don't rock the boat"* as she walked through the corridors of the Colosseum leading the Christians to the arena full of lions. It got to the stage when all I had to do was put my hand up, to be told to be quiet. This became a problem occasionally when I only wanted to be excused to go to the toilet.

I remember during her religion classes, she always said that out of everyone in the world, God would always love us. I often thought that if this were his version of love, I could do without it, thank you very much. My image of him was of an old man in a white flowing garment sitting on a cloud high above us with an army of angels singing and playing harps while He looked down benevolently on his minions. He must have been so far away that He couldn't see all the pain and suffering that was going on in this cold, uncaring world He'd created.

* * *

School was conducted in the front room, which I had glimpsed my first night. Two rows of desks faced the front and led away to the back of the room with a small walkway between rows. At the front of the room was a blackboard and our behaviour was recorded on it for all to see. Any slight infringement of rules and a cross would be placed against your initials on the board and woe betide any child whose initials attracted three crosses. That would definitely ensure a visit to Mr Pinky.

The nuns' strategy for ensuring good behaviour can be summarised by one word: bribery. In the orphanage, where luxuries were almost unheard of, children would turn themselves inside out to earn 'holy cards', which were pictures and stories of popular saints. After receiving one, we would swap for favourites the same way children do now with basketball or baseball cards. Holy cards were one of the few items we were allowed to keep as personal possessions. For Sister Philomena, discipline was as simple as black or white – holy cards or Mr Pinky.

I saw the back of Mr Pinky on several occasions during school, more often than not for talking, but occasionally for more creative misdemeanours.

We all soon learnt to distinguish the sound of Sister Philomena walking down the corridor towards us. Heard above the warning "shush" was the clicking of the black beads that served as a belt around her waist and dangled in front of her habit. By the time she appeared in the doorway, we had all turned into angels, sitting quietly with our hands folded on the desk in front of us. But on one particular occasion, I missed all the warning signs.

A child's mind is bound to wander if their interest isn't caught and held and Bible reading was not always the most exciting subject to an eight-year-old. One morning I remember sitting hunched over, enthralled by colouring all of my fingernails with my lead pencil, until it dawned on me that I could hear the scratching noise I was making above the silence. Startled, I glanced up to find everyone staring at me while Sister Philomena stood in front of me with her arms crossed over her ample bosom and her lips pursed. My eyes widened in fright when I saw the look on her face and I knew I'd earned a visit with Mr Pinky. With resignation I walked stoically to the bathroom, like Joan of Arc on her way to be burned at the stake.

"For your sin of vanity, Patricia," she said as she held the brush high above her head. "You are nothing but gutter trash."

Trash. The word hung in the air as she stared down at me. To an eight-year-old who had been brought to Nazareth House with no reason given and virtually forgotten, the word came with a dreadful realisation. My eyes widened and I gasped as my mind rushed back to the trash lying around in the courtyard at home. The connection shocked me. *Trash was just bags of stinking, unwanted garbage. You abandoned trash. You threw it away. You didn't want it. That's what I was? Unwanted, abandoned, stinking garbage?*

I know. They're just words. Words spoken in anger by a woman devoted to God who had probably never imagined doing such a vain thing as colouring her fingernails. But I won't pretend the words didn't have an effect on me. Tears stung the back of my eyes and a lump formed in my throat as my mind reeled. But even as my tiny heart was breaking, I somehow knew not to let her see how much her words had damaged me. I gulped back the sobs and gritted my teeth and tried desperately to still my shaking body and quivering chest as I repeatedly blinked back the tears pooling in my eyes.

As if unaware of the pain I was suppressing, she stared me in the eye and continued hitting my hand with the brush.

* * *

Religion took up the vast majority of the morning, but afternoons were spent on more conventional studies. I can remember learning to write in copybooks and having the occasional spelling competition. Daily, we all sat hunched over our desks trying to copy the lovely writing shown in our books. To us it looked beautiful and perfect like a priest had written it. The spelling competitions usually ended in a hotly contested battle between Monica, who had become a close friend, and me.

I remember winning most of these competitions and I was rewarded at the end of the year on Speech Night with a prize for being top of the class. Practical prizes in the form of sewing boxes, pencil cases or books were all we received, despite longing and praying for a doll of any description. Prizes were liberally given to all the girls, with categories ranging from best shoelace tier and cleanest girl, to a variety of academic achievements. No one ever missed out.

These personal prizes given for individual achievement were promptly reclaimed by the nuns at the end of Speech Night and placed in a toy locker. This locker, inaccessible during the week, was opened on Sundays when toys were displayed, and returned to the locker again at the end of the day, until the following week. Any other toys brought back from outings or holidays were duly placed in the locker as well, to be shared with everyone.

The joy of Fridays, when school ended, was marred by the distribution of the regular dose of Cod Liver Oil. (A follow up of Castor Oil on Saturday night, was given to us 'to clean us out'.) Still, we all looked forward to the weekends except for Saturday mornings, which were reserved for floor polishing, a very time-consuming chore assigned to the older children. There were three dormitories and every weekend two details of girls would be given rags, one to wax the floors and one to polish them. After breakfast, one group started at the first dormitory where we would drag all the beds (on castor wheels) down to one end, then place a rag with wax on it under our right foot and proceed to wax the floorboards from one side to the other until we had reached the other end. The second group had clean rags under their feet to shine the floors.

We all stood in a row lengthways, arms around each other's waist, as we glided on one foot to the other side and back again, singing the latest popular song of the time. The song that sticks in my mind is 'Moon River' and I have no idea how all of us knew the words as we sailed over the shiny floors. We would then move on to the next room and repeat the process, thus filling our first morning off after the school week.

The afternoons were reserved for hair washing and everyone would line up on the grass near the laundry, where huge tubs of water had been placed. After a quick check for head lice, we would take turns having our heads dunked in the water and washed. Then we were let loose to run like a pack of animals in the paddocks and grounds or allowed to play on the nearby swings until our hair dried. Sometimes, a nun would take us on a supervised walk up to the front gate. We would go in pairs, hand in hand, up to the gate and back through the paddock, trying to avoid the many soft cowpats that dotted the grassy slopes.

The last day of the week was reserved for church, rosary saying and confession.

Confessions for us were not purely based on our actual misdeeds for the week. Instead we found ways of enlivening these supposedly deeply religious moments that were not much more than a time-filling exercise for most of us.

We had several visiting priests from Iona or Villanova Colleges, two of the local Catholic boys' schools, but our usual confessor was Father Rudolph, a stooped grey-haired man of about eighty. He was almost deaf, causing a certain amount of amusement when he took confession. The private conversation whispered from behind closed confessional doors ended up being shouted and echoed throughout the chapel, with all present hearing everything being said including details of any sins confessed.

It was on one of these occasions that Pat Williamson went into the confessional to be heard. Pat was one of the older girls who was seemingly always in some sort of trouble as well.

"Bless me Father for I have sinned. It's been one week since my last confession," could be heard quite clearly by everyone present.

"What are your sins, my child?" bellowed Father Rudolph.

"I've been smoking cigarettes and stealing cars!" was the fictional confession that reverberated loudly around the chapel, bringing titters from all the children.

Pat had also been the one who'd taken soap powder from the laundry and put it in the holy water fountain, guaranteeing a lot of her time being spent with Sister Bernard Mary and the strap.

I had very little to do with Sister Bernard Mary, a small nun with a distinctly pear-like body shape. She always seemed to have a frown on her face as she bounced down the corridor on some mission or other. She was in charge of the older girls and was only at the convent for my first year before being transferred to another institution. She seemed to be a moody and bad-tempered sort of nun as well as the one prone to using the strap and her hand, according to some of the girls who had been at the home longer than I had.

The first Sunday of every month was a special day for all of us. We would dress in our best dresses and wait for our families to arrive. Each child waited quietly in the playground, either drawing or playing with the toys from the locker, hoping for a nun to come outside and call our name, announcing a visitor. When a nun walked through the doors to the playground, we all held our breaths, hoping against hope that she would call our name, pleased for the one who had been called but sad to be left behind.

I hated those Sundays. They were interminable as I sat among the handful of children not collected. As I waited, I came to realise that Nazareth House was just a place where parents dumped you and then forgot about you. Just like trash. Garbage.

And yet, despite the hurt, there was a sense that no one could replace my parents. There was confusion and fear that escalated into terror at times, but the over-riding feeling was grief at the loss of them. Despite the anger and the pain, a part of me never stopped loving them. Wanting them. Desperately *needing* them. Longing for the intangible loss of stability and security, however tenuous, and the sense of belonging that puts the jigsaw puzzle together and builds a home, a true home, or to at least offer some sort of control, however small.

I can't remember how much time elapsed before my father first visited me. Almost a year, I think.

The first time my name was called, I thought I had heard incorrectly. I just sat there stunned, believing I'd heard incorrectly, until my name was called again. Astounded, I was led to the office where I was told to wait for my father. I'd hoped, dreamed, prayed, for that moment for so long and when it finally arrived, I just couldn't quite believe it. I felt like I was waiting for a stranger to come for me. By then, Dad existed only in my memory.

When the door of the office opened, he stood in front of me, dressed in his best suit, shirt and tie. He held his hat in front of him with both hands and that wonderful smile of his split his face as he knelt down on one knee and held his arms out to me. My heart swelled as I ran to him and I thought my heart would burst with happiness. As his arms engulfed me and I rested my head on his chest, tears welled in my eyes. I took a deep breath and the smell of cigarette smoke from his clothes wafted over me, smelling as lovely as perfume. I felt myself go back in time to our squalid little flat. I saw my peg family waiting for me on my bed and I saw my blue string bag hooked over a doorknob. The memory was so strong, I even thought I could smell tea and toast.

In my ecstasy, I never noticed how much he had aged since I'd last seen him, just one year, and I didn't notice how he had to stop and catch his breath, even after a short walk. I was happy just to see his smiling face and hear the soft rumble of his voice again.

Over the next few years, on those rare occasions, we would go for walks to the beach, a long way for him, and me, but done without any complaint from either of us. Once or twice, we just sat in the play area with the other children who had no visitors, happily drawing and talking for hours before he left to go home. After such visits, I came to learn that all the nice things in life are everyday things.

His budget didn't provide for many special treats, but a train ride to the George Cinema in the city to see *'King of Kings'* starring Jeffrey Hunter as Jesus, was one I'll never forget. We had lunch afterwards and then headed back to the home by train again. I had a tremendous crush on Jeffrey Hunter for years after seeing that movie.

As the years passed, there were a few visits from my father, but never any visits from my mother, and I would wonder many times why not. One visit from my mother was all I wanted. By then, I somehow knew that I would never be going home with Dad because of his bad health, but Mum was a different story. The only time I'd seen her unwell was when she'd come home drunk at night and woken up sick the next morning. I remember as she lay in bed with a washer over her forehead, I would make cups of tea and walk as slowly as I could with them, slopping tea over the top of the cup. By the time I reached her, the cup was always half empty and a trail of tea led from the kitchen to her bed.

Every month, I waited for her to come and see me. Deep down, I had a feeling she was ashamed of me and I wanted to say I was sorry for always being dirty and breaking things. These childish frailties always seemed to annoy her more so than they had Dad. I wanted to say that I would try harder, and then everything would be all right and she'd love me again and take me home. Your mother should love you, shouldn't she?

But she never gave me the opportunity. She never came and I soon stopped asking for her.

Instead, my need for love transferred to my father and I longed for visits from him so intensely it hurt. He came as often as he could, not regularly, but I remember those times so well. I never discussed with him why I was at Nazareth House because firstly, I already knew the answer. He was sick and Mum had gone again. Secondly, I would never interrogate my father. If I'd learnt nothing else from the nuns, I'd learnt to keep quiet. Be the perfect child. Be lovable. Don't create waves. Don't ask questions. Don't rock the boat. According to the nuns' rulebook, if you said a word out of line, you would be punished. Therefore I remained silent. We were all effectively brainwashed into submission and I was too damn scared to say anything in case my father's infrequent visits ceased completely. Then I would have absolutely no one at all.

So I never asked him why I was there and he never told me. Rightly or wrongly, I accepted my fate. Instead of asking myself 'why?' I asked 'how long?' reasoning that I had been taken back home once before when I was young and I would be again. It was just a matter of time. Surely that's all it could be. Time.

But time stretched on and I remained with the other children, waiting and praying for a miracle.

There was one memorable day that stands out in my memory. I remember it was a Saturday and for some reason, perhaps it was school holidays, I'd been allowed to stay with Dad for the weekend. It was Exhibition time, Queensland's largest country fair, and once a year it comes to Brisbane.

A fair or carnival is always a treat for children, so Dad had planned a surprise trip for me. The main arena with its displays of farm animals, the horse and buggy races and fireworks combined with the noise and fun of stomach-churning rides at side show alley appealed to everyone from two to eighty-two. Sample bags and every type of junk food a kid could want were all readily available. At eleven years old, I thought this place was heaven.

We walked around most of the day eating hotdogs and drinking strawberry milkshakes with two other adults, a man and a woman, who I suppose would have been in their early twenties. I had no idea who these people were, but they seemed to be friends of Dad's. They walked around with us, while the lady held my hand through sideshow alley and I stared up at the rides, wide-eyed and thrilled.

Dad left me with them that night but returned the next day to take me back to the home. I don't remember doing much in particular during my stay besides walking around their small garden and hanging over the fence looking at passing cars on the busy street. Sunday looked to be like a sleep-in day for them, so I kept to myself, which I really didn't mind at all. Survival for me meant being unobtrusive and keeping a low profile anyway. I was away from the home and that was a treat in itself.

Days later, back at the home, we were told that those who'd gone out for the weekend could write a letter of thanks and it would be posted for us, so I bent my head to the task. I poured my thanks out effusively trying to ingratiate myself with the couple I'd visited in the hope of future weekends with them or possibly permanent placement. I couldn't remember the couple's names or where they lived but that didn't faze me. I simply addressed the letter to *'The man and the lady who live in the white house on the corner of the busy street at Milton.'* Sort of like writing to Santa Claus.

Amazingly, it seemed to work. A week later in the playground, during mail delivery, my name was called. In all the time I'd been at Nazareth House, my name had never been called before. No one had ever sent me a letter or even so much as a birthday card. Never.

Sister Philomena stood at the front, holding a small bundle of letters in her hand. As I walked up to her with a huge smile on my face, I looked around at the other children to see if everyone was watching me collect mail from someone who cared enough to send me a letter. I saw envious faces, expectant faces and some unhappy ones who knew there would be nothing for them. Some children looked bored, simply shuffling their feet wanting to go back to what they'd been doing.

She handed a letter to me in an off-hand manner and continued looking around and calling names. I clutched mine preciously to my chest and walked back to my place, anticipating the moment when I could sit down and read it alone. I couldn't stop myself from glancing down at the envelope to see who loved me enough to send me this prize.

My happiness evaporated when I saw the words 'Return to Sender' stamped across the front of the envelope. Not wanting to believe what I'd read, I tore open the letter and sure enough, I saw my own writing on the pages I unfolded.

Cautiously, I looked up to see if anyone was watching me, while keeping a smile firmly planted on my face. I didn't tell anyone. I wanted them all to think that I was loved and wanted. Even though the pain was immense, if my secret were ever found out, nothing would have been worse than the humiliation.

I remember glancing up at Sister Philomena as I fought to hold back the tears stinging behind my eyes, thinking that she would have been better off looking after lepers than raising children. She never even looked at me. There was no flicker of emotion, nothing that would have softened the blow for me. Hadn't she seen the front of the envelope? Surely she'd seen 'Return to Sender' stamped boldly on the front. Would it have been so hard to have pulled me aside later and explained to me why it had been returned? Perhaps even just destroy it without showing me?

I never found out whether she was really as cold-hearted as she seemed or whether it was just a veneer of aloofness. I avoided her as much as I could as I hardened my own heart.

These days, as I look back on that day, I can afford the luxury of giving her a little latitude. What seemed like coldness could actually have been detachment. I've often wondered if any of the nuns initially became too involved with the plight of the children but eventually learnt to distance themselves from their emotions, a strategy that a child would see as uncaring. I've often tried to put myself in their situation and I think it would have driven me crazy. Like working in an animal refuge and watching pain and suffering day after day.

What the nuns didn't realise was that all we wanted from them was love to make our lives bearable. Nothing more, nothing less.

ONE OF THE few relatives I visited once was Dad's cousin, who I called 'Aunty Mary'. She lived in one of the outer suburbs of Brisbane in a house that looked as if the next gust of wind would blow it over. What fascinated me the most was her outside toilet, situated in a small building in the backyard and called an 'outhouse'. It didn't have a chain to flush like the one at Nazareth House. Instead on the floor was a box full of sawdust to scoop into the toilet that got emptied once a week.

The one time I saw her, Aunty Mary clasped her hands together and smiled at me as she said, "Look how much you've grown. When I last saw you, you were two years old. You looked like a little doll barely tall enough to walk, but instead you ran everywhere."

When Dad took me back to the home after that visit, I was silent. The joy of the visit had deserted me and all I wanted to do was run back to him and be loved again. I wanted to feel his arms wrap around me as I lay against his chest forever.

He looked down at me and asked, "Do you feel all right, Trisha?"

How could I tell him how I felt? How could I tell him I felt unloved? Unwanted? Rejected?

I wanted to say to him, "Please don't leave me." But I never said those words. Instead, I smiled a watery smile and gulped back the tears in silence as he left.

These occasional personal outings with Dad supplemented the rare group outings at Nazareth House, which were available only for the ones deemed to be 'well behaved'.

Once every couple of months, we would all line up in pairs, like little soldiers, and walk for what seemed like miles, but was actually only about 400 metres, to the local train station for a ride to Wynnum Central, the hub of Moreton Bay. It was then only a short walk from the train station to the busy main road, Edith Street.

This metropolis had two blocks of small shops and offices facing each other across the road, separated by little service alleys which ran around the back of the buildings. There was a barbershop, a doctor's office, a couple of jewellery stores, some coffee shops, one lady's and one men's outfitter, and the main grocery store, Woolworths. On the street, there was no protection from the blazing sun or the rain. Only empty benches waiting forlornly to be used.

We had been given one shilling (today's equivalent of about a dollar) back at the home and on arrival at Wynnum, we were set loose in Woolworths with strict instructions on conduct, behaviour and meeting time. When our money had been spent on bags of lollies, we returned as instructed, ready to head back to the home with our treasures.

We became very astute buyers, only spending our pittance on boiled sweets that could be sucked indefinitely, thus lasting longer than the much-coveted chocolate. We also learnt to ration ourselves when eating our sweets because no one knew if they could stay well behaved enough to be included in the next excursion.

The untimely demise of a prominent local Catholic religious figure, Archbishop Duhig of Brisbane, had provided us with an unscheduled trip to St Stephens Cathedral in the city. The fact that this visit involved viewing an open casket, for those who were inclined to pay their last respects, resulted in a slightly reduced level of excitement for me.

It was on this occasion that my friend Monica and another girl, Christine, and I were told that we had been chosen as the best behaved and would accompany Sister Philomena and two other nuns in the convent station wagon to view the mortal remains of Archbishop Duhig. Over the years, I had stopped bashing my head against the wall in rebellion and started conforming to the day-to-day rules of the nuns. I was, however, still surprised to find that I could be classed as well behaved.

There we were, lined up in our Sunday best (our school uniforms were pronounced not good enough). Our underwear had been sniffed and our good shoes inspected. A large hole had been found in the sole of one of my shoes, so a piece of paper was quickly coloured black and placed inside my shoe to ensure that when I knelt in the pew, the person behind me would not have an offensive insight into my 'sole'. It was obviously important that I was 'un-holey' on this holy occasion.

On arrival at St Stephens, we made our way forward slowly in the queue, finally arriving at the casket to look at someone who, on the evidence available, clearly had not yet gone to heaven. After all, hadn't we been promised that when you die, and if you have been good, you go to heaven? Archbishop Duhig obviously had not been as good as he should have been because there he was, looking sound asleep and certainly not in heaven yet.

Just then, a nun next to me leant over, gave me a nudge with her elbow and whispered, "Kiss him, Patricia."

My eyes snapped open in horror.

"But he's dead," I stated with a quaver in my voice.

"The ring," she sighed in an exasperated voice. "Kiss the ring."

I looked down again. I noticed that his arms were crossed over his chest in the shape of a cross, just like mine were every night, and I wondered if the black dogs followed you into heaven too if you didn't cross your arms.

With a jab in the back, I duly kissed his hand then turned and sat down, waiting for the rest of the entourage to pay their respects. While I waited, I looked around and remembered my time here at school when I lived with my parents. To the left of the entrance was the baptismal font where I had been baptized in Grade 1. I remembered walking up the aisle wearing my white communion dress and lace veil, lent to me by the nuns on my first communion day. I remembered smiling serenely and shyly at my parents, sitting close together in one of the front pews beaming back at me. As I walked past them up to the altar, my hands had been pressed together in front of me in prayer like a little saint. I glanced over to the beautiful stained glass-windows and saw the playground in the background where I skipped rope with friends. It all seemed so long ago. My world had changed since then. I had gone on to another life.

All too soon, we were on our way back. At the home, we were the centre of attention. The three of us related stories to the other girls and basked in the attention until after lunch, when we discovered to our amazement that everyone else would now be going to the cathedral in the school bus while we had earned the dubious privilege of being left behind to clean up everyone's dirty lunch dishes.

As I washed and Christine and Monica dried, I turned to them and said quite seriously, "I'm never being good again."

Aside from these rare outings, yearly concerts were performed close to Christmas for relatives of the children and provided us with another break in routine. Although I can't remember any Christmas decorations or trees during those years, I can almost hear the buzz of excitement as we went about our daily chores until the holiday foster parents eventually appeared.

We would practise our Irish jigs and sword dances daily, with our hands clenched and arms glued to our sides, while being encouraged to 'lift those knees' by Sister Philomena. Performing surprisingly nimble steps for someone her size, she would stand with her right heel tucked into her left instep forming a 'T' and proceed to hop from toe to toe with veil flying and a rosy glow in her cheeks while keeping perfect time to the music. These were practically the only times I saw her smiling.

As well as this dancing, a select dozen girls between the ages of five and sixteen were chosen for the choir. Marilyn, a girl who arrived when I had already been there a year and who left a year before my own departure, was the eldest in this group, and as such was chosen to lead the choir.

On arrival at Nazareth House, we had each been given the regulation near-military haircut, but Marilyn's, for some reason, was even more severe. Her hair had been long and wavy, but the nuns had shaved it so close to her head that she had to wear a babushka until some semblance of recovery growth had started. It was fairly obvious that none of the nuns were hairdressers before joining the convent. All of us sported short uneven hair and looked more like convicts than little children.

Marilyn, in charge of the choir, took her role seriously and promptly took on the task of giving singing lessons to the youngest ones, something we all could have used, even her. It was in these early years that my love of music surfaced and I became aware of the joy and happiness it could bring. Even today, Irish ballads bring tears to my eyes and a lump in my throat.

Just prior to our Christmas extravaganza, the event everyone looked forward to was a picnic on the beach organised and paid for by the local parishioners. Boxes full of swimming costumes, all of them old and tatty, were dug up from the bowels of the convent and distributed amongst the children with little consideration being given to colour or size. We usually spent the first hour after receiving our costumes trying to adjust them by tying the straps in a knot on top of each shoulder or tying the backs together with anything we could find, in an attempt at modesty.

We would all be taken to the beach at Wynnum, such as it was, where Santa arrived on the back of a trailer distributing bags of lollies to everyone. We were given soft drinks and cake, unheard of at Nazareth, and played for hours in the concrete enclosed saltwater pool on the beach or on the swings nearby. None of the others knew how to swim so we simply splashed around in the water. We were also allowed to walk to the end of the jetty where we could see the fishermen coming in with their catch. Ugly wet fish hanging on the end of lines.

At the end of the day, we went back exhausted, sunburnt and happy after this break in routine. Such wonderful events were enjoyed by all of us but were very few and far between. All too quickly we were back to the reality of life in an orphanage with all its associated order and discipline.

For all the nuns' teachings of an all-loving, all-forgiving God, and for all the infrequent flashes of normalcy in our routine, what we craved more than anything in those years were physical affection and love, both in short supply at Nazareth. They seemed to be short on warmth and long on Jesus.

Outward signs of affection such as touching and holding hands were forbidden: even sisters were separated and discouraged from spending time with each other.

This caused real heartaches for children already trying to attune themselves to their new way of life. While I tried to make the most of my situation, I had no other choice, some children never adjusted to this institutional life. A set of five-year-old twins, Marianne and Antoinette, could always be found sitting together holding hands in out-of-the-way corners, hoping the nuns wouldn't find them. If they were found together, each nun had her own way of disciplining the children.

Sister Bernard Mary was very physical, choosing to discipline with a strap or the back of her hand as Pat Williamson had found (via a burst eardrum and subsequent partial deafness in one ear) and although Sister Philomena could produce Mr Pinky on any occasion, her main technique was psychological. She preferred to prevent wrongdoing with demonic tales that instilled terror in young impressionable girls and guaranteed good behaviour no matter what the situation. This was her way of teaching us not to be greedy, vain or jealous of each other and that as long as we repented our sins, God would forgive us. As for Sister Magdalene, she was simply an angel.

THE CHAMELEON

"Have you guys done your homework?" I asked, putting the last of the shopping away. Both boys had their eyes glued to the television, engrossed in their sit-com.

"It's Thursday, mum," Mark turned and answered over his shoulder. "It's sports day tomorrow, so nothing's due until Monday. We've got all weekend to do it."

"Oh, haven't I heard *that* one before," I laughed. "Don't get mad at me on Sunday night when I nag you to do it then."

Tony turned around to look at me. "Oh, I forgot to tell you, mum. Dad rang while you were shopping," he said.

I was on fairly good terms with my ex-husband, but it was now 8.00 pm, my feet were screaming from standing on them all day and I was looking forward to a glass of wine and just spending some time with the boys watching mindless television shows with them. Maybe even a good book later in bed.

"Do you know what he wanted?" I asked.

I didn't really want to call him back but if it was important, I knew I would probably have to.

"He didn't say but I told him you were shopping and he said he'd call back later."

"Any idea how much later?" I asked.

"Nope."

Just then the phone rang and I reached over to answer it. The voice on the other end of the line was my ex-husband.

"Hi Trish. It's me," he said.

"Hi, Rad. Tony said you called earlier." I held the phone between my shoulder and ear and opened the fridge door. There was an opened bottle of white wine on the middle shelf and I reached in and took it out. "Is everything alright?"

"Yeah. Look, I'm calling because I had a strange phone call tonight from someone who said her name was Sandra Stewart."

There was silence for a few seconds while I took a glass from a glass cabinet above my head and began to pour myself a generous glass of wine.

When Rad didn't continue, I stopped pouring and asked, "Okay. And?"

"I don't know how to say this, Trish."

I sighed, continuing to pour the wine. "Rad. We've been divorced for five years now but I can still remember that in all the fifteen years of our marriage, you were never short for words. Please. Just say it. It's late and it's been a long week. I'm tired and my feet are killing me. I just want to put them up with a glass of wine and a good book. So please, just tell me."

I took a sip of the wine and waited.

He sighed uncertainly. "She said she's your sister."

I stood dumbfounded, the wine glass halfway to my lips. I didn't know what to say.

"Wha...what?" was all I managed to stutter.

* * *

I REMEMBER the first time a sister was mentioned to me. It made no sense at all, but then again, my whole life had seemed to make no sense.

It was a period of my life when I had almost given up. Those years held rejection, pain, hurt and anger, and those emotions have never really left me. Thirty years of suppressing memories have made them a little hazy, and yet, trying to fully rid them from my mind is like trying to scoop mercury up with a fork.

Those few spoken words from Rad made them all come back in horrid vividness and clarity.

If asked if there was one thing I would change about my time at Nazareth House, it wouldn't be the lack of visible and physical love. It would something more sinister.

At the time of a child's life when they're fast becoming aware of themselves and others, the selection of suitable foster parents is crucial. In the 50's and 60's the process did not have the stringent controls that have in place these days. Today, there are interviews with prospective parents, visits from social workers, checks done on financial status, not to mention an interminable waiting list before all of this even begins. But in those days, being a Catholic was assumed to carry with it all the requirements for being a suitable foster family.

Sadly, some foster parents were unprepared for the psychological problems that many of the children carried inside them as a result of the situations they came from. There were children who had come from shattered families where one parent had died, leaving the other parent unable to cope with one or more children on their own. Putting them in the home was the only way of handling this situation, with the understanding that it was only temporary. Marilyn had been one of those girls. Others, like me, had other stories to tell.

Practising Catholics who are taught from an early age *'to give rather than to receive'* and that *'the heart is happiest when it beats for others'* were asked, or volunteered, to take orphaned and abandoned children into their homes during school holidays for periods of up to six weeks. By and large, these teachings are wonderful tenets to hold in life, and have often inspired other Christians to help those who were not as well off as themselves.

For the most part, some people believed they were doing an unselfish Christian deed by breaking the day-to-day monotony for the children and giving them something to look forward to.

Some had other agendas.

By eight years old, I understood I would never be going back to my own home. With a father who I rarely saw and a mother who had virtually disappeared, my chances of returning to them were negligible. Without being told, I knew my only hope for leaving the orphanage was to be fostered. As terrible as it felt to admit it, I knew that was the sad truth.

Although many of us harboured feelings of abandonment and rejection and most of us lacked self-confidence, what was common among all of us was a craving for acceptance. These holiday visits turned me into a little actress, thinking I was on display for people who were choosing a child to stay with them permanently. I knew that as I grew older, it was more and more unlikely that someone would want me since most people wanted small children who could be passed off as their own. I had seen this happen on numerous occasions and I knew my chances of being chosen were becoming less and less. I had no idea of where my future lay. The future for me was tomorrow or the next day.

I went to a series of holiday foster homes until I was nearly twelve, each time put into a 'do or die' situation where desperation overshadowed the happiness that these people had intended for me in the first place. I went with high hopes, wishing desperately that they would see something in me that they liked and therefore decide to keep me.

Once inquisitive and happy, my growing uncertainty about my future made me a quiet and insecure child who would initially sit and watch, listening for any indication whatsoever of the kind of child they preferred. I learnt to watch hard and long, observing, noting and calculating while trying to interpret every possible nuance from the way they talked or even looked at me. With this in mind, I changed more often than a chameleon.

If they wanted a bubbly, outgoing child – I would be exactly that. If they wanted a studious child who read quietly and stayed out of the way – fine by me! If they wanted a cute little girl who played with dolls and had tea parties – no worries!

I changed my personality with every foster family and tried to mould myself into their perfect child. I carried with me more personalities than a politician, ready to ingratiate myself into their lives. I was undemanding, tidy, always clean, and always a happy, laughing child, doing all my chores without complaint. Nothing was too much for me. I was the child anyone would want.

One small but terribly important piece of information not passed onto the children by the nuns was that these people only wanted to have a child for the holiday period. Not knowing this, it seemed no matter how hard I tried, I just wasn't good enough. I was always returned.

At the end of every stay, we would pull up at the main entrance of the home and I would be out of their car and walking stoically up the stairs to the doorbell with my head held high before they had even closed the car door. I made myself hard. I forced myself to never look back at them, to never let them see the pain bubbling up inside my chest. Even when I heard the sound of shifted gears, the revving of the engine and the crunch of tyres on the tiny stones of the orphanage driveway, my steely pride would not let me look back. I would keep my eyes trained forward, my heart hardening like lead in my chest, as I walked through the door.

I tried to show them all I didn't care, but I can't pretend it didn't hurt deep down because it certainly did. It was yet another rejection and it hurt like hell. Every time I was sent back, I died a little inside, again and again. Nobody wanted me. I *was* unlovable. I *was* gutter trash like Sister Philomena had called me. I was starting to feel like I was going through a revolving door, no sooner out than back again.

I was first introduced to some of the seedier characters of this world at the age of seven.

The Conlon's were once my parent's landlords, and as such, were one of the early foster parents selected for a visit since I was already familiar with them. Mr Conlon was married with a son a little younger than I was and in the back of my mind, I remember a time when the two of us, aged between five and six, sat huddled in a small wooden outhouse near my courtyard, taking turns of puffing his father's cigar. Of course, we were both violently sick afterwards but we had giggled and laughed until we cried.

For a little while, the attention Mr Conlon gave me was very welcome. He would offer to wash and dress me, until even at that young age, I started feeling uncomfortable with the detail and extent of the washing routine.

One night, as dinner was being prepared by his wife and Mr Conlon read to his son and me on a double bed, he tried working his hand down inside my pants.

My only thought was, *This is a bad touch*. I wanted it to stop, instinctively knowing this shouldn't be happening. I crossed my legs tightly to prevent further exploration.

Through all of my young life, the only people I had ever been afraid of were the nuns who had my respectful fear, but never 'normal' people. That is until Mr Conlon put his hand up my skirt and hurt me with his fingers.

I ran into the kitchen clinging to Mrs Conlon. My visit with them was suddenly cut short and I was returned to the home shortly after the incident, never visiting them again.

What I was left with was a feeling that I was the one being punished and consequently should be ashamed of myself.

It seemed as if a pattern was starting to form when at another home bathing the children was again done by the foster father. He would wash me last, insisting that 'all my crevices' were properly cleaned, eventually sending me into fits of tears every afternoon when bath time was announced.

Another time, I remember waking up in the middle of the night to find the foster father standing at my bedside naked. His only comment was *"Just touch me"*. I turned my back to him and prayed desperately that he would go away as I lay curled up in a foetal position, too scared to move, listening to his breathing. Eventually I heard his footsteps retreating back to his bed.

I barely slept for the rest of that night. I lay awake until I saw the slight change in the shadows that meant dawn was approaching.

Over the years, after similar instances with other foster fathers, a change in me gradually started to set in. I'd tried to be good, but somehow I knew that good behaviour wasn't what they wanted. I'd gone to them all, scared and afraid, having been deprived of every liberty and associating the 'home' with abandonment and neglect, and all I received in return was a worse type of abuse.

I became angry and bitter, a picture of pure defiance and filled with a dark rage, something that didn't go unnoticed by the nuns. Sister Philomena's solution to this was more work. It was decided that I was now old enough to help change the bed linen in the aged section of the home every afternoon when school had finished and again every Saturday morning, on top of my other chores, which included bathing the younger children at night.

I became a tough, cynical eleven-year-old and a handful to control, but by then I'd seen too much to care. I'd learnt to shut down and not react any more – just like a circuit breaker. When nothing could be relied upon, when everything could change at a moment's notice, I learnt to build a shell around myself of non-caring, coldness and defiance. I now know that what I was feeling was pain at the impermanence of my life and the frustration of helplessness.

This was the sullen, angry, defiant child who greeted the Andersons during the Christmas of 1967 when I was twelve.

Theirs was to be the last foster home I would live in. Deep inside, I was hoping, praying, this was the day that someone would care enough about me to hold me so tight that all my broken pieces would come back together again.

That's what I was hoping for anyway.

DEADCLIFFE

The Andersons lived on the Redcliffe Peninsula, about thirty kilometres north of Brisbane and more affectionately known to the youth who lived there as 'Deadcliffe'. It was mainly a retirement area in those days with very few facilities for the growing young population, just a pebbly beach sheltered from the surf by nearby islands. Its only saving grace was it was cooler than Brisbane in the summer and a little warmer in winter because of the ocean breezes.

After crossing over a bridge called the Hornibrook Highway, we drove quite a long distance to a suburb called Scarborough, turning left into Bennett Street and driving a short distance before pulling into a driveway.

Hugging the small case containing my three changes of clothes to my chest, I stepped out of the car and looked around.

The house had a small front yard, closed in on both sides by a six-foot fence. A low white picket fence at the front shielded a row of annual flowers. Small stones had been used as a border between the coarse grass and the flowerbeds. Overhanging the front yard was a Poinciana tree, not as big as the one at Nazareth House, but greener and bushier, obviously better cared for. The house was high-set with stairs that led up from the side to the front door.

Once inside the front door, a huge grand piano dominated one half of the L-shaped lounge room while lounge chairs and a television dominated the other half. Sitting in the kitchen was a table with four chairs.

As I was led through the compact house to one of the three bedrooms, I remembered Sister Philomena's final words to me, her lips pursed in that familiar no-nonsense way of hers. As I stood on the steps of the orphanage, she said, *'Be good this time. This could be your new home.'*

I didn't tell her I knew the length of time I'd be there would just be a repeat of the others. Soon I'd be packing up, saying goodbye, moving, unpacking and starting all over again. My only thought was *Don't get too comfortable. You'll be gone soon.*

A couple in their mid-fifties may seem a bit old to be fostering hard-to-handle adolescent children but the Andersons had somehow managed to step around the system. I was to find that both had been married before and the only child from either marriage was from Mrs Anderson's former marriage, a son who was married with children of his own.

Mr Anderson worked for the Brisbane City Council and travelled daily to Brisbane, an hour each way and back, arriving home at 6.30pm to a meal on the table by 6.35pm. He was a nondescript, portly man at only five-foot four, with only a little grey hair left on his balding head.

Mrs Anderson was a very patient but firm woman. And she needed to be if she was to handle me. She gave me chores to do like helping to prepare meals every night, doing dishes and helping with the ironing and laundry, all of which I had already been doing in the orphanage, so it was just a matter of course for me. My days were filled, and at night I was allowed one hour of television if all my chores had been completed, and then it was into bed by 7.30pm where I could read if I wanted.

As well as myself, a Malaysian boy by the name of Adam lived with the Andersons. He was a sweet-natured child, adopted at birth and now five years old. He won me over on my first day by smiling and winking at me whenever he caught my eye. We both regarded the Andersons as grandparents more than parents, not just because of their age, but because Mrs Anderson's grandchildren were all my age or older.

In the next few weeks, I learnt a little about Mr Anderson. He fussed over small things. The towels on the bathroom rack had to be perfectly straight. The kitchen sink had to be dried completely – all suds and water were to be mopped up to leave a gleaming sink. When I dusted, all items were to be placed exactly where I had found them – dead centre. And he was so proud of his handwriting. It was neat and precise, and he laboured to make every stroke perfect. Now, I would call it pedantic, which matched his personality completely.

Many times, he would sit with me on the stool in front of the piano keyboard to teach me how to play. He said I had the perfect hands for playing the piano, long fingers that could easily span a full octave even at my young age. As much as I would have loved to learn, the thought of sitting on the stool close to him (or anyone) every day for an hour or more was something I couldn't bring myself to do. I cringed at the touch of another person. I wouldn't even let them kiss or hug me goodnight.

The Andersons had been unaware of what had happened to me over the past few years, only observing that I was withdrawn, distrustful and suspicious of everyone, and that I saw ulterior motives in everything done for me. I had built a barrier around myself believing that if I kept everyone outside it, I wouldn't be hurt anymore.

I was this strange enigma. Despite my desperate need to be loved and cared for, my intense longing to be wanted, there were times when an unwanted demon popped his head up for no reason at all and I reverted back to the uncontrollable, angry child I had become in the orphanage. In my head, I could hear Sister Philomena saying, *'This could be your new home'* and as much as I wanted that to be true, something deep inside that I couldn't control sometimes emerged and I became a furious little creature full of pure anger. I had this *feeling* that something as good as this couldn't really happen to *me*. I was unworthy of any such thing as love and it would be snatched away from me yet again and I'd be sent back in the home. Again.

Maybe I presented a challenge to the Andersons because by the end of that Christmas break, they decided that they would try to keep me. It came as quite a surprise because with them I had decided not to try at all.

Out of the blue, I was faced with a problem I hadn't anticipated. *What if Dad goes to the home and I'm not there? How will he know where I am?*

It seemed that there was nothing I could do about it because the Andersons had set the paperwork in motion.

I became aware that they had previously fostered three other girls before me and all had left at early ages, never to be heard of again. The exception was Jennifer, who had married young and lived thirty minutes away. She'd never had any children of her own but she had a toy poodle that she regularly dyed apricot and treated like a baby, dressing it in pretty coats and putting bows in its hair.

Because of my small selection of clothes, Jennifer took pity on me and gave me dresses and shorts that she no longer wanted. I remember thanking her and being so happy to have so many lovely things to wear. The fact that they were all too big was totally lost on me. Most of the dresses hung down to below my knees, accentuating my pigeon toes and bandy, skinny legs. But they were so pretty and the colours were bright.

Mrs Anderson adored Jennifer, and we went to see her quite regularly. Shortly after I started living with the Andersons, Jennifer gave me some insight into my near future.

Looking at me seriously with her hand on my shoulder, she looked me in the eyes and said, "Listen to me. I want you to come to me straight away if anything ever happens that you don't like. Anything at all."

I wish I had understood then what I was to understand all too well later.

***

My seventh school year at the only local Catholic girls' school in Redcliffe, Saint Bernadette's, turned out to be very difficult for me, resulting in a basic pass as I struggled with a curriculum that was vastly different from that of Nazareth House.

I could recite freely from the Bible, knowing parts of it almost backwards, and I knew all about the lives of many of the canonised saints, but I could barely add two numbers together and arrive at the correct answer. It seemed that teaching, as well as hairdressing, was deficient at the home. Many nights, before exams, were spent sitting with Mrs Anderson while I repeated the 'times table' over and over until both of us were thoroughly exhausted.

Still wary of everyone, making friends at school was a problem for me. As always, my survival routine was to make myself an island: seemingly indifferent and uninterested in everyone. When schoolwork was given, I took advice from the teachers, but I was reluctant to stand up and ask if I didn't understand something. I preferred to work and worry it out myself. At lunchtime, I ate my food alone and when it was time to go home, I walked by myself. At night, I lay with my eyes open staring at the ceiling until exhaustion took over and I fell to sleep. Then the routine would repeat itself the next day.

Mrs Anderson suggested that I call them Mum and Dad now that they intended for me to stay with them permanently. But I couldn't. Other foster parents had asked me to do the same thing and I'd done it just to please them. I'd called so many women 'Mum' in my short life, I just couldn't bring myself to refer to yet another woman by that name. I didn't want these people to be my parents so I simply waited until they looked at me before I spoke.

I used to look around at the other girls laughing and smiling with their mothers, holding hands and looking so happy. Inside, my heart would clench. It wasn't as if I didn't have a mother. I did. Then I would look at Mrs Anderson. I didn't want this old lady to be my mother. What I wanted was my own mother.

As for Mr Anderson, he had no hope of living up to my father.

It was at this time that I discovered the library, becoming an avid reader of any whodunits I could lay my hands on, starting with Agatha Christie. Her mysteries held me spellbound. Then one day, by accident, I saw a book with the face of a beautiful woman on the cover. *Rebecca*. I deviated from whodunits to read it and was transported into a world of mystery, love, romance and passion. From there, I couldn't stop. *Jane Eyre. Little Women. Lorna Doone.* The magical *Wuthering Heights*, the magnificent Heathcliff and the beautiful Cathy. The trivia of Mills and Boon romances did not interest me. I needed something with substance. I'd sit quietly and read for hours, totally absorbed in the story, oblivious to anything that was happening around me. It was another world to live in and it felt good pretending to be someone else in another time and place. I never felt alone or lonely while I had a book in my hand. I was never happier than when I lost myself completely in the life of the hero or heroine and dreaming of a life that was anything but the misery that mine was.

Surprisingly, I passed my exams in Year 7 and progressed into Year 8, commencing at St Bernadette's 'sister' high school, Soubirous College, yet another Catholic School for girls. This was again a close religious atmosphere, barely different from Nazareth House, with Brigidine nuns for teachers and mass held three times a week. I soon learnt that possibly like most institutions, rules were rules and if you obeyed them, you would be fine.

I was again perceived as a 'loner' and drama class was the choice of the nuns to bring me 'out of myself' and into a group atmosphere where I could learn to interact with other girls. Although I had no trouble remembering lines and cues and I loved the idea of pretending to be someone else, (in reality I'd had enough practice), one major obstacle stopped me from doing well in this class: I was extremely shy and lacking in confidence. I preferred to be a 'beige' person, blending into the background rather than bringing attention to myself. I still wasn't prepared to open myself up to what I thought would only be criticism or ridicule, so I found it safer to just sit and watch, hiding my inner turmoil.

The nuns had other ideas.

It was discovered during this class that I could also hold a tune. I was no prodigy, but I had good pitch and I loved music. The nuns instantly enrolled me in the choir, where I could blend into the drama group and sing as well.

As distressing as the whole situation was for me, on reflection, it was probably the best thing that could have happened to me. It was the first step towards making friends at the school and blending in.

Of course, I was terrified. The words would blur and flutter on the page like demented flies as I stammered out the words, my voice croaking painfully as I willed myself not to look at the faces floating in front of me.

"You must persevere, Patricia," the nun said. "And dear, please make sure to wash your hair before coming to school in future."

I stood aghast and stuttered. "But..but..I do. I wash it every night."

The nun looked at me as if I was lying and shook her head.

"But I do!" I stated tearfully. "I use soap every night."

She tutted at me. "Use shampoo, Patricia. Not soap. Soap will just make it greasy."

The words stuck in my throat. *I didn't have shampoo. The Andersons only gave me soap and baby talcum powder.* And there was no way I was asking them for anything. I'd rather go without than do that.

It was then I began dusting my hair with talcum powder every morning and the effect was wonderful. It lightened my hair even more and I felt...changed.

Finally, I began to feel accepted, giving me the badly needed confidence that I'd lacked and I began to laugh again. From there, I was asked to join sporting activities such as swimming, tennis and athletics.

Everyone had been allocated to different sporting teams, called 'houses', that were named after religious themes. Bon Secoeur was blue, Lourdes was red and Fatima was yellow. I was a Fatima girl, and even though we were the loudest supporters, we never failed to come anywhere but last.

Everyone competed enthusiastically in all sports but the school favourite (though not mine) was definitely swimming, with training being held daily between 5am-6am and 4pm-5pm. We all regarded this harrowing schedule in addition to school studies and homework as a form of torture devised by the nuns, and surely best left for the truly dedicated or talented. It soon became obvious that I was neither.

Mr Cusak, our swimming coach, would walk up and down the side of the Olympic size pool, barking out instructions to improve our swimming form or in my case, lack of form. While he was renowned for his patience and persistence as well as attaining extremely good results from most of the girls, I'm sure he had never seen the likes of me before. He soon found out that I was certainly no Shane Gould.

Freestyle I could cope with, but I never seemed to gain much forward momentum with breaststroke and would be left far behind in the pool as the gap between the others and myself widened. Fortunately, there were no lifeguards at our swimming meets, as I'm sure there would have been an attempt to rescue me during my butterfly display and my directionally uncontrollable backstroke. Lane markers as well as other girls were always in danger of being sideswiped as I invariably skewed all over the pool while performing both of these strokes.

My friend, Therese Pilgrim, and I would swim our hearts out for our house while also having a private competition between the two of us. She persistently won the bet by coming second-last, but no matter how hard I tried I always came last.

I was finally saved from the starting blocks when Mrs Anderson noticed that my fair hair was getting a decidedly green tinge from the chlorine in the pool and that unfeminine Atlas-like shoulders were forming on my small frame.

Maybe there was a God after all, because I much preferred the newly allocated ball sports to swimming. We were all encouraged to participate in everything no matter what sport we preferred but tennis was my favourite. A club was organised where weekend games were played at different schools, (Catholic girls' schools, of course), but during the week the lunch bell produced a scurry of twenty or more girls all struggling to be the first onto one of the two tennis courts near the play area. None of us took the time to change out of our school uniforms and into our sports clothes before the game, so in summer, sweat-soaked armpits and an invisible cloud of body odour made it obvious who had played tennis and who had been smart enough to sit in the shade near the tuckshop.

The agreed rules were that the first two girls on the court for that lunch period, be it little lunch or big lunch, could choose their own partner and had the court for all or part of lunch, at their own discretion. As soon as the bell sounded, we forgot all the lessons the nuns had taught us about being refined young Catholic ladies as we turned into screaming harridans, pushing and shoving everyone out of our way and waving our tennis rackets high above our heads yelling, "Me first! Outta my way! Get lost!"

The irony of this was that the class immediately preceding lunch was 'Deportment and Etiquette'.

* * *

I WAS ALWAYS COMPETITIVE, striving to do my best in everything, and schoolwork was no exception. I tried very hard to receive good marks in all my subjects, eventually coming consistently in the top ten of my class after deciding to take an academic course. I was told this course would give me more of a range of future professions. Although Latin (which I hated) was my best subject, I can truthfully say that none of my subjects gave me too much concern, except for Physics, which, contrary to popular belief, seemed to have no logic whatsoever.

By the end of year 9 and with the equivalent of an 'A' today, I decided to change from Latin to Typing, concluding that the latter had more scope and practicality for me. This decision caused Sister St Jude to place both hands over her heart and stare at me in utter disbelief while exclaiming, "Oh no! Not TYPING, Patricia."

I had been her pet because I'd achieved such high marks with her beloved Latin but from then on, whenever she saw me, she would shake her head and frown disbelievingly at me.

More important than any school subject was a woman's attributes. A figure, manners, deportment, elocution. All of these would guarantee a quality marriage. In those days, that was the best a young woman could hope for. After all, it was a man's world. I grew up with these sorts of values, where women were judged like that.

I participated as demanded but inside I felt gauche, stumbling, unappealing and unattractive. *I have no hope* I decided. *I am plain and dowdy and unlovable. Gutter trash.*

All studies and sports were designed to ensure we had healthy minds and bodies. To balance this with a healthy soul we had Father Frawley, our parish priest, who was usually assisted by a 'trainee priest' (a curate). In the few years I was at Soubirous College, curates seemed to come and go quite rapidly.

On one occasion, a young, good-looking, fair-haired curate, Father Kennedy, more like a movie star than a priest, arrived at Soubirous, and sent the college full of young pubescent girls into a head spin. He must have been the hardest working priest in Queensland with each girl going to confession three times a day with sins concocted to shock him. This, I am sure, enlivened his life and generally raised the temperature in the confessional box.

During his sermons, we all sat looking at him dreamily, none of us hearing a word he said. He could have told us Jesus was a Martian and we would have believed him.

If the hierarchy had thought more about it, they would have realised that ours was probably the wrong school for him. After only two weeks, Father Frawley realised it too and sent him away to avoid continued disruption, none of which was really his fault. His replacement was an elderly priest who wouldn't send our hearts and newly developed hormones racing as he glared at us over his spectacles. He left no doubt that he would not stand for any such behaviour, assuming we even wanted to engage in it.

* * *

ALONG WITH RACING hormones came the onset of my menstrual cycle, all of which brought many confusing emotions as rules and restrictions became extremely stringent at home.

At school, we were given lectures, shown movies, and a nurse even visited our class to explain what would be happening to our bodies. Everyone had been given a sample pack of sanitary napkins to take home so that when this 'happy and blessed event' occurred, we would all be prepared. Even though I was aware of this forthcoming process, its actual arrival came as a shock, and for some reason unknown to me then and now, my feelings were that I was dirty. For me, this event was something to hide, not rejoice in.

I'd had three menstrual cycles before Mrs Anderson discovered blood on my knickers one washday and the truth finally came out. On previous occasions, to buy pads at the corner shop on the way home from school, I'd had to secretly take money out of her purse, adding more tension to an already stressful situation because I was now waiting to be found out for that as well. The sword of Damocles always seemed to be hanging over me.

She was very hurt and confused about why I had hidden this from her. Even I didn't know why, but she diplomatically dropped the subject.

With the onset of my periods came other changes in my body that I didn't like. My puppy fat dropped off me almost overnight it seemed, and my body started filling out everywhere. All my clothes became loose in some places and tight in others and for the first time I had a waist, rounded hips and breasts, something that bothered me rather than pleased me. I felt conspicuous and was sure people were looking at me.

One person certainly was watching me. Mr Anderson.

It's hard to say exactly when everything began to change because it was such a slow transition. In actual fact, it was puberty that let me down. One day he was forcing me to hold his hand in public and the next day he would pass me in the small hallway and reach out to touch me as we passed. As he touched my breast once, he would crudely said, "Your headlights are on."

At the time, I couldn't believe he was doing something that I thought was so blatantly obscene. The next time he touched me, the reaction he got was certainly not the one he expected.

I had no idea where the fear came from. It started like a fist in the pit of my stomach, clutched at my heart then bubbled out hysterically as I screamed and flailed my arms around my head, yelling, "Don't touch me, just don't touch me!"

Mrs Anderson had no idea how to console me. She left me to sit alone in my room, my back against the wall, knees up to my chin and my forehead resting on them, sobbing uncontrollably as my heart pounded in my chest.

I had been confused and shocked at the intensity of what I was feeling and had no idea of what was happening to me or why. I just wanted to be left alone. I closed my eyes. Somewhere out there, life made sense.

Mr Anderson didn't dare come near me for a while. I made my face hard as I looked at him and it was enough to make him lower his eyes and walk quietly away.

That glimpse of my future sent a chill through my heart and a shudder through my body.

Soon after this, I was not allowed to visit any friends who had brothers. I'd protested that most of them were only younger brothers, but that didn't matter to Mr Anderson. His decision had been made. They were free to come to my house, but I was never allowed to go to theirs.

This seemed so very unfair, both to the few friends I had and to me, and naturally the invitations soon died away. Therese, my friend from swimming, convinced me to join the local youth group made up of only school-age Catholics from Soubirous and De La Salle College (a Catholic boys' school), seen to be a safe place for young men and women to meet while avoiding the parental distress over drive-ins and other seemingly seedy places.

This was where I met Michael Banner, a Year 12 boy whom everyone in my circle thought was quite cute. Not too long after I started going to the club, a night was planned for everyone to visit Toombul Ice Skating Rink and Michael asked if I would like a lift in his car (the front seat, mind you). Adhering to all the rites and rituals required of these young men, he presented himself at my house to ask permission to take me.

Mr Anderson talked to Michael quietly alone in the lounge room while I sat in the kitchen. His request was apparently granted and the outing proceeded, although I do remember thinking at the time that Michael appeared a little cool towards me, unlike other times at youth meetings when we'd gotten on quite well.

I didn't hear from him for almost two weeks after that, but I jumped every time the phone rang. Eventually, I dug up the courage and did the unheard of – I phoned him. With my heart in my mouth and hands shaking, I made my voice sound happy. "Hi! Remember me? Have I done something wrong?"

After a slight hesitation, he asked me, "Did your father tell you what he said to me on the skating night?"

My heart sank. He hadn't, of course.

"No," I said. "And by the way, he's not my father. But tell me anyway."

"Well, he said that I was to stay away from you after that night and if I ever contacted you again, I would be hearing from his solicitor. Look, I don't know what the problem is, but my Dad will kill me if I get in any sort of trouble. I'm sorry."

Michael had nothing to do with me from then on and my heart broke for the first time. I remember gulping to stop myself from crying.

Needless to say, my chances of having a boyfriend were destroyed at the same time as the weekly visits to the youth club ended.

* * *

Mr Anderson's interest in me was a slowly ever-worsening situation.

He began sporting bright, shiny satin shirts of luminous greens and purples with snug fitting chequered pants as well as a new toupee that didn't quite match his own hair colour (however little there was left). Sometimes it would slide sideways during sudden turns of his head, leaving it balancing precariously on his smooth dome, as I folded my lips together to stop from laughing.

When he started showing favouritism towards me over Adam with little gifts of a chocolate bar or a book brought home from work, I knew this to be a bad sign and started to refuse the gifts, eventually quite rudely, to get the point across to him. I wanted no part of it.

I hated him with a passion and avoided him constantly so there would be no conflict. Then, to my horror, Mrs Anderson commenced working at the local drive-in theatre three nights a week, most times taking Adam with her, leaving me to deal with him alone.

Coming into the bathroom to wash me became his next ploy. A locked door finished that approach but started him insisting that I sit on his lap where he would run his hand up my leg, asking me when I would be his 'big girl' or saying, "You belong to me. No one wants you, but I do." He said he would show me how to please him and show my gratitude.

I hated the feel of his cold hands on my legs but clenched my teeth together and sat as still as I could. In my mind, I floated above the ground. Above whatever was happening below. I flew through the windows out into the night, under the stars. I wasn't *there*.

The sleeping arrangements changed as well at this time with Adam, then aged seven, sleeping every night with Mrs Anderson and Mr Anderson moving into Adam's room.

One night when Mrs Anderson was at work, I'd only just gone to sleep when the feel of a hand touching my body woke me. Mr Anderson was lying in bed with me.

Nothing in my life so far had prepared me for this. His hands were resting on my hips, kneading them, and the feeling of revulsion rose from the pit of my stomach like I was about to be sick.

I flung the covers back and slapped his hands away hysterically. Trying not to fall over the tangled sheets clutching at my feet, I ran to the corner of my room screaming, "Get out! Get out!"

For hours afterwards, I felt an almost overwhelming urge to be sick, but I was too scared to leave my room and go to the toilet. I knew I was crying because my hair was damp from tears, but I wasn't making any noise. Instead, I stayed curled up in a ball in the corner of my room.

As I sat, I retreated to my dreams for the first time. I imagined myself walking barefoot along a beach. I could smell fish and seaweed, and salt in the air. No one else was on the beach with me and I stood with my feet in the water while my toes dug deep in the wet sand, which felt like sugar beneath my feet. The water receded with a dragging feeling almost over-balancing me and then splashing up my legs as it came back in again. It was hypnotizing. I felt calm and at peace as the breeze blew my hair around my face and my dress hugged my body and legs. I sat down on the sand and hunched over my up-drawn knees, squinting at the ocean as the sun blazed down on me. I scooped sand up in my hand and felt the coarse grains filter through my fingers. I could see white-topped waves crashing on the beach, their regular rhythm merging with the sound of the seagulls that flew in circles, wheeling and crying, flapping their wings. So peaceful.

I remember a sound from outside my door suddenly disturbed me and the image disappeared. I was back in my nightmare again.

I jumped up and locked my bedroom door and did so every night from then on. I became a very light sleeper, jumping at the occasional scrape of a tree limb against the window or the sound of the house timbers settling, listening to the tap dripping and the clock ticking.

I imagined my life to be just a nightmare. Something I'd wake up from in my own bed at home. It would be the morning that I hadn't smelt tea and toast – the morning I'd gone to school by myself. This time, I wouldn't go. This time

I would hide like I had other times and no one would be able to find me. Then that night, Dad and Mum would come home and we'd be a family again. My life would be different, and I wouldn't be here now. It amazed me to think that the course of my life may have altered by making that one simple decision.

If I'd been asked to draw a picture of my world, it would have been black. The innocence that every child deserves was lost to me forever.

* * *

THE BUILDING BLOCKS of my life had already been laid at previous foster homes so this attention from Mr Anderson was nothing new. Sadly though, he had taken these building blocks and added to them in ways that a thirteen-year-old girl should never have to experience. That last visit into my bedroom, after everything else, was the straw that broke the camel's back. I'd had enough. The nightly insistence I sit on his lap so that he could touch and feel me would never happen again, I vowed.

His anger must have gotten the better of him because physical beatings started soon after, supposedly as punishment for being rude and ungrateful. The first time his hand came into contact with my face, my vision exploded with light then blurred and the sound of bees buzzing in my head filled the air as I leant against the kitchen wall holding my face.

Jennifer's words came back to haunt me. *Had this happened to her as well?* I thought. She'd said to go to her straight away if anything happened. But if I had, I'd have been there every week. I longed to tell her what was happening. I ached to have someone know and understand the extent of my agony, but shame stopped me. And even if I did tell her, wouldn't Mr Anderson simply deny it?

* * *

MY LIFE BECAME a chaotic mix of conflicting emotions. While I felt vulnerable and desperately wanted someone – anyone – to help me, I just couldn't ask for that help. No one would believe me. No one even cared enough to help me.

The only way for me to cope with this new nightmare was to block it out of my mind. To put an imaginary brick wall around myself. And I learnt how to never show my feelings or emotions. No one would know how much I was hurting inside.

My frustration turned into uncontrollable anger: anger at my life, anger at my parents and anger at both of the Andersons. Surely *she* knew what was happening. She must have seen the bruises and cut lips. Why did she ignore them? Didn't she know what he was doing? Did she just choose to ignore it? Why? They had adopted other girls before me and two had never been heard of again, could this be the reason? Surely that was too much of a coincidence. Why did she keep allowing this to happen? Didn't she know that by ignoring him, she was giving him permission to continue? She was actually condoning his behaviour. I hated her as much as I hated him. She was no better than he was. Only that week at school, I had read that on the way to his execution, Sir Thomas More had said to Henry VIII, 'Silence is consent'. Now I knew what he meant.

The mind is a cruel thing. In my pain and anger, I turned the hurt and agony around and I blamed myself. Wounded children have this rage, this sense of failed justice that burns in their souls. And what do they do with that rage? They turn it inward. They become the target of their own rage. They repeat in their thoughts the same harmful words that were spoken to them. *No one wants you. You are nothing but gutter trash.* And they want to lash out. But the only one weak enough to attack is themselves.

Looking back now, I realise that at fifty-five years old, in those days, starting a new life alone would have been difficult for a woman. It was easier for her to turn a blind eye to everything and have her life stay as it was. In those days, women believed that they needed a man in their lives. Nowadays, women can go anywhere and find a job far more easily than a man can. We can waitress or do clerical work and the options are endless. But it was different then. A woman needed a man especially at Mrs Anderson's age. So it was easier for her to go along with what was happening. This weak man was probably better than no man at all. Even though he was a failure at everything in his life, a loser, he was better than nothing.

This weak woman's choice to ignore what was happening condemned me to a life of isolation and aloneness. Outwardly, I looked like a sullen, angry adolescent but inside, I was screaming.

* * *

AFTER AN INCIDENT one night that left me with a broken finger and a swollen, bruised cheek, (I was certainly getting used to the coppery taste of blood in my mouth), I asked for something that I never thought I would. I asked to be sent back to Nazareth House. I was thirteen now and the prospect of returning to life at the orphanage was far better than staying with the Andersons.

I remember glancing at the kitchen table looking for something to hit him with. *Don't worry about what happens. You can do it. Grab the plate. Do it.* I could actually see myself hitting him. *He might hit me harder. He might even kill me,* I remember thinking. *So what?* another voice asked. *You feel dead already, don't you?* I felt like there were two people inside me having a conversation: one strong, one weak. For all my bravado, in reality, I was really just a scared little girl.

"You asked for it. You know that, don't you?" he sneered. "No one wants you back at Nazareth House," he continued. "No one wants to ever see you again and by the way," his eyes were fixed on me, "you'll never see your sister Robyn either."

My strength vanished with that one sentence and I remember feeling frozen. *A sister? I don't remember any sister. It simply couldn't be true. This must be just another way to hurt me.*

Still, his words stayed in the back of my mind.

Robyn was an Irish name. If he was lying, why hadn't he chosen a name like Mary or something equally as common? Why an Irish name like Robyn?

By then, a huge argument had erupted. It was then I was told that at my father's request, an appointment had been made for me to see him in a fortnight's time at the Children's Services main office.

In retrospect, this appointment was probably the reason for the tension that resulted in the fight that night. Mr Anderson was more than likely worried that I'd tell Dad what had been happening.

The remark about a sister was pushed to the back of my mind with this wonderful news. I was ecstatic. *He actually wanted to see me?* It had been well over a year, maybe two, since I'd last seen my father and I dreamed of begging him to take me with him – anywhere - as long as I was with him. I'd tell him everything that was happening and he'd take me away. Everything would be all right again. I would look after him and we would be together, just him and me.

For the first time in over a year, I went to bed happy.

When I woke up, my face was stiff and for the next few days, I could hardly see out of my eye. No one seemed to acknowledge what had happened except that my finger was taped up and I was told to stay at home and not go to school. For the next five days, I simply sat in my room and read.

Solitude became a friend that I welcomed at this time.

Again, I went to my beach.

* * *

THE NEXT TWO weeks dragged as I waited impatiently for the day to arrive.

The June holidays had finished, and it was suddenly well into July. Like any thirteen-year-old anticipating a happy event, I was dressed and waiting hours before we left on that cold, windy winter's morning.

The appointment was for midday, but by 11.30am we were sitting in the waiting room, my enthusiasm bringing smiles even to Mrs Anderson.

Midday came and went.

One o'clock, then two o'clock and then three o'clock.

As the clock ticked on, my worst fears crept over me like a dark shadow. He wasn't coming at all.

What could have been so important that it kept him from showing up to see me?

Suddenly, the shill ringing tone of the phone pierced the silence. The clerk answered it then listened for a few seconds before glancing over at the three of us waiting. He mumbled, "Thanks" then put the receiver down and called Mr Anderson over to the counter. For a few minutes, the two men whispered.

I sat quietly, still in my own private hell desperately wanting to know why my father had not arrived. That was when Mr Anderson came over to me with a clipboard in his hand. He handed it to me and said, "I should have known. Your father isn't coming." He held the clipboard out to me, pointing to a line at the bottom of a page attached, and said, "You have to sign here. And date it as well to say I brought you here today but your father didn't attend. The date is 25th July. Write it there, and sign it here," he pointed.

Crying all the way home, I eventually sobbed from the back seat, "Why didn't he turn up?"

The vision of Mr Anderson turning around in the passenger side of the front seat will burn in my memory forever.

"Your father was drunk," he said brutally.

His explanation was delivered like a slap in the face. Anger and bitterness surged through my body as I realised once again, my father had betrayed me. When we arrived home, I stormed into my room, refusing dinner and any consolation. All I wanted was to be left alone.

And there I stayed, alone with an aching heart and a vow never to let anyone hurt me ever again.

* * *

THE NEXT YEAR PASSED UNEVENTFULLY. I closed myself away from everyone, going to school during the week and staying in my room when I was at home on weekends. It was the only way I could function.

Every Sunday, Mr Anderson, smiling and nodding to other parishioners, would still take Adam and me to church, displaying us in our very best outfits for everyone to see. I could barely keep the contempt from showing on my face.

I gave up smiling and I never prayed any more. Praying was like wishing and wishes never came true.

I was told that on several occasions the Andersons had applied to adopt me. At fourteen years of age and in Year 9 at school, I couldn't understand why they even bothered any more. I certainly wasn't the loving daughter they supposedly wanted when they decided to take me out of Nazareth House. I didn't love them, and I gave them very little to love.

This provided little consolation because now, almost twelve months after the failed meeting with my father, I was told that my adoption papers had been duly signed. By my mother. All that was needed was my signature.

I was crushed. *My mother signed the papers? Where had she been all this time? Had she suddenly turned up so that she could permanently give me away? And where was my father? What had changed his mind?*

This was the final rejection. The last straw. My mother was always drunk and had never even bothered to visit me in the home and my father couldn't even stay sober long enough to see me after having made the appointment. Now after another year, both of them were getting rid of me just like everyone else had. So, gritting my teeth and snatching the pen, I signed the papers.

* * *

I HAD A PLAN IN MIND. I would finish school at the end of Year 10 and start work, doing anything. A job came up for a junior at a local bank, making coffee and doing menial jobs, so I took it while waiting for the results of a Public Service exam that I sat for in school.

The first two pay cheques from the bank were spent on a small suitcase I hid under my bed; the next ones were set aside for bond money for a flat. After paying weekly board money to the Andersons, I had almost $100 saved in the bank.

Fate must have been on my side the day the results of the Public Service exam came in the mail. The house was empty when I arrived home and I absently collected the few letters sticking out of the letterbox.

My name jumped out at me from the top one and my heart did a little somersault. It was the second letter I'd received in my life, if you counted the one marked 'Return to Sender' at the orphanage. My eyes raked the white envelope stamped with Commonwealth Government logo on the right hand side and I knew it would be the result of the exam I'd sat for at school. With shaking hands, I dropped the other letters on the kitchen table and took the one addressed to me to my room.

When I read the results, I smiled sardonically. I'd passed the exam with flying colours and the Commonwealth Government Public Service had a job for me doing clerical work at a hospital. Greenslopes Repatriation Hospital. The same one I'd visited with Dad ten years before, sitting on the slopes playing with the toads. The irony of the situation did not escape me.

One Saturday morning, I waited until the Andersons left to do grocery shopping before reading the section in the paper advertising 'flats to rent'. After phoning and accepting one sight unseen, I packed my bag with my few possessions and left a note simply saying, "Good-bye."

Three years of fighting off the bastard was enough. I was fifteen now and I could survive on my own.

As I stepped out of the house with my suitcase in my hand and walked towards the cab I'd called, I glanced towards the heavens, silently asking a God I suspected didn't exist, *So, what's next? Another flood? A plague of locusts? Do your worst, I don't care. I'm free!*

I could see a light at the end of the tunnel. I only hoped it wasn't a train coming straight at me.

* * *

My flat wasn't exactly what I'd imagined when I'd planned on starting a new life, but it was in a good position and only a twenty-minute bus ride after a thirty-minute walk to work. I put up with the smell of cooking food wafting day and night from the take-away restaurant across the road because in the same block there was a laundromat as well as a corner store that sold bread, milk, tea, coffee, papers and the sort of things people forget when they do their weekly shopping. This shop was ideal for me. I needed very little to survive.

The flat contained two rooms: a kitchen with only a fridge, gas cook top, one square table and two chairs as hard as church pews; and through a set of French doors, a bedroom with only a single bed and a small wardrobe. An uncurtained window let in some light, filtered through the trees, but not enough to warm up the cold linoleum floor in winter. The bathroom, used by all residents, was at the end of a hallway at the back of the house and I would tiptoe up to the tiny room once a day with my bag of toiletries clutched tightly in my hands. Inside the bag were my treasures. Deodorant! Shampoo! Cashmere Bouquet soap! I would close my eyes and hold the treasured soap up to my nose and breath the beautiful scent in deeply. Visions shifted through my mind of Nana Mooney's scowling face, Dad's mouth stretched into a beautiful smile and the corner of Mum's mouth twitching, trying not to laugh.

My life was very spartan, but these luxuries were as much as I could afford now that I was a lowly Clerical Assistant Grade 1 working for the Commonwealth Government. There were no pictures on the walls, no knick-knacks to dust, no vases of coloured glass or souvenir ashtrays to accidentally knock over. I hadn't even thought to decorate my rooms. It never occurred to me. All I had, and needed, was my growing pile of books in the corner of my bedroom. I'd heard people referring to themselves as poor and I guess that was me too in my day-to-day struggle to survive. But the alternative didn't bear thinking about.

I saw myself standing in the dirt in front of the 'ladder to success', not even on the first rung yet, but single-minded, concentrating only on my job and putting everything else out of my mind. At least I had control of my own life and no one would demand any explanation from me that I might not be ready to give.

This was to be my home for the next three years. What I remember most about those years were the simple things. The immense happiness of being able to cross the road from my flat to the take-away shop, buying the food and bringing it home to eat. The first meal I ever bought for myself. Bought with my own money. Eaten in my own flat. No one could take this away from me. My early years had made me afraid of hoping for contentment but now I had it, plus stability and peace. Sure, I was lonely, but in comparison to what I had come from, things seemed bright and promising. I needed very little money. I lived simply.

The nights were blissful. I could lie in bed and hear the swish of cars driving past, the distant music of a radio playing somewhere or sometimes the soft patter of rain on the roof. No longer did I have to lie awake, alert to any sound in the night or listening for quiet footsteps at my door. For so many years, I'd wandered between reality and fantasy but now, to my surprise, some degree of contentment and purpose emerged.

In my whole life, I'd never done anything remarkable or looked at myself seriously or valued myself. I'd always been very private, almost apologetic. A skittish, shy creature. Getting through school, learning, growing up. Throughout those years, I was barely hanging on. But I knew somewhere inside me there had once been passion. A fire burning. And I was hoping there was still an ember glowing, just waiting to be fanned. Like most of the kids at the orphanage, I thought of myself as just an accident. But something made me want to stand up and be counted. I didn't want my life to be insignificant. I wanted to shout out "Hey, I'm a nice person and I *am* worthwhile."

I started thinking more and more about my mother and the reasons why she gave me up and I realised that I could think about her differently now that I had started a life of my own. It couldn't have been easy for her to do such a totally unnatural thing, such as giving up a child. Unless of course, she felt she had no other choice. My mother had been an alcoholic and today, alcoholism is regarded as a disease. It changes people and turns them into total strangers doing things they wouldn't normally do. I knew that. But what had put her onto that path?

I started reading books and articles written by psychologists on early childhood and I was amazed at some of the insights they offered.

A Dr Robertiello said that most girls are products of their mother's love, whether the mother is aloof or smothering. What we must do is break down the specific components of our mother's love. We must analyse exactly the ways she did not love us but also the ways in which she did. Did your mother give you a kind of basic security, a structure of stability, shelter, nurturing? Did she give you admiration, a genuine feeling that you were worth plenty in your own right? Did she give you warmth and physical affection, cuddles, hold you and kiss you? Did she really care what happened to you and accept you – her daughter, right or wrong? These are some of the components of real love. When a tiny child doesn't get the kind of satisfying affection and love, they do not evolve emotionally. They grow older but part of them is still looking for that closeness and when they find it, they fear it will soon be snatched away.

As I read the words, I was in a mild form of shock at the...*correctness* of it. How could he possibly have known?

I read on quickly. His theory was that the deprivation of love stamps a woman for life. Such women have missed something vital from their mothers, and they grow guarded and distrustful. Even as their husbands and lovers tell them that they love them, these women still believe that they will leave and reject them. They take a civil service job instead of a more demanding career and never believe in themselves. They work in bursts until, having achieved success, they look around and say, '*What does it all mean?*' These 'impoverished infants' are still emotionally impoverished as adults, despite their worldly success.

I couldn't believe it. Every one of these traits was mine! I'd often wondered that if I was as strong as I thought I was, why was I haunted with fear that I wasn't good enough? All my triumphs meant little to me as I endeavoured to do better and better again. I strived to be a winner, but my idea of a winner was someone perfect and, as we all know, none of us is perfect. I had been good at schoolwork and sports, liked by people after I'd come out of my shell and I had succeeded in my working life, but negative feelings still overshadowed all my accomplishments.

At times like this, we often think of the different courses that people cut through life. For some, it seems so simple. They don't hesitate. They are beautiful and intelligent, and life opens up to them as the Red Sea opened up to Moses.

Others have a constant struggle. They are shy. They stutter. They stumble. They never lose their self-consciousness. They talk when they should be silent, or they are silent when they should speak up. When they hear laughter, they assume it is directed at them. Though smart, they feel stupid. Though creative, they feel dull. Their path through life resembles a person wading through mud. All these characteristics were mine.

Then an amazing thing occurred to me. I tried to imagine myself in her place: loving and living with a married man, a small child in tow and

Nana Mooney's cool aloofness. And despite the hurt she'd caused me, I actually started feeling sorry for her. I remembered Nana Mooney's scowling face and wondered if that had been reserved for me or if my mother had lived her childhood seeing it as well. I had no idea.

Because of my youth, she and I were never able to talk about our feelings. I could have come to terms with her angers, disillusionments and other emotions, if I'd been older. I would have understood that while my mother loved me, other emotions impaired that love. Instead, I was left feeling that *I* had caused the problems at home.

How lonely she must have been at times, with no one to turn to. I knew the emptiness of being alone. I knew that being loved and wanted was what I needed more than anything. She would have been no different to me in that respect.

I shut the book and sat back, stunned, looking around me at my tiny existence. Once again, after all these years, I found myself alone and lonely. Looking at the whole picture of my life, I knew something was missing.

Then, for some reason, I suddenly remembered Mr Anderson's spiteful statement about a sister.

I would rather have walked over hot coals than contact Nazareth House, but seeing no other way, I picked up the phone and rang, hoping they would have some usual information.

With my heart pounding in my chest, I explained to the secretary what I wanted. Sounding friendly, she said, "You would have been here when Sister Philomena was in charge. How wonderful. She's here right now."

Before I could scream out *NO!!!!* the familiar Irish brogue was on the other end of the line with a "Hello Patricia."

I know I gasped. *She remembers me?* I recall thinking. *Had I been so unforgettable?*

I felt like I was ten years old and in trouble again. My legs turned to jelly and my hands started sweating as I shakily sat down and stammered my way through my prepared dialogue. With my eyes closed tightly and a pulse pounding in my throat, I repeated what I had told the secretary.

"Hello Sister. I'm sorry to bother you, but I was wondering if you remember from my records if I had a sister. I was told by my last foster parents that I had one and I really would like to try and find her."

After a hesitation, I heard the sorrow in her voice.

"No, Patricia. There was never anything in your file and no mention of a sister. I am truly sorry."

There was a small silence and then she said, "What are you doing with your life, dear?"

"I'm working now. I have a good job," I replied.

"And you're happy?"

"Yes, Sister," I lied. "Everything is good now."

"Oh, that's lovely, dear." The words were simple, meant to be reassuring. But I could hear something in her voice. A hesitation. Was there something she wanted to say but wasn't sure how to say it?

"Patricia," she started slowly. "Time heals all wounds."

There it was. Her great revelation. In my heart, I knew she was trying to soothe me but instead, I felt annoyed. Time heals nothing! It's what we do with our time, the choices we make, the people we surround ourselves with, the life we create. *That's* what heals us. It's the hope in our hearts and minds that heal. Not time!

For so many years, I longed for a life I could control. I wanted a home decorated with pictures, soft cushions and scented candles. I wanted shelves full of books of adventure and poetry. I wanted to wake up every morning, excited for what was to come. I wanted to feel healthy and strong. I wanted to feel satisfied with my life, not ashamed because it was empty. I wanted friends who could teach me how to live. I wanted to feel alive. Instead, I felt like a broken little girl who had to learn how to get back up and to never depend on anyone.

We chatted for a few minutes, talking about my job and what I was now doing with my life. I finished my call to her feeling drained, empty and terribly disappointed. I hadn't told her that I hadn't been to church since I was fifteen or that it was hard for me to accept the theory of an 'all loving, all giving God' who watched over us when He had been decidedly absent in my life up to now. I didn't tell her that I couldn't see why not attending church was a 'mortal sin' for all Catholics, when prayers could be said equally as well at home. The concept that I would go to 'hell' for this, no matter how good a person I was, left me feeling very sceptical of my religion. I believed then, as I do now, that the main thing is how good a person you are, not how many times you go to church. Praying can be done anywhere and at any time.

In my life, I had seen enough to turn me completely against the regimented religion that Sister Philomena represented. I'd known people who had gone to church regularly but who had left their religion inside that church when they went home.

After talking to her for that little time, I'd started seeing her through the eyes of an adult and not as a child. I started to wonder, *Could I have been wrong about her all these years?*

It only occurred to me then that the nuns had probably done the best they could with the resources that were available. Although I'd never disagreed with the basic premise that discipline was necessary, the extent of that discipline, and the methods used, were different matters.

Still, the nuns were untrained, trying to do a difficult job and more than likely thrown into their situation the same way the children were. It was like telling a group of carpenters that they were now brain surgeons. The nuns had possibly never wanted children of their own, joining the convent to embrace religion, and there they were, responsible for fifty or more children as a part of their daily life.

They were segregated, imposed with values and responsibilities that are not part of a normal life, and had to learn to suppress normal desires and needs that conflicted with their newly chosen path. When I actually thought about it, the worst emotional scars of my childhood did not come from these institutions but from other individuals whose care I was put in. Some of these people were wrongly assumed to be virtuous purely because of their religious background, making those foster homes an even worse nightmare than what I had been wrenched away from.

Anger slowly surfaced again as I remembered Mr Anderson's lie told to hurt me. I felt like I had been running around in circles looking for something that just wasn't there. But I'd given it my best shot and pursued all avenues I could think of. It was time to move on.

I decided that from then on, Darwin's rule that the fittest will survive was going to apply to me. Life keeps on moving. I saw myself as just an ordinary person who, having been tested, had to ask myself, 'Will I crumble, give up and fall down in a heap, or will I rise up out of these circumstances?' I could sit on my backside and wonder why all of this had happened to me or I could just get on with things. From the rubble of my life, I would survive. I was damn sure I would.

After this mental shake-up, I decided I'd had enough time to think things over. It was time to move on, not throw my arms up in the air in defeat. After all, life is all about moving on, and change can occur at random and sometimes at unpredictable intervals. This was my chance to prove it.

* * *

AT THE BEGINNING, I kept to myself, not making friends and not caring. All I wanted was to work and to be left alone. But it left me feeling empty inside. A dead leaf drifting in the wind, devoid of emotion. I found little things scared me. I was scared of getting on a bus heading in the wrong direction. Terrified of being even one minute late for work. Sometimes I would put my head in my hands and cry for no reason at all. I was panicked by small noises. I jumped at the phone when it rang at work. I was suspicious and afraid of strangers. Nervous. Anxious. Panicky. "You can do it," I would chant to myself as my heart fluttered inside my chest. "You can do it. You can do it. You can do it." I was like a frightened little girl wearing women's clothes, pretending I felt comfortable in my new role.

The first six months of my new life was spent in the file room of the hospital, obeying all the rules and wanting to obey. Wanting to blend. Desperately needing acceptance. Every day, I was given a list of names and my job was to collect the files and take them to the various wards and departments who requested them. With the list of names in my hand, I wandered the isles picking out files for inpatients and depositing them back again once the patients were discharged. It was the perfect job for me. I didn't have to talk to anyone, and I was left alone to do my job.

Slowly I began to heal.

Then one day, while retrieving files in the G section, I came across my father's name. Ernest Joseph Rudolph Gourgaud. The bold lettering of his name fairly jumped out at me.

I reached in and pulled the file out slowly, glancing nervously over my shoulder to see if anyone was watching me.

I must have stood for two or three minutes with the file in my hand, just holding it and reading the name over and over, surprised I'd never thought to do this before now. Should I open it and read it? Was he in the hospital…now? Would he even recognise me if I ventured up to his ward?

Anger suddenly took hold of me. It gripped my heart like a vice. Of course I wouldn't open it and I certainly wouldn't go to his ward and visit him. He couldn't spare the time to visit me when I needed him most so why would I visit him now? He could rot up there for all I cared.

I shoved the file back into its place and stormed off to do my job.

Of course, looking back now, I regret not opening it. But every day spent at the Andersons flashed before me as I held his file in my hand. It was anger and frustration driving me. It was pain and hurt and the feeling of abandonment all rolled into one. And of course, there was my intense love for him that he hadn't bothered to return.

* * *

AFTER THE OBLIGATORY six months in the file room, I found myself promoted to Ward Secretary in Ward 12/13, the Chest Ward, the exact ward where I had played outside years ago while visiting my father.

I remember looking around the grounds, reliving the nights sitting on the grass with the toads. Those times had seemed so happy and I remembered with a heavy heart all the hugs and kisses my father had given me, once upon a time.

Why had he deserted me? What had I done to make him not want me anymore, just like my mother?

I remembered how tall he seemed to me and how blue his eyes were, the concave part of his back where his left lung had been removed and the hat he always wore whenever he had come to visit me.

God, I'd loved him so much. To this day, his resemblance to Humphrey

Bogart, with his hat perched jauntily on his head, sends a sharp pang through my heart.

My recovery was slow, and I sometimes thought it would never be complete. Even though my life was vastly different now, my inbuilt shyness made it difficult for me to make friends. At first, no one spoke to me. I didn't know what to say to them anyway. Eventually, they started to ask questions, wanting to know about me. *How could I open up and tell anyone about my life?* I thought. Besides that, I thought no one would have believed me anyway. And I certainly didn't want anyone's pity or sympathy. I was trying to move on from all of that. So in the end, I kept to myself.

Eventually I was able to move on although I still couldn't stand anyone touching me, not even brushing past me in the corridor. I would press my back against the wall, my heart hammering in my chest, as they walked past, sometimes glancing sideways at me.

I was asked out occasionally in the beginning, but the offers soon stopped after I overheard a young man commenting to another one that I was, "Too quiet. A cold fish."

His words brought a sharp pain to my chest and a lump to my throat. My pride had felt a twinge of hurt, but I said nothing. After all, that's what I'd been told to do by the nuns. *Don't rock the boat.* But I wanted to scream as loud as I could, "I am NOT a cold fish! I was pushed to the limit and I survived!"

If I'd had the courage, I would have cried out that everyone deals with unimaginable pain in their own way, and everyone is entitled to that. He would not want to endure what I have endured. While he sees me sitting quietly and coldly, looking like a calm ocean on a sunny day, I wanted him to know that while the ocean may seem calm, in another place in the very same ocean, there is a colossal storm. If I'd been brave enough, I would have told him my trauma was valid. Even if it happened a year ago. Even if it had happened many years ago. Even if no one knew at all. I was simply struggling with the magnitude of it all, processing and trying to unload some of the pain I carried. And I was allowed to do that! Nothing and no one should take that away from me because they thought I was a 'cold fish.' I had endured. I was lost but there I stood, still moving forward, growing stronger every day. I would never forget my past. The memory of it held me together and kept me moving, even though I felt like I was shattering. Like Humpty Dumpty. Where all the kings horses and all the kings men couldn't put Humpty together again. That was me. Broken. Except I was healing and getting stronger.

Instead of saying all these things, I held back the tears and walked quietly away.

I tried imagining what it would feel like to feel normal. I would walk down the hospital corridors and people would stop and smile and ask, "How are you, Trish?" and they'd really mean it. They would ask me to go out in their group to dinner or someone's house and be so pleased when I said yes. I would be liked and sought after as their friend. I would *belong*.

They were lovely dreams. In reality, all I could manage was a quick nod, and then I would drop my head and walk on silently. My fear of men almost had me believing I had a vocation to be a nun. Then I remembered Sister Philomena and the thought disappeared in an instance. Instead, I worked and saved my money, choosing not to spend anything on my small flat, instead buying much-needed clothes.

For the first time, I could buy what I wanted. Probably a little foolishly, I followed the latest trends of the early 1970's and bought short dresses and high wedge shoes. Looking back now, I realise I actually bought many bad outfits. All of a sudden, I began to change again.

Maybe because the frilly underpants are such a powerful childhood memory for me, I started to think that femininity began in an outward way: girls dressed in girly dresses, played with dolls, brushed their hair and preened themselves while dreaming of knights in shining armour. The clear message to me was that girls should be elaborately fragile and doll-like.

So, I changed yet again, this time into what I imagined was a demure young lady. The complexity for me was that while I had once been inappropriately hostile, the frilly pants told me that I was supposed to be perfectly passive. Such is the power of memory. Now, I know that my ability to look at and feel good about myself lies embedded in my own early emotional truths.

And then I had my hair cut into a fashionable Farrah Fawcett style and I almost didn't recognise the new person that emerged in front of the mirror. Up until then, my hair had been in no particular style, just pulled back into the ponytail that I'd always wanted. It hung lifelessly down to my shoulders and the overall result hadn't been what I'd imagined at all.

My hair was now soft and feathered around my face, after the light perm I'd had, and it took my breath away. My mother's green eyes stared back at me and I could see a little of their long-forgotten sparkle shining through, although fear and disquiet still lingered in their depths. Like a deer caught in the headlights, I was held there by my own gaze, wondering if this person was really me. I had always believed that my nose was too large but as I looked at the transformed face before me, the softness of my hair seemed to minimise it. *Would this be the change I needed? Would I now find someone who would love, understand and accept me?*

On reflection, the new clothes that I bought were totally unsuitable for my job as the Ward Secretary of a heart and chest ward. But no one said anything to me. I can still remember clomping along the wooden veranda in my mini skirt and platform shoes, oblivious to everyone staring at me. I must have been regarded more as a health risk than a help to the poor old gentlemen who had been sent here to recuperate.

This became my awakening period. My transformation, if you want. I began to feel like a worthwhile person, to actually *believe* it for the first time in my life. Bad memories started to fade as my life opened up for me. It seemed so inconceivable, so impossible, that this could happen. But it did.

I loved my job. I loved everything about it. The independence, the security and especially being a part of a group and not alone any more. I discovered that if I wanted to talk to someone, I could. If I needed to be alone, that was no problem either and I couldn't remember being happier.

When I'd arrived at Nazareth House, I transformed from that happy little girl and I became someone else. Possibly not even someone else: a group of people in one body. I changed my personality so many times in the hope of being wanted, I didn't know who I was any more. But now, I was starting to find out.

As time went on, I grew more confident in myself and I started to change even more. The fire of my youth returned, and I now felt strong enough to say no to things that I had given in to for so many years. I was able to experience everything at my own pace. I thawed and learnt how to interact with other people while I grew and developed as a person.

I was eighteen when I met Rad. My first boyfriend. I guess I liked him enough, but trust? That would maybe come later, I thought. He was very charming and I was very needy. I needed to be wanted and loved so desperately.

When I first started to date him, I thought it would never come to anything serious. I was too short, reserved, and felt inadequate for stupid reasons. Breasts not big enough, nose too big, legs too skinny. But six months later, I jumped at his offer of marriage. I was far too young, but I believed I had found love, when what I really needed was to *be* loved. I remember feeling so grateful. He was so wonderful and good-looking, and he wanted me. ME. My own mother hadn't, why would anyone else?

I'd never eaten in an outdoor restaurant before or been away on a holiday. I'd never slept with a man. I did all three on my wedding night.

After my marriage, the next few years of my life seemed fairly normal. My previous life had been hard and chaotic. Now I had to work at making my new life, one that was full of peace and happiness.

Between the two of us, we had enough money saved for a deposit on a small house, in an average suburb, paying off a mortgage like so many other young couples. The only furniture we could afford was a double bed, a fridge, two beanbags, and a small black and white portable television sitting on a second-hand coffee table. All washing had to be either done by hand or up at the local laundromat. But we were happy. We both had jobs and life seemed pretty sweet. Over the next few years we saved for other items of furniture and my husband's family helped us as much as they could. These things were all new for me and I moved in a daze of happiness.

My husband's family were European and as was the custom in many Mediterranean families, the women's needs seemed to take a back seat to the men's wishes. It seemed that the women's sole purpose in life was to look after the men, almost as though the men were a different species from them. This virtual subservience didn't sit very well with my newly found independence and arguments popped up out of the blue more and more frequently. But still I was love-struck.

As my home life flourished, I made more friends at work, one very important friendship.

David was a hospital orderly working to pay for flying lessons when we met. His job was to bring patients down from the wards to have their X-rays taken. By that time, I'd had a promotion to Clerical Assistant Grade 3 and was working in the X-Ray Department. David had been one of my first friends at Greenslopes Hospital, one I needed desperately, and we'd clicked immediately. He made me and everyone else laugh. That was his great gift. And he liked me just for me. No ulterior motives.

I introduced him to a girlfriend and the four of us became great friends, going out at nights or evenings at home full of laughter and card games. Eventually, they married and after David joined the Air Force, they moved away to start a new life. It broke my heart to say goodbye to them.

Eventually, after many hints from my husband's parents, we decided to try for a family of our own. While I looked forward to the prospect of motherhood, I was also terrified by it. I would be totally responsible for a little baby. Totally. I hadn't so much as held a baby, let alone fed or changed one. I knew I could depend on my mother-in-law for help, but I couldn't rely on her for everything.

After five years of marriage and one miscarriage along the way, I finally fell pregnant again. I hadn't realised it would take me so long. Here I was trying desperately to have a baby while fifteen-year-old girls were having sex in the back of cars for the first time and falling pregnant straight away. Where was the logic or fairness in that?

Finally, on Friday, July 13th 1979, my eight-pound baby boy was born with bruises down one side of his face and his nose pushed out of shape from the difficult birth. I named him Mark and he was the most beautiful baby I had ever seen in my life. And he was mine.

He slept well and rarely cried and I found myself sitting for hours with him asleep on my chest, just so I could hold him longer. His early dark hair fell out at three months to leave him totally bald but very soon, a fine growth of white hair started to grow on his head. I knew his colouring came from me (his father was dark haired with an olive complexion) but I had no idea where our fair hair came from. Both my mother and father had almost black hair.

He never crawled but went straight to running at ten months old. How had my mother given me up after going through all the happiness of watching a baby grow? Before I knew it, he was three years old and I was pregnant again.

When a second boy arrived, my husband's family decided amongst themselves that this one should have a family name. An old uncle in Yugoslavia was called Tony so that would be the new baby's name.

Again, this baby was perfect, but he was so different from Mark it was hard to believe they were brothers. Mark still had his white-blond hair, light brown eyes and a gorgeous, mischievous grin while Tony had almost black hair, my green eyes and a 'melt your heart' smile.

I had stopped full-time work after the birth of Mark in order to raise my small family, working only part-time as a function hostess with a wine distributor until falling pregnant with Tony so things at home were starting to be more and more strained as we found it increasingly difficult to maintain our family on a single wage. When Tony was a one-year-old, I resumed part-time work as a waitress in a local restaurant chain, until after four years I felt my family could cope with my working part time again. Over the following three years, I rose through the ranks by working hard and completing a management course, until I was managing a branch on my own.

I loved this job despite the long hours. I found myself working most nights until midnight, oblivious to the effect it was having on my family. With both of my boys still in primary school, the reality of my commitment to work was brought home to me one night, when after awaking from a nightmare, Tony called out for his father instead of me.

I realised then that I had come full circle and had put my children in the same position I had been in when I was a child. I had always said that I would be 'there' for my children, but I had turned into a lousy mother, just like my own.

I could try to justify my reasons for working most nights. I was unskilled with little education. I was doing it for my family. We needed the money. All true, but the result was still the same. I had put myself ahead of them and was unknowingly pushing them away. In fifty years time, the type of car we drove or the amount of money in the bank wouldn't matter. But it would matter to my children that I was with them while they were growing up.

I resigned from my job the next day.

By then, I was no longer the unassuming, cowering wife who gave in to all arguments just to keep the peace and was strong enough to stand up for myself and what I believed in. Possibly because of this change, together with the long-term effects of too many nights working while my husband stayed at home minding the children, Rad and I finally agreed our marriage was over. Marriage at eighteen had seemed right at the time but we had definitely been too young, neither of us had had the chance to experience life before settling down with a family. In the early days of our marriage, my innocence had saved us. But after fifteen years, I had turned into a totally different person.

ALL I'D EVER WANTED

"What?" I asked Rad, dumbfounded. "My sister?"

"I know, Trish. I know. But that's what she said."

His voice sounded as shocked as mine.

I managed to calm myself even though my heart was hammering inside my chest. With those few words, everything came back. The pain. The loneliness. The years of cocooning myself so no one else could hurt me. I'd wanted a sister so desperately, but it wasn't true. Sister Philomena had told me that. It was a cruel lie invented to wound me at a time when I was so fragile and near to breaking.

"Rad," I whispered, suddenly exhausted. "You know my history. You know I called Sister Philomena and you know she said it wasn't true. You know this is not possible. I don't have a sister."

"I know, Trish," he repeated. "I told her that. But she was pretty insistent."

I took a deep breath to calm myself. "Look, thanks Rad. Really. Thanks. I appreciate you calling me first but can you do me a favour, please? Can you call her back and say she's mistaken? I don't know anyone by that name." *It's just not possible, I thought.* "Thanks for not giving her my number but please can you call her back and say something, anything, to get rid of her? I've just never heard of a Sandra Stewart."

There was silence for a few seconds before he finally spoke.

"She said you might say that," he said a little tentatively, "but Trish, she said to tell you that you might know her as Robyn."

I started shaking, shivering on this warm summer night. I could feel perspiration popping out on my top lip but I also felt cold and clammy. My chest was so tight, I could barely breathe. I spun around to put my back against the kitchen bench for support as my eyes filled with burning tears. As I turned, wine slopped over the top of the glass and spilt down the front of my top.

Rad continued. "Trish. She said she was thirty-eight and had been adopted at birth, but because her adoptive parents are both dead now, she decided to try and find her birth parents. When she received her original birth certificate, she found out that her parents' names were Ernest Joseph Gourgaud and Merle Rose Mooney and that she had a sister by the name of Patricia Gourgaud, aged four."

"Oh my God," I whispered as tears overflowed. "OH MY GOD!"

Robyn? Was it true? Had Sister Philomena lied all those years ago?

"I have her number, Trish."

I gulped in a few breaths before stuttering, "Oh. Yes. Hang on. Let me get a pen."

I fumbled around in my junk draw, the third one down, and found a pad and a pen.

I wiped the tears away from my eyes with the back of my hand. "Okay. Go ahead."

I wrote the phone number down and thanked him, shakily taking more deep breaths. I was nervous, confused, excited and scared all at once.

After all these years, was it possible? How the hell could this be happening?

"Are you all right, Mum?" Mark called out to me. Both boys had turned around on the lounge and were watching me.

"You're not going to believe this, guys," I said to both of them, not quite believing it myself. "Your father just had a phone call from a woman who says she's my sister. How about that?" I said in a tremulous voice.

Both boys looked at me in amazement. The only comment was from Mark. "Cool."

Wild eyes gazed back at me from the reflection in the kitchen window as one word repeated itself over and over in my mind. *Robyn. Robyn? ROBYN!*

Eventually I turned towards the phone on the wall. It took my shaking fingers three attempts to dial the correct number, but after a single ring a woman's tremulous voice answered. "Hello?"

Seconds ticked by in absolute silence as I sucked in ragged breaths, realising that I hadn't even thought of what I was going to say. My mouth had gone dry and my heart was pounding.

In the silence over the phone, I heard a tentative, "Trish?"

That single word was all I needed to start tears streaming down my cheeks again, and with a lump the size of an orange in my throat all I could croak out was, "Yes…Oh God…Yes." I sobbed as I said, "You just don't know how much this means to me."

"Did you know about me?" she asked. I could hear her crying softly as well. "Is it really true?"

"I think so. Yes. At least, I hope so. I tried to find you years ago, but everyone said that you didn't exist. I can't believe this!" I choked out the words. "Please, you talk, I can't. I'm sorry." As I babbled, I was searching for the tissue box. "How did you find me?" That was all I could manage to say.

"God, I don't know where to start. Okay. When I was twelve years old, my father told me that I had been adopted. My mother died of cancer when I was four but my father died only a few months ago."

She took a deep breath before continuing. Struggling with the emotion in her voice she continued. "I went through all his things and Jill, she's my sister who was adopted as well, found her papers but I couldn't find mine. We looked everywhere but they weren't around. I guess it was then that I decided to try and find my real parents, more particularly, my mother."

She took a few shaky breaths. "I rang Children's Services and they sent out a booklet and a form to fill out so I could get my adoption records. They also sent a form that gave me the authority to get my original birth certificate."

I could hear how hard this was for her, so I simply said, "Please. Go on. I'm still here."

"Anyway," she started again, "these departments take forever to send you anything but eventually I received the authorisation form to take to the Registry Office. I'll never forget that day. I opened the letter and for the first time, I saw my parents' names. Ernest Joseph Gourgaud and Merle Rose Mooney. But not just that. It said that I had been named Robyn Ann and I had a sister by the name of Patricia Therese who had been four years old when I was adopted." She sniffled before continuing. "The paperwork said that both my parents were dead now, but you were alive."

My heart broke a little at the news that Mum and Dad were both dead. But what had I been hoping for? Dad had always been so sick. As for Mum. Excess alcohol does terrible things to your body and I knew that had been Mum's weakness.

"All I could do was to go outside and cry for ages," she sniffled. "When my partner came outside and asked if I was all right, I couldn't even talk. All I'd really wanted was a mother and now I had a sister."

Sounding a little more comfortable now that she was into familiar territory, she continued more confidently. "The next day, I went into the Registry Office to apply for my original birth certificate from the Births, Deaths and Marriages department. They don't just give it to you over the counter, did you know that?"

"No," I said. "I've never had to get one. Please, go on." I was greedy to know everything.

"Anyway, I went back the next day, which was Friday, to pick it up and sure enough, my birth name was Robyn Ann and your name was listed as a sibling on the certificate. On Sunday night, my partner and I were talking and wondering what nationality Gourgaud was, so we opened the phone book and there were three listings. He said to me, 'Why don't you ring? There's only three in the book and it's not a common name. Maybe it will be her.'" She gulped. "I was so nervous. I said to him, 'No, you ring for me.'"

She was talking so fast now I had to really concentrate so I didn't miss anything.

"He took the phone from me and I went outside. I didn't want to hear what was being said. I didn't want to know that this was just a mistake. When he came back, he said, 'I spoke to a woman and told her a quick version of the story. The name is French. Ring her back and see if they know anyone by the name of Patricia.'"

She sniffled again before continuing. "So I did. I wasn't sure what to say or how to start the conversation so when a woman answered, I just blurted out, 'Hi. My name is Sandra Stewart and my partner just rang up asking about the nationality of your name. I was adopted and I just got my birth certificate and I wanted to know if you know an Ernest Gourgaud?'"

"The first thing she said was 'Is that you Robyn?'"

Sandra started to cry again but between sniffles she said, "I couldn't help crying. Someone actually knew who I was. You know, everything was happening so fast."

She stopped to take another deep breath and collect herself. "She said her name was Paula and that Ernie was her father. That meant that she was my half-sister. Yours too. Did you know that?"

I had been listening with my mouth opened in amazement. I had no idea who Paula was. A half-sister?

"No, I didn't," I whispered. "If she knew about you, did she know about me?" I asked.

"Yes, she did. She mentioned something about going to the Exhibition with you when you were just a kid."

I gasped. "I remember that! I didn't know she was my sister, though. She was just someone who was there with Dad and me. She was there with her husband, or boyfriend, I think. Oh my God. That was Paula? She walked around with us all day and I had no idea who she was."

"Well, she knows you. Anyway, after getting my birth certificate, I had to go back to the Registry Office to try and find out if you were married and what your name was. Since your name was on my certificate, that was enough proof of identity for me to get your records. They only do searches in five-year slots and they charge you for every slot. I took a guess and I was right the first time. That was so lucky. The same guy served me again and he went out the back and came back with your married name. He said if I wanted your address, I could find it at the Electoral Office. He was really nice. I've been in there three times and he's served me every time. He knows as much as I do," she laughed.

"When was this?" I asked trying to get the time sequence straight in my mind.

"Today! Just today! As soon as I found you on the Electoral roll, I ran to the nearest phone in Queen Street Mall and phoned my partner. All I could say was, 'I found her! I've really found her!' I was so happy. Earlier tonight, we looked in the phone book again but I couldn't find your name, so I tried directory assistance and they said your number was unlisted. There were only a few people with your surname in the book, so I rang the first one. Your husband answered, well, your ex-husband answered. When I told him the story and asked if he knew you, he just asked, 'Who is this?'"

"I had to go through everything all over again from the start. I finished by telling him my name was Sandra Stewart, but he was reluctant to give me your number. When I said that you might know me as Robyn, there was a long silence before he said, 'I'm her ex-husband. I'll give Trish a call and see if she wants to talk to you.' I'm so glad you rang."

"I just can't believe it. I have to see you. Where do you live?"

"I live at Mt Warren Park, in Beenleigh," she said.

That was only half an hour away from me, but I would have driven to the moon to see her in any case.

Amazed at the closeness of her house, I asked, "How long have you lived there?"

"I've lived in Brisbane most of my life," she replied.

Glancing up at the clock on the wall, and trying not to push too hard, I asked, "Can I come now? It's only 8 o'clock. Would you mind if I came right now?"

"Yeah, sure," she said nervously. "I don't mind. You know, you can come tomorrow if you want to." She sounded tentative but that was understandable. I was feeling nervous myself.

"I want to come now, if that's all right." I had to see her. I'd waited twenty-five years for this moment. I didn't want to wait any longer.

She gave me the address and I hung up.

I turned to the boys and said, "Guys, I'm going to see her now. Can I trust you two not to kill each other while I'm out? I'll be back as soon as I can. Don't wait up. I'll tell you all about it tomorrow morning."

I ran into my bedroom and quickly changed out of my work clothes. I didn't have time for a shower, so I sprayed some perfume over my clothes. I ran to the front door and yelled out, "Bye" as I grabbed my bag and keys off the table near the door. My tiredness had totally disappeared.

Unmoved in any way by tonight's events, Oscar was still blocking the busiest thoroughfare in the house. As I stepped over him, I said, "What do you think about that, Ossie? You've got an aunty."

He barely lifted his head as he tried to focus on me with his crossed eyes.

I scratched him behind an ear. "Don't get too excited, sweetie. It's not good for you,"

And then I was gone.

THE DARK YEARS

The inconvenience of nightfall was lost on me as I sped along the freeway towards Mount Warren Park.

Is all this really happening? kept echoing over and over in my head. I'd wanted something like this to happen for so long, but I'd basically given up looking. Now it had come out of the blue.

It had been almost twenty years since I'd last spoken to Sister Philomena. Seven thousand three hundred days. Plenty of time for wounds to heal, you'd think. But I've come to realise that even emotional wounds need to be dressed and attended to. After hearing her voice, restless ghosts walked around in my head clanking their chains. Over the years, recollections of the orphanage have become fewer and fewer but still, occasionally when my mind is idle, memory bubbles from those days slowly rise to the top before I have time to burst them.

In all those years, not a day had gone by when I wasn't wishing that she had made a mistake and I did, after all, have a sister. Since that phone call, my life drifted on through good times and bad. I finally became strong enough to date. I married Rad, happy to think that *someone* wanted me, but fifteen years later, the marriage collapsed and once again, I found myself lonely. I still had my two boys, but what I craved was adult companionship.

As I sped along the freeway, dark memories juggled with each other to the surface.

* * *

My main objective in life after the divorce was to put my past behind me and forge on to a better future. I was determined this was going to be *my* time. A time to find myself. I had allowed my life to be like a Ferris wheel, full of ups and downs, so at thirty-five I was determined to make a fresh start. I wanted to do something with my life although I had no idea what that 'something' was. Most of the time, my life felt like a dream but not one from which I would awaken gently.

Don't rush into anything, everyone told me. *Have time by yourself,* they all said. What is it that makes you think you're smarter than everyone else? That you know more than all of them combined? I know now I should have listened to them, but hindsight is a wonderful thing. Somehow, I believed everything would be all right. And yet...

The 'and yets' of life are what slow us down. A wild rabbit casually grazes on clumps of grass by the side of a road and yet you hear rustling among the leaves and ferns as if it's not alone. People seem happy and open, and yet sometimes we have a feeling they're only wearing masks and that deep down a lot of them feel as lost as we do.

Soon after the divorce, I found a job and the boys and I moved into a house in the Redlands, an area of Brisbane like many others, standing guard between Moreton Bay and the city. A sentry almost. There was no mystery or excitement in my new home, just the security I needed.

Within months of the divorce, I realised I was doing my chameleon act again. Trying to change my personality, I laughed too hard at jokes when I really didn't see anything funny at all. I changed my appearance and tried to show the world, *See. This is the new me,* even though I had no idea who 'me' really was. I wanted to be outgoing and bubbly, but I had no idea where or how to start. I felt depressingly ordinary and inadequate. For thirty-five years, I had a miserable tally of assets.

On the night I met Michael, I was poised exactly between the things of life I wanted to do and the things I needed to do, and I was hoping like hell they were the same. It seemed logical for me to assume that by now the odds would be stacked in my favour. Surely, it was *my* turn. After two drinks that night I truly believed that. You see, I thought I understood the nature of evil.

You'd think I'd have known better.

It was during the drinks at the end of the conference that a manager I vaguely knew came over to me.

"I have a friend who'd like to meet you."

That was it. No build up. No talk about how this friend thought I was so attractive. No flattery at all, just he'd like to meet me.

He pointed Michael out to me and still I wasn't impressed. Michael was sitting in a booth by himself nursing a drink, an almost sullen look on his face.

"I don't think so, Miles."

The party was in full swing by now and I hadn't even had a chance to get around to all the people I already knew. I was in a great mood and his friend's dark, surly James Dean look has never really appealed to me.

"Yeah," he said, swaying a little on his feet. "I told him you'd think you were too good for him."

"What?" I was flabbergasted. The statement was ridiculous. But then, hadn't I heard others I worked with say that they thought I was a snob in the beginning? They'd had no idea that it was shyness, not snobbery, which made me keep to myself.

Faces swam around me, people I didn't know and some I'd *never* know. All of my life, because of those five years in the orphanage, I'd been closed up like a locked door, which hadn't helped my fifteen-year marriage. Happiness and contentment seemed a forbidden world to me at this stage.

"Make a liar of me and have a drink with him."

Miles hiccupped and staggered away leaving me standing by myself. I peered through the mass of people. Michael was still sitting by himself.

It's not like Michael was so strikingly handsome or that he stood out in the crowd, because he didn't. To tell the truth, I hadn't even noticed him until Miles pointed him out. Even then I wasn't impressed.

Most of us are only aware of the superficial aspects of another's behaviour. We see the polite part, the public part, and may not give a thought to what exists beneath. If the surface is conventional, we assume the rest is the same. And even though Michael looked moody, he also seemed conventional. He had almost black hair, he was a little too thin for my liking and his nose had a little bend in the middle that hinted it had been broken at some time in his life. But he looked, well, *normal*.

Recently, I've read that eyes are the window to the soul and if I'd known that back then, when I looked into his eyes that never quite looked at anyone else's, I would never have walked through hell for a year and a half.

'If only' comes to mind as I write this account. If only I hadn't stayed for those drinks after the meeting. If only I'd stopped at *two* drinks and gone home. Or if only I'd had one *extra* drink, I'd have been puking it up in the ladies and I'd never have walked over to sit with him at all.

Sometimes, even now, I dream of that moment. Of what would have happened if I'd decided not to go over to his table. And sometimes in my dreams, I do actually walk out of the party to my car, and then, if I'm lucky, I don't wake up screaming.

But, oh no! Fate had to step in and sit Michael in a booth and then send his friend over to bait me. And then I had to walk over to Michael and sit down to talk to him.

Even then, I was unimpressed.

So why did I give him my phone number, you may ask? To this day, I don't know. Maybe I thought I could change that surly expression on his face to a smile. It was a challenge, I suppose. And I love challenges.

And so I tumbled headlong into the void that was Michael. Twelve months later, I was to remember that night as the start of my downward slide into pain.

THE REVELATION

"And where have you been?"

My tone had been playful. I wasn't afraid of him at that stage. In those days, I didn't go over his every word in my mind looking for hidden nuances. I didn't analyse everything he said for fear of him turning what I said into a roaring argument. We'd only been seeing each other for a couple of months, after all. We hadn't developed a strong bond of friendship yet, but he was flatteringly attentive, and I was needy.

What is it that psychologists say? There are none so vulnerable as those who want to be loved? I guess you could say I was on my way to being happy even though we were an odd couple, Michael and me. He was intense and serious. I was always trying to please and understand everyone – the right, the wrong, the good, the bad, the cruel, and the selfish. He saw everything in black and white, the absolute, and judged quickly. I was prone to colours and shades and sometimes didn't judge at all.

When he didn't answer me straight away, I turned and looked into his eyes and my smile disappeared. His dark eyes shone with anger, his face was pale and pinched. His hands clenched and unclenched at his sides.

How do you describe someone who looks less than human, even deadly?

Later on, I blamed myself for his violence and angry outbursts. Don't we all? I made myself believe that I deserved it, that I had created this series of events, inexorable as an avalanche. Somehow it was *me* who fuelled his anger until he exploded. Something in *me*, not him. Something in *my* past that made me question anything and anyone who showed me even the slightest bit of affection. So yes, I deserved what I got.

All garbage, of course. Real victim mentality. It's obvious to me now as I think back. But I'm not stupid so I don't know why I didn't see what was coming in the future or why the alarm bells in my head weren't ringing like crazy.

I remember stepping back in surprise, almost expecting his hands to fly out at me although he'd never done anything like that before to me. My hand flew to my chest and I whispered, "What's wrong?"

In a second, he crossed the space between us and brought his face so close to mine I could feel his breath moving the fringe of hair on my forehead as I blinked rapidly.

As he leant towards me, the room suddenly darkened and I glanced over towards the door seeing storm clouds drifting and colliding across the darkening sky. An omen of what was to come, I would say, as I think back.

His eyes darted to his right as if to see what I'd looked at but then swung back. His gaze held mine again. For a moment, I thought he was going to tell me he'd lost his job or someone had run into the back of his car. Something like that. But the look of contempt on his face astounded me. Almost evil.

Far-fetched? Maybe. But I don't know how to describe that moment. I knew instantly he was someone I couldn't reason with. A predator almost. Someone whose mind was incapable of normal human emotion. And this made him dangerous.

But I'm racing ahead of myself because this feeling was so fleeting. It was there one second and gone the next. All I was aware of was that something had changed this man I thought I knew into.... I don't know. A stranger. An alien. It was enough for me to hold my breath while he spoke.

"Don't you EVER talk to me like that again."

Spittle sprayed from his mouth. I could see droplets moving slowly in the air, almost suspended, as they made their way towards my face.

"Don't you DARE treat me like one of your bloody children!"

I could see the muscles rigid with anger beneath his shirt and as I looked at him, I saw him as if in a negative of a film where everything was the same but different. I knew this man, but I didn't. The essence of who I thought him to be had disappeared becoming this malevolent substitute.

Something, an instinct, told me not to answer him. What would I have said anyway? I forced myself to look away, *tore* my eyes away, back to the dishes I'd been washing, only then realising that I'd been holding my breath. I could feel the anger emanating from him in waves, it took all of my strength not to run from him and put a locked door between us. But not with my two children sitting quietly in the lounge room watching The Simpsons. And at this stage, I had nothing to base my fears on except this sudden urge to flee. Nothing concrete. He'd never hurt me before.

I always try to lighten tense moments. I hate tension, always have, so I was tempted to turn around and force a smile on my face and punch him lightly on the arm while saying something witty or silly. Something to make his anger leave. But what to say to someone who was barely holding himself together? I couldn't even trust my voice to come out in anything except a croak indicating my fear.

So, fighting to keep my voice even, I said, "We've already eaten but I have leftovers if you'd like some." Sweet as honey. The heroine in a movie. A real convent girl.

He didn't answer for a moment but in my peripheral vision, I saw his shoulders slump as he stared broodily at my right shoulder. I wanted to ask if he was alright, even began rehearsing how I would start and began to play a little scene over in my mind, when he suddenly turned and walked away, heading towards the bathroom.

"Hey," I turned around and managed to say to his back. "Do you want a glass of wine?"

I kept my voice soft. I wanted to know what had caused this extreme reaction but decided not to push it. I didn't want to know what minor mishap had changed him into this *being*. It was easier to just blame myself for pushing him in this direction. Easier to say it was my insensitive question at the end of a long day.

Unfortunately, low self-esteem has always been my driving force. I still had no sense of self-worth, which made me a sitting duck for anybody with a kind word. You probably know other women like that. Emotionally dependent. I had to be the agreeable one. Never the one to say no. Everyone had to like me. Don't rock the boat. I couldn't stand to be disliked. Instead, I was the one to adjust, to change. In actual fact, this was my weakness but instead, I saw it as my strength.

He gave the wall an abrupt nod and said in a strangely hollow voice, "Yeah," before slowly undoing his tie and turning back to me.

"What happened?" I wanted to ask but changed my mind. Instead I nodded. "OK" was all I said. Then, "How was your day?"

"Fucking DROP it, will you!" he snapped.

His outburst made me jump, in surprise not fear.

"All right," I muttered, halfway between conciliatory and annoyance. "I was only asking."

"Then don't, you stupid......" His voice choked off as he snatched up his tie and stormed out of the house onto the veranda.

What would my life have been like if I hadn't been stupid enough to run after him? But if I began thinking like that, I'd never go out of my house again. So of course, I went after him. I even caught up to him and grabbed his arm.

"Michael, please. Talk to me. What have I done wrong? What's happened?"

Then he did a scary thing. He slowly turned to me and began jabbing me, about five times, in the chest. It's amazing how much just one finger can hurt. If done hard enough, each jab leaves little round bruises between your breasts for days afterwards.

With each jab, he said, "Go (jab) away (jab) and leave (jab) me (jab) alone (jab)."

His mouth was set in a rigid line as he stared down at the five angry red circles on my chest.

I pushed his hand away and found the courage to yell, "*You* go away. Go on. Leave!"

His eyes jerked up and he looked at me, all anger suddenly gone. They seemed to glaze over and became blank and staring. At first no sound came out but then he murmured, "I'm sorry. I'm not good enough for you. I don't deserve you."

Before I could say a word, he crossed over to an outdoor table and chairs set up in the corner of the veranda and sat down without inspecting the seat first to see if the cat was asleep there. His hands hung between his legs and his head dropped forward forlornly, chin on chest.

What was I to do after a statement like that? I glanced over towards the door to see if my boys had heard the commotion. Nothing.

It's odd, I suppose, when I think back over all that happened at that terrible time, little unconnected memories are the first things that come to mind. I remember the almost inaudible creak of the wooden swing in the yard. The maple tree in my front yard dropping its fiery red leaves on my front lawn. Thousands of tiny sand flies hovering around the outside light like a grey cloud. I remember it had been a long, beautiful summer and it was only weeks away from what was officially winter. But in the mornings, the sun still had a gentle warmth even if the sea breeze had picked up the oncoming chill.

I turned back to him. He was staring off into the distance, the whites of his eyes shining in the half-darkness, taking no notice of me. All I could hear was the buzzing of mosquitoes and my heart beating. He'd lost more weight of late and the shadows gave his face a corpselike look. He opened his mouth but all I could see was darkness.

"Are you going to tell me what's wrong?"

I said the words more bravely than I felt. I was anxious for him to leave but I wanted him to justify his outburst to me. I waited but he was silent.

"Michael?" I repeated.

"We used to play together all the time," he began. "When it snowed, our mother would collapse cardboard boxes and place them on the ground, and we would imagine we were on sleds."

He'd never told me anything about his childhood back in England always saying that it was history and to concentrate on the future. These two sentences told me he had a sibling, a sister or a brother, I wasn't sure which.

If the roof had suddenly fallen in, I doubt if he would have noticed. In the warmth of April in Brisbane, I shivered a little and told myself it was the oncoming rain. Michael's story had made him oblivious to his surroundings and I had no want to stop him talking. His tone was flat and his body motionless.

"One day, after a particularly heavy downfall, we were told that we wouldn't be going to school, it was closed because of the snow, and we were to stay inside and play quietly. I wanted to go outside and play, desperately wanted to, but I sulked in my room instead, while Thomas stayed in his."

He glanced up at me briefly, then looked down at his hands. "Thomas was two years older than me, nine years old at the time, and he was my hero. If he said the sky was green, I would have believed him. He was the favourite. I thought so anyway. He always got the new clothes and I always got his hand-me-downs. Mother always laughed at his antics while mine always ended up breaking something. He always got a terrific report card while I struggled to pass most subjects. But I loved him."

He sighed deeply. "This day, I looked out of my window, down towards the front step that led onto the footpath and the road beyond. And there he was, sitting on a sheet of cardboard in the snow while I was sitting in my room. It sounds silly now, but when you're seven, seeing this unfairness especially when you've been longing to do just that all day long, sent me into a temper. I ran to my closet and took my own cardboard sheet out, panting with anger. I ran all the way down the stairs and flung open the front door. I stood there for a few seconds to see if he had the gall to turn around and apologise for excluding me, scared to go outside because I'd been told not to, but determined not to miss out on any of the fun either. I could see snow covering the steps so that their shape was gone, and in my imagination, it looked like a ski-slope. Thomas was sitting on his sheet of cardboard but at the sound of the door opening, he turned around and smiled at me. Anger filled me. I turned and shrugged on my coat, then ran outside to put my cardboard down behind him. As I sat down, I kicked his back with all of my might."

His chest shuddered. "The pressure of my feet plus the smooth surface of snow sent him down the steps, out of control. He reached the bottom but continued onwards across the slippery footpath and onto the road."

I gasped. I couldn't help it because I knew what was coming. I was mesmerised by his story. Michael, of course, didn't even register my reaction. He wasn't here. He was back thirty years ago when he was seven years old and about to relive an ordeal that he would never forget for the rest of his life.

"Thomas didn't see the car coming. He was concentrating on where he was going and holding onto the cardboard. But I saw the car. I saw the eyes of the driver open wide in alarm as Thomas flew out from the footpath into the path of his car. He had no chance of stopping, of course. None whatsoever. And neither did Thomas."

Michael sighed and shifted uncomfortably in his seat as if to indicate that the story was over.

"I nearly killed my brother that day. Thomas was in hospital for twelve months after that and he has never walked since." He stood up and sighed again. "And I was sent to boarding school at the end of the school term for the next eleven years. Thomas hasn't spoken to me since."

He glanced over at me. "Today is his birthday. I had to make you understand, but it's not easy." He sighed. "You're so formidable, you know. Aloof and arrogant."

Me? I gaped in shocked at his picture of me. I knew I was secretive. That was my nature. But arrogant? Never! Aloof? Perhaps. Reserved, yes. Sometimes weary, tired of insincerity and triviality and unwitting cruelty which was a throwback to my days with foster parents. Definitely. But he'd seen me as something else. Cold. And that wasn't me at all. Defensive was probably more like it.

Why should I care what he thought, you ask? After all, I'd only just started seeing him. Now, all these years later I have the luxury of saying *'If only I'd been like Rhett Butler'*. If only I hadn't given a damn, I'd have saved myself a lot of pain and sorrow in the future. But I didn't want to be hard. I didn't want to be encased in an impervious shell and I didn't want to be arrogant.

"You've never been afraid that everything could come apart," he continued.

I sucked in the air through my mouth.

Never been afraid.

I didn't look at him. I wasn't seeing him. I was seeing myself as an eight-year-old, abandoned and feeling so disposable, as my father sadly walked away from me, leaving me once more in the hands of the nuns at Nazareth House.

Never been afraid.

I was feeling the emptiness that enveloped me, cold as a shroud, when I realised I'd never see my mother again. I was too young to remember much about her before she abandoned me to the nun's care in the orphanage, so she remains an odd, shadowy collection of smells and impressions. In my teens, I used to search the crowds hoping to catch a glimpse of someone I thought looked like her, something that looked familiar in a stranger's face. Those moments soon passed but I remember the fear when I realised she was lost to me.

Never been afraid.

I breathed out slowly between pursed lips in the shape of an O.

We faced each other, each of us quite alone.

"I know how it feels to be afraid," I whispered softly. Yes, I knew. I knew how it felt when life was like a small boat caught in huge waves and everything on the deck slips and slides. I knew what it felt like to be just one scared child among fifty others crying out for attention, love and acceptance.

"Now you know my big secret," he sighed. "A conversation stopper, wouldn't you say?"

There was utter desolation in his voice; it almost broke my heart to see someone else in so much pain. And it was a link we shared. We were both broken.

So, I walked over to him and put my arms around him. "Oh Michael," I whispered. "Oh Michael."

The next morning before leaving for work, I called his flat but there was no answer. I admit I was disappointed, and a little resentful that he wasn't there waiting for my call when I was so caught up in this new role of friend and confidante.

I let it go another day then called again, frustrated that I couldn't contact him and he hadn't thought to contact me. *Maybe he was busy*, I thought, *and just didn't have the time to call me. If that was the case, I reasoned, I should be pleased that he'd managed to forget the ordeal he'd told me about and begun to repair his life.*

I *should* have been pleased, but instead I found myself being a little offended. What did that say about me? Was I self-centred? Was I clingy? I didn't think so, but then again not many of us are aware of our own faults, are we? If we were, we'd try to fix them.

What I *did* feel was that we were both damaged goods. I had always thought *I* was the vulnerable one but here was someone else who was just as susceptible to bruising as I was.

I sat and brooded the next night, willing the phone to ring and finally thinking, *'Blow it'*, and went to bed.

The next day dawned clear with bright sunshine filtering through the trees that only yesterday had shown signs of the coming winter. I lifted my face to the sunshine and relished its warmth that was calming and soothing. *The day could be anything you wanted it to be*, I thought. *Anything is possible.* The air smelled fresh and my mood lightened considerably despite what I regarded was an obvious snub from Michael.

I had an easy run to work that day. Every day it seemed, unremitting roadworks spurred on by an up and coming election created hellish traffic as a result. This month it was storm-water drains just in time for the dry season. Usually, smug men in luminous yellow vests, one man working while five others stood around watching, seemingly oblivious as the traffic formed and idled in bumper-nudging intimacy.

Whether it was because the inevitable road works had been completed or because the workers had all decided on an early coffee break, I had no idea. I was simply grateful for the respite that morning and sat on 75kms/hour the whole way.

Michael called me that day and the horror commenced.

THE FIRST TIME

"Talk to me, Michael."

We were on our way back from a friend's place - Lewis and Sue's – and my ex-husband had my boys for the weekend.

Sue was one of the few people I call a close friend. We gravitated towards each other years ago through a mutual friend and because we were both shy, we immediately bonded. During my divorce, we became closer and this was to be the first time she and her husband were to meet Michael after three months of us seeing each other. It wasn't a great start to the evening because he wasn't keen on going in the first place and it added tension between us before the night even began.

"They're *your* friends, not mine or even *ours*," he argued petulantly before we left. "And tell me, do you always dress like this?" He looked me up and down condescendingly. "Is it because you're disinterested in fashion or is it because you've just got no taste?"

There it was. The classic sign.

What was wrong with what I was wearing? I remember asking myself. I was wearing a pair of designer jeans and a black cashmere pullover with knee high boots and I thought the contrast of the dark material against my blonde hair made me look almost pretty. As I talked to him, the cloth began to feel scratchy and prickly against my skin. Why was it that everything I did went wrong even when I tried to do what was right? Michael always made me feel so inept and unsure. Unsure of how I lived my life. Unsure of myself. Too fearful and then not fearful enough. Everything.

If I'd only taken notice of that first sign, everything would have been different that night. Actually, I *had* seen the sign, but I didn't put it in the right category and when I did, it was too late. I had allowed him to be fully ensconced in my life by then, like some tick under my skin or a mosquito in my ear, and I was beginning to accept his criticisms, no matter how petty or unfair.

Before we even left to go to the party, my stomach had become an instant knot of trepidation because I had no wish to be embarrassed by trying to placate my sulky new partner even if it was at my oldest friend's house.

"But they could be our friends," I persisted; dismissing his caustic remark and wondering who *his* friends actually were because I never saw any. "I've wanted you to meet them for weeks. I want my friends to be yours and vice versa."

"So I can sit there and have them appraise me like a prize monkey?"

"They're not going to appraise you. It's a party, for goodness sake. You're being ridiculous."

It was one month past the *revelation* as I called it to myself, and we were still finding out things about each other. Every now and then, I'd tried bringing up the incident but he always brushed it aside saying it wasn't important.

Except it was. To me anyway. What happened that night created a presence between us, and I thought we needed to talk about it. It obviously still preyed on his mind from time to time like a slow release poison.

Later on, I blamed myself for what happened after the party, reasoning that I had handled it badly. I don't know why I couldn't leave well enough alone and I convinced myself that if I had, things would have been all right. It's only now that I realise his predisposition for violence was *his* problem not mine.

His head made a small darting turn to look at me after my 'ridiculous' statement, and the consoling smile that was rising on my lips disappeared when I saw the look in his eyes. It was enough to make me suck in a surprised breath until he spoke again.

"Don't treat me like an imbecile," he said quietly. Menacingly. I watched his jaw clench and unclench so I shut up and said nothing more on the subject. Somewhere in the recesses of my mind, I sensed that Michael, already angry, would neither listen nor believe me while he was in this mood.

"And what is it with you Australians anyway? Someone asks you to a barbeque and you take drinks, food, the lot. In England, you throw a party and it means just that. *You* throw the party. You don't expect it to be a BYO *everything*."

He was one of the few people I've known who, despite cloudless skies and brilliant sunshine, hated barbeques. While most people enjoy grabbing a bottle of wine and a bowl of salad to take to a friend's house for a sit-around-the-barbeque on any given day, Michael much preferred going to a pub and watching football on the television; rain, hail or shine.

I wanted to tell him to stop being so pathetic, to stop acting like a spoilt child but I couldn't quite bring myself to actually say those words. The thing was, even at this early stage, I was wary of this man, as unfortunately I've always been wary of men. I know it was apparent that he just didn't want to go, throwing a tantrum actually, but it didn't mean that I wasn't also aware of his open aggression. Despite my uncomfortable feeling, I shrugged and let his comments slide.

In spite of the shaky beginning, the night went well, or so I thought. Michael put on his James Dean persona again and said very little, but I put that down to first-meeting jitters. On the way home, his mood darkened more.

"Are you OK?" I asked, feeling quite light-headed and contented.

He just stared out the taxi window. I could see he was angry but I had no idea why.

"Michael?" I murmured quietly so that the taxi driver couldn't hear what was being said. "What's wrong?" I asked as I leaned towards him and touched his arm.

He mumbled something as he wrenched his arm away from me.

"Pardon?" I asked. There was no response. "I'm sorry. I didn't hear what you said."

He looked at me and I could see him trying to control his anger. "Nothing," he said between gritted teeth.

"Something's wrong," I stupidly persisted. "Have I done something wrong?"

Why didn't I just shut up?

"Don't tell me you don't know."

"But I don't. I really don't."

He stared at me with such contempt and I squirmed a little in my seat. He had this little habit of tilting his head to the side when he was considering what he would say. So, he gave me his tilt and said, "Crap," between clenched teeth before turning away again.

The word hung in the air like the sound of a slap and I could have sworn my scalp receded against my skull. Warning enough? Not for me.

I was shocked at the vehemence in his voice. All the words I had inside to compromise evaporated before they were spoken. I wasn't so drunk that I didn't know what I'd said or done. As far as I knew, I'd behaved well. I'd paid Michael attention all night, introducing him to whoever I knew. I'd included him in all the jokes told. I'd only had three drinks, so I was aware of everything that had happened. Michael wasn't Lewis's cup of tea but give Lewis his due, he gave Michael his best shot. Good food, lots of good wine and good company. What could have gone wrong?

He refused to talk to me so when the cab pulled up in front of my house, I asked, "Are you coming in or are you just going home?"

He got out of the cab and threw $10 on the front seat of the cab, half the fare I noticed, and walked towards my house.

Now I was starting to get angry and if it weren't for the cab driver, I would have yelled at him then and there. I handed the driver another $10 and thanked him before following Michael up the front stairs.

"What the hell's going on?" I shouted at him. I was more than a little piqued that he was treating my house like it was his own. I'd never been to his flat even though I'd hinted several times that I had no idea where he lived, so watching him walk confidently up to my front door really got my back up.

He stood back silently as I unlocked the front door, thanking God that it was my ex-husband's weekend to have the boys. I had no wish for them to see Michael in this mood.

I turned to face him. "Michael, this is mad. If I've done something wrong, just tell me."

He turned to me then with a look on his face that would be all too familiar to me in the coming months. Contempt with frightening anger.

"Are you stupid, or what?"

I could feel the anger building up inside me. "No, I don't think so," I said breathing slowing to control myself. "But if I've done something wrong, I'm sorry."

I waited for him to answer. I shrugged. Waited again.

"I hate being made a fool of," he said. "You made me feel unimportant in front of your friends."

I gaped at him. "I what? When did I do that?" I honestly didn't know.

His face twisted into the parody of a conversation. *"Michael doesn't work for the advertising firm anymore. He works for a company selling cleaning products now,"* he said in a falsetto voice mimicking mine.

Then the realisation dawned on me. I *had* said that, but it was a part of a much bigger conversation. We'd talked about how hard it was to find work these days if you didn't want to do shift work. I had found it hard to find decent work and having enough money to pay the bills was hard enough much less having any spare cash for luxuries.

I almost laughed. *That was it?*

"Oh come on. You've got to be joking. *That's* why you're angry? Everyone knows how tough it is to find work these days."

He said nothing. He just stared at me, his eyes deadpan.

"I'm sorry, Michael. I didn't mean it to be derogatory. I was just stating a fact. It may have come across as insensitive, but I meant nothing by it." I knew how hard it had been for him to make the transition from assistant manager to a low-grade salesman and maybe it was those three drinks that had made me relax my guard, but I honestly hadn't meant to hurt his feelings.

"I'll make us some coffee," I mumbled.

I felt bad for having upset him but at the same time I knew it wasn't anything that was too awful although as I walked into the kitchen and filled the jug with water, I began to remember with an uneasy feeling, snippets of the conversation that night.

Lewis to me "...remember the time when..."

Sue to Lewis "...you always were a show off..."

Me to Sue "...this trifle is marvellous..."

But not a word from, or to, Michael.

It was only then that I sensed him behind me as I pushed the 'on' button of the kettle and began to reach for two coffee mugs. Positive that he was coming over to make up, I half turned towards him with a smile on my face when I saw something flying towards me. I had no time to put my hands up to protect my face before something connected solidly with my cheekbone.

Pain exploded inside my head and I went down like a ton of bricks. I remember thinking I'd hit my head on the overhead cupboard as I put my hand out to stop myself from falling hard. Either that or something had fallen on top of my head. I even remember hearing the sounds of mosquitoes buzzing in the vortex around me, like an electrical short in the rain.

When I looked up through the haze of stars, I saw Michael looming over me. I put out my hand thinking he was there to help me up. And that's when he hit me again.

My lip burst like a ripe tomato and I felt pain in every cell of my brain. I have an idea I tried to move away from him and held my hands up to shield my face, and I think I shrieked in surprise. Brightness flooded my eyes and I realised he'd walked away because the brightness of the kitchen light was piercing my vision.

After the initial shock, I felt a terrible starkness that pierced and stabbed. I lay there for a while, my heart racing, not sure of what had happened.

It was the end. It had to be, I thought. I'd always vowed that if any man hit me, I'd end the relationship instantly. No questions. No apology. No turning back.

Even when I'd spoken those words to friends, I never really thought it would happen to me. I gave myself far too much credit than to start a relationship with someone who was capable of hurting me. If I met a man like that, I would know immediately what sort of man he was.

Except I hadn't. And there had been no warning except for that minor hint one month ago after his 'revelation'. This had come out of the blue with amazing suddenness. He had brought violence into my home and the result was shocking and devastating to me. What were the rules now?

I pulled myself up into a sitting position, a huge effort of will, tasting coppery blood inside my mouth. My face felt heavy and I ran my tongue over my teeth gingerly to see if any had been loosened. Everything seemed fine. I was lucky. Ha! Lucky!

I looked down at my pullover and saw blood from my lip. My head swam dizzyingly so I leant back against the cupboards feeling sick with every throb of pain inside my head. *Had he left?*

I strained my ears for sounds but could hear nothing. *Good. He's gone. He's saved me the trouble of telling him to leave.* Even as the words formed in my head, I knew I was too scared to actually say those words to him.

I dragged myself to my feet, grabbing a tea towel from the bench to catch any blood dripping from my mouth. Hunched over, I made my way to the bathroom and looked in the mirror. A dishevelled stranger with a split lip and a swollen cheek stared back at me. A cold compress would reduce the swelling on the side of my head, although I could see a bruise already forming, and the lip looked only a little worse than when I had a cold sore. I spat and noticed there was blood in my saliva.

I splashed water on my face gently and dried it gingerly, noticing that the bleeding had almost stopped. As I walked out of the bathroom, I heard a muffled sobbing from the veranda.

I was sure it was for my benefit and I should have been pleased to hear that sound. It should have made me stronger and more determined to face him, show him what he had done, and end it right then and there. But it didn't. What I felt was something deep inside me that said I couldn't walk away from someone who was so unhappy. A type of pity probably.

I walked outside and stood watching him for a moment. He was sitting in the same chair he had one month ago, in that very same position, head bent with his hands dangling between his legs. He looked up at me, stricken.

"Trish. Oh God. I'm sorry."

When I spoke, my voice was thick. "You hit me."

His shoulders shook in the darkness and I heard the sobs again. "How can you ever forgive me?"

"I don't know if I can." My voice had gained some semblance of control.

"I'm so sorry." I remember him saying each word clearly. I remember a lightning flash at that exact moment and waiting for the thunder to follow. I remember hearing the soft ping of raindrops on the tin roof. I remember everything.

He started to cry softly again. "I lost control. I thought everyone was making fun of me. It's not a good enough excuse, I know. I'm so ashamed of myself. I'll never do it again. I promise. I can't live without you, Trish."

So many of us complain that men run away from commitment, so to find one so utterly devoted was too good to be true. To have a relationship with someone who appeared to want no one but me signified that I might just have attained that female romantic ideal of getting and keeping her man even if the attention was overpowering. Like millions of other innocent girls throughout the last fifty years, when I hit puberty I fell in love with novels like Wuthering Heights, Rebecca and Gone with the Wind. I wanted to be someone just like Cathy out of Wuthering Heights, loved by men like Edgar and Heathcliff and live rather melodramatically ever after. Of course, being rich, beautiful and endlessly resourceful, not to mention triumphing over adversity, held my attention as well – and lots of stories have feisty heroines, didn't they? But what had special meaning to me was perhaps the proximity of love and passionate attachment to Cathy by the men in her life.

Women nearly always see the extent of men's passion for us, initially anyhow, as positive examples of female desirability and male devotion. We start out believing that this must be evidence of the perfect relationship. They cannot live without us. They want to be with us as much as possible. They have eyes for no one else or they cherish every part of our being.

And so I went over to him.

I know. Bloody idiot! What I didn't know at that stage was that apparent devotion is often really just there to disguise jealous possessiveness that could only lead to domineering, controlling violence and abuse. But the fool that I was went over and made mother-hen noises as if *he* was the one with blood all over his clothes and bees buzzing around inside *his* head. He cried and I felt sorry for him when I really only wanted someone to feel sorry for *me*.

What I should have been was angry. Angry that he had used me as his punching bag. Angry that he had such little regard for me. But instead, I doubted myself. I blamed myself for releasing this demon. Yet again.

"I'm not good enough for you," he whimpered. "I don't deserve you. I'm such a shit."

Deep inside I wanted to agree with him but seeing him so full of repentance, I was compelled to let it go. I didn't tell him it was all right, because it wasn't, but I foolishly thought this was a breakthrough for us. It was like someone softly calling 'Cathy' across the moors.

In a way, I thought that his explanation might be true in some way. Any explanation was better than nothing at all, so I grabbed it.

Maybe I had drunk too much. Maybe I had humiliated him and just couldn't remember. Rationalising, it's called. Making excuses for him was what it actually was. It was like I had two people in my head talking to me. One was saying, *'If you don't run, you're crazy.'* The other was saying *'Talk to him. Find out what caused his anger.'*

As I stood there looking down at him, pity was the only emotion that I had the energy to summon. So stupidly, I gave in.

It's amazing how wrong you can be. I'd actually turned into one of the stars from the soapies that I scoffed at for being foolish and blind.

THE WHIRLPOOL BEGINS

My life was changing and I remember expecting to see the world changing too.

Instead, the next day was like every other day. Everything was the same but now it was different and I didn't know how to bring it back to the way it had been only three months ago. I'd entered the relationship expecting it to develop healthily and I was surprised at where I found myself.

I've often wondered why I let things go as far as I did even though it wasn't anything I did consciously. I'd read horror stories of women who end up with burn scars, broken limbs and dead children and like everyone else in a situation like this, I thought, *'That'll never happen to me.'* But before you even realise it, you're a statistic with no way out that you can see, living in a nightmare. There isn't one day that goes by that I don't have the harsh taste of regret in my mouth.

At the time, I was so flattered that of all people, Michael chose *me* to tell his dreadful secret: a tragic accident with tragic consequences that he always blamed himself for. So I kept quiet about my own situation. I went through terrible agonies to keep the truth to myself and away from others because I didn't want the few friends I had seeing me as less than perfect.

Stupidly, I focused on what other people will think of *me* instead of focusing on Michael's lack of respect, even control.

I'd only been divorced for nine months by this time and here I was in a worse situation than I'd walked away from. I even imagined my friends putting two and two together and blaming me for the break-up of my marriage. And I didn't want to be like other single women: divorced and bitter. In the end, if you can believe it, it was easier to justify Michael's actions than to admit I'd made yet another mistake. After all, don't all the psychologists say that no one is born evil; they are simply moulded by their experiences?

I suppose shame kept me quiet although, as I look back now, I don't exactly know what it was I was ashamed of. Sometimes, too often perhaps, we refuse to put our fears into words because the words will make them concrete, inescapable and overwhelming. For some of us, the fear of naming also includes the fear that we will have to do something about the abuse once we admit it's happening. I don't remember being conscious of this, but I suspect it was there. Contemplating any kind of a change was frightening for me.

I felt confused most of the time. And Michael confused me. Most times, I didn't know what he was going to do next. Mostly, he was like everyone else, and then he'd do something perverse, like hiding my car keys for the fun of it and refusing to tell me where they were. I never had a sense of what he would do or why he would do it. I couldn't see how his sense of cause and effect operated. He was like the surface of a lake. Something was stirring underneath but I didn't know what.

It seemed easy to find myself in this situation but not so easy to find my way out again. I guess even at that stage, I realised that most people have no sympathy for a woman who stays with a man after several beatings and abuse and I didn't want to wear that label. After all, we don't live in some part of the world where woman's fathers sell them off to their husbands and where they have no way to survive on their own.

It seemed finding out *why* I let this happen was just as important as finding the fix and I made myself think seriously about it. Two things kept coming back. One was the message I received in the orphanage. We were brought up to be seen and not heard. They didn't allow us to have our own opinions or to make our own choices. Everyone else's feelings came first and, in any case, other people – especially the nuns – always knew better. Some version of this message was received and translated into the belief that if my feelings counted at all, they came last.

Not only did this have the potential to undermine my self-assurance, it made me feel as if I didn't exist at all. I was brought up without a sense of self-worth or individual identity, and without the skills or the confidence to make decisions, I was left without the means to stand up for myself. If I'd been able to just stand up once and voice my inner feelings about what I felt, then I might have been able to stand up to Michael.

The second thought that came to me was the circumstances of my marriage. Besides the fact that I'd married far too young without experiencing life in any shape or form, I also remembered my overwhelming emotion at that time as being one of surprise that someone, anyone, would actually want *me*. After all, no one else had, not even my parents. I remembered the many times I'd been delivered back to the orphanage by so many different foster parents who hadn't wanted me. So, to stop that pattern of being 'thrown back' yet again, I tried to mould myself to be what my husband wanted me to be. *Willing* myself to be the perfect wife. With no basis for comparison, I made myself subservient, obeying and unobtrusive yet aware of his every need. The problem with that, of course, is you lose sight of your own needs.

So how could someone like me act in such an uncharacteristic way and accept his dreadful behaviour? Because I thought it was *my* fault.

In the months that followed, I would sometimes lay awake listening to the moths hit themselves against the fly screen, annihilating their wings as they tried to reach the light. Why would they destroy themselves in order to fly towards a bright white orb that would kill them anyway? When I had those thoughts, I covered my head with my sheet because I didn't want to know the answer. I knew I was no better than those stupid moths.

Everything began to accelerate downhill after that party at Sue and Lewis's. Michael changed overnight, it seemed. His moods became an exhilaratingly high one day and an unhappy dangerous low the next. He began to riffle through my drawers, read my diary to know where I would be on any given day. I would have to tell him exactly where I had been when I was away from him. He even checked the mileage of my car after I'd used it. And then there was the amount of milk in his coffee, what I wore, how I did my hair, his impatience towards me and the amount of alcohol he drank. All utterly ludicrous reasons to assault anyone but those were the sort of excuses he used.

Why did I take it? Because I didn't know how to stop it, I suppose. And my pride wouldn't allow me to think of myself as abused because I wasn't the cowering type. I suppose it takes most women a long time to believe that someone they've chosen could turn out to be abusive. I found it hard to believe that something with so much potential could turn into *this*. Such an immensity of difference. It was like standing in a desert without shade while the hot sun beats down on you. How could it once have been an oasis?

But I knew I was in trouble. *That* I *did* know. I had already begun to alienate most of my friends and there was no one to help me, so I learnt to know what set him off. I knew what subjects to avoid and I smiled to cover up the knots in my stomach. It was better to change myself than to fight the unfairness and suffer the consequences. I would do better next time. It's *my* fault.

It sometimes seems like our capacity for self-blame is limitless. Not only did I expect myself to be vigilant, if I slipped up even once, I blamed myself. As in a storm, I could sometimes feel the tension rising, building, and I began to read his moods and see warning signs appearing on the horizon: words, glances, intimidating gestures. Sensitive to these warning signs, I got very good at avoiding the oncoming onslaught by staying out of the way. Well, most of the time. Even peaceful situations turned so suddenly that sometimes I was left amazed by the abruptness of his change. One minute we'd be sitting quietly watching TV and the next he'd backhand me for simply talking during it.

So, as hard as I tried, I could never escape. I even began to believe that I was lucky to have anyone want me at all.

"You can't even keep your friends," he would say to me.

"But I *do* have friends," I cried back.

"You're mad if you believe that. So tell me, where are these so-called friends?" he'd ask.

On the tip of my tongue, I wanted to say, "I don't see them anymore because of you." It was the truth of course but I was wise enough to know what would happen if I spoke those words. The storm would arrive. So I said nothing. I agreed with him until I eventually began to believe him.

Then amazingly, he would smile brilliantly at me and say how wonderful I was. All the tell tale traces of his anger, his frown, his lips pressed tightly in a harsh line, disappeared and once again, pleasure transformed his face.

Don't gag when I tell you this, but he could sparkle when he wanted to. There would be glimpses of the happiness I yearned for, like a window being opened in a sweltering room and a puff of cool air blowing in. Patronising kindness followed his cruelty and left me doubting my own sanity. I would then begin to think I had imagined everything. That I really *was* going mad. Then, days later, lulled into thinking things had changed, I would turn and say something that would make him furious and the cycle would begin again. I remember thinking it would be wonderful to say something suddenly without testing it on my lips first, but if I tried harder and was more careful, everything would be all right.

He knew my vulnerable areas. He knew my boundaries and he picked away at the little confidence I had until I wasn't sure of anything anymore. It made me so dependent on him that I had to ask his opinion of everything and *that* eventually angered him as well because I was so ineffectual. I just couldn't win.

I regard myself as intelligent but why I stayed with Michael for twelve months when we had so very little in common, nine of those months were when he was hitting me, is the million-dollar question. And why was it that I protected and covered up for that violent man in my life?

The answers are complex and varied but none the less pathetic. My answer was I'd opened up the can of worms and let them out and it was my responsibility to put them back again. You see *I* was the wrong ingredient. The bad mushroom. Without me and with someone else, wouldn't he have been a happy well-balanced person? I can almost see you shaking your head in disbelief but as sorry as the reasoning was, it was true.

In the beginning, I never saw him as cruel or violent. I saw him as a victim of his past where every now and then he had to release the poisons inside him to survive. And outwardly there didn't seem to be anything hostile about him. The abuse crept in slowly and subtly.

With every passing day, I felt like I was walking on eggshells wondering whether today he would be *normal* or would he be sullen or irritable.

Manipulation can be subtle. It confuses you and can even make you doubt yourself and your own sanity. Things you say are twisted and then the mind games begin. You see the best way to control a person is to confuse them. Instead of giving you confidence in yourself, they take it away and make you doubt yourself. Control is the key word here.

Sue was the only one I ever mentioned my dilemma to. She would look at me disbelievingly and shake her head when I showed up with bruises.

"Michael the Moron?" She'd taken to calling him that after the first couple of times I turned up with bruises. Whenever she saw him, she looked as though she was riding in an aeroplane and it had hit an air pocket. "Get rid of him, why don't you," she'd say.

I used to ask myself the same question but after that first revelation of his, I don't know. I felt sorry for him and blamed myself for being callous and insensitive. I honestly thought it was my fault for not being what he needed or what he wanted me to be. It was *me* who'd brought this out in him and it was up to *me* to get rid of it.

I knew he was capable of a kind of tenderness and he was always sorry after he hit me (in the beginning, that is). But my emotions changed from day to day and nothing was ever black or white. It was the typical ambivalence of a survivor of domestic violence. They say love is blind, but it can also be pathetic. It reduces us to act like idiots or the sort of people who infuriate us in soapies as we sit back and shake our heads and say, 'What a fool!'

It's not that I didn't believe in love. I did. I longed to feel the 'pangs of love'. I just never had so far and in my mind I thought love was something that came eventually after getting to know the other person's faults as well as his good points.

And then came the straw that broke the camel's back.

BREAKING THE SPELL

It was a night like many others.

We were quietly watching an old black and white movie; Gregory Peck in some thriller, but the name escapes me. My boys were with their father, so I'd given in and gone to Michael's flat. I'd only been there a couple of times because I didn't really like it. Not because he didn't keep it clean, but it was something in me. I never felt relaxed or at ease there. I acted like a schoolgirl sitting in front of the principal – still and uncomfortable just waiting for the worst to happen. Probably subconsciously I felt safer at my house although it didn't seem to matter when or where Michael's rages began.

So there we were, sitting in front of the TV when suddenly he stood up and switched it off.

"Hey! Why'd you do that?" I asked.

"I'm tired and it's a crappy movie."

During the beginning of my 'Michael period', I had begun to censor myself. It got that bad. I'd begin to say something, let things slip out at times and instantly regretted it. I had to train myself to keep my mouth shut instead of speaking out loud. But I hated being careful of what I said and I didn't want to spend my life holding things back. It was this imbalance between saying what I wanted and keeping it bottled up that made me say, "No, it's not. It's a classic and I want to watch it."

He raised his can of beer to his mouth and watched me over the bottom of it while he drank, staring with a cold appraising gaze. Cats, both wild and domestic, watch their prey with unblinking regard, alert for the smallest variation in posture, the minutest shift of attention, ready to jump at any sign of weakness. He had that intensity.

Holding tight to my composure, I watched him with equal care. His narrowing eyes, his thick dark hair, his compressed mouth, that tic of his. There was no other emotion. No other reaction. Until he lifted his half-finished can and threw it at me. When I turned away, he grabbed my hair and yanked me back.

"I said it's crappy and we're going to bed."

Can you see what's coming? Yes, so could I. But by this stage, I'd been beaten and bullied so many times I'd be damned if I was going to trot demurely off to bed with him just because he could hit hard or because he didn't give a fig about my needs or opinions.

Fair enough? I thought so, too.

I'd been able to avoid the last few beatings he'd almost administered but not this one.

I won't go into the argument. I'll spare you the details because it was similar and as inevitable as all of the others. Suffice to say, I ended up with Michael hitting my head on top of the TV and mushing my face into the screen. When I opened my eyes, it was as if in slow motion. I saw his fist rise, then I felt the usual pain as it connected with my face, splitting my lips yet again. Then he walked away and went to bed leaving me on the floor dripping blood onto the carpet.

As I slumped on the floor quietly sobbing, I felt the usual sinking inevitability. But this time, something had changed. I thought of all the times he'd done this to me and all the times I'd excused him and forgiven him. I remembered all the vile names he'd called me and almost believed. But not anymore. The straw had finally broken the camel's back.

The thought leapt into my head that enough was enough and a surge of adrenalin energised me. Shakily I stood up, licking my lips and tasting blood, and reached out a hand to brace myself against the wall.

As I cleaned myself in the bathroom, I kept expecting him to come in at any time mumbling an apology or at least admonishing me for not wanting to go to bed with him earlier, hence the argument. But there was nothing.

I steadied myself before walking into his bedroom. There he was, sound asleep in bed, snoring softly. The first few times he'd been remorseful but now he was just indifferent to the pain he caused me.

I watched him sleep, expecting him to sit up and see what he'd done. I wanted him to, so I could see the look in his eyes as I told him I was leaving and not coming back. I felt strong enough to do that now.

But he kept sleeping peacefully.

I wondered how I had come to be this pathetic creature, trying to make right out of what was so wrong. How could this person be me? I was the one who was always so strong. Why had I left all my defences down? I felt like a child lost in a strange dream.

I remembered stories told to me in my childhood about the bogey-man. There was no such thing, I'd been told, and so he can't get you. But I knew better. Experience had taught me that the bogeyman *did* exist and he can get you at any time. He is not afraid of anything and he doesn't respect boundaries.

Gradually, I began to be realistic about Michael and me. Sure, there were highs and lows in every relationship, but the highs were becoming fewer and fewer and the lows were just plain soul-destroying. Like a flash I knew our relationship had been doomed from the start and that I actually hated him. It simply fuelled my resolve to walk away. I suppose up to now, what I felt was a strange kind of passivity at the results of his abuse. Like Olive Oyl on Prozac. But now I had to take action.

I picked up my bag weighing it in my hand to see if I could hit him with it hard enough while he slept. I clenched my hands and grit my teeth while I breathed heavily, and my heart pounded so hard I was sure he'd wake up.

I even thought of leaving him a note, but what would I say? Thank you for making the last twelve months of my life a misery? I will not miss the cruel words you utter to me about my mother being a whore and me not much better? I will not miss the tantrums and the weekly fights over nothing? In the end, I decided not to write anything at all. Without a word, I turned and left.

I felt like I was running clumsily, as though my legs were stuck in thick mud, dragging me down. Panic rushed through me. Against him, I had no chance at all. I stumbled, staggered, gasped and cried and I ran as quietly and quickly as I could to my car. I slowed momentarily as I glanced apprehensively behind me to see if he was coming: but I was safe.

Relieved, I picked up my pace again, seeing my car not twenty feet away. In seconds, I'd be there. Ten feet. Five.

I struggled to open the car door, and then sat quickly down pressing the nub to lock the car door down at the same time. I sat panting, half sobbing, trying to fight down the nausea in my stomach for several horrible moments while I fumbled for the key and tried to fit it into the tiny lock with trembling hands. I was in no fit state to drive but that was the last thing that I was thinking about. I don't believe I was thinking at all.

Relief mingled with a sense of loss. I'd wasted twelve months of my life, tried so hard and the result was no different than it would have been if I'd walked away from him the first night of the 'revelation'. All I'd managed to do was prolong the agony. But just as I'd done when I was fifteen, I took the opportunity to close off a period of my life that was like an open wound.

On the drive home, my lip throbbed and my head ached but I felt a soaring joy at my newfound resolve never to see him again. I was struck by a sense of realisation that I'd decided once and for all to move forward with my life and have nothing to do with Michael. It jolted me and filled me with excitement. I was going to walk away from him and leave him to sort out his own problems. I'd done it! I'd broken the spell I was under.

Working on these plans made me feel in control of my own life again, giving me a stronger sense of self. I wouldn't give in this time. I *wouldn't*. I could even visualise my new life. My children, happy and carefree again, not skittering out of the room like frightened crabs whenever Michael walked in. Socialising with friends again. Even just the pleasure of smiling once more. I'd been brainwashed and conditioned to think that I was of no value to anyone but by God, that was going to end! He'd damaged my self-image and esteem but not irrevocably.

Suddenly, I was alert like a subject who has been under a hypnotist's spell. I'd been speeding, letting my autopilot take me home. I lifted my feet off the accelerator and the car slowed down.

A TRAPPED ANIMAL

*I*magine being alone in a house at night and hearing a floorboard creak and a door softly opening. The mind at once interprets what it might be something benign. The wind or the house resettling. You wait for another sound. You hear the humming of the fridge, a clock ticking. Lists of alternatives run through your mind. If you feel scared, you imagine the worst. If you feel content and safe (but what is safe?) you might try to return to sleep. Then comes another noise.

Glancing at the clock I saw it was 2am and instantly I knew it was Michael.

To say I felt sick, scared, vulnerable and totally alone is probably an understatement. I curled up into a foetal position and wrapped my arms around my body and cried.

Eventually, I opened my eyes and caught the remains of a fading shadow. So fragile. Like the shadowy pattern of leaves on the lawn. I almost whispered 'Dad?' but stopped myself. The streetlight caught and elongated the shadow for a moment. *Maybe Michael is right. Maybe I am unbalanced*, I thought. *If I am mad, there is a wonderful liberation in my madness.*

I wanted to do what I did when I was a child. I used to travel many miles in my mind to a great rolling ocean, full of power and strength, rising and heaving. Then suddenly, for some reason, the ability to do that left me.

I lay motionless, trying to make myself relax, trying to uncurl my body and breath slowly. I noticed that I'd crossed my arms over my chest as though it was the most natural thing in the world to do, the way Sister Philomena used to say protected you from evil. My hands were clenched and even my legs were crossed. It was a typical defensive pose, I suppose. Bracing myself against another attack and making myself as small a target as I could. I might be a victim, but I hated looking like one, retreating like a turtle inside my shell. At one time, I became aware that my hands actually hurt because I'd been clenching them tightly into fists for so long.

I tried to let all the negative energy flow out of me. That's when I knew something terrible was there in the darkness. Something nearby. I could hear my heart beating abnormally fast. So fast it reminded me of a tiny sparrow I'd held not so long ago that had fallen out of its nest. I'd cupped its furry body in my hands and felt its heart beating so rapidly it seemed like a constant vibration rather than a heartbeat.

Then I felt the bed move as Michael sat down beside me.

In my mind, I could still see him lying peacefully in his bed, softly snoring.

"I'm sorry, Trish," he whispered. "You made me so angry. I just lost it."

I managed to turn over and look at where I knew he was. Slowly my eyes adjusted to the darkness and I could see him.

"How many times do you think I can forgive you, Michael? How long can we go on like this?"

"I know. It won't happen again. I promise."

Yet again, I could tell that he really meant it. His voice was so soft I began to shake.

I looked straight at him, willing him to look at my split lip, and his eyes obligingly dropped down but quickly rose back to mine again. In all the times he'd hit me, it always surprised me that he could so easily dismiss the result of his rages. Somewhere in the labyrinth of Michael's brain was something that allowed him to forget the damage he'd caused or the pain he'd administered.

"Open your eyes, darling, and look at me when I'm talking to you."

I managed it.

"There you are. Not so hard is it? I'm not going to hurt you."

He picked up a pillow and lifted my head gently to position it for my comfort.

He walked around to my side of the bed and knelt down beside me. "You shouldn't try to make me angry, you know. Should you?" he said looking down at his bruised hand.

I didn't answer.

"SHOULD YOU?" His voice rose.

"No," I whispered. Tears were rising in my eyes again and began to trickle out.

"Oh Trish. I never want to hurt you. You know that. I'll run a bath and then pop you in bed with a nice hot cup of tea."

I heard him go away and then water running in the bath. He lifted me and stood me by the bath then gently undressed me before helping me into the bath.

The water was beautifully warm and slowly I began to stop shaking.

He sponged me with infinite tenderness and then towel dried me gently. After helping me to put on my nightie, he walked me back to bed and tucked me in.

"Now for that tea. And maybe some Panadol."

It seemed only a minute later that I felt his hand behind my head as he directed a cup to my split lips and helped me drink through a straw. Then he gave me two Panadol and stroked my hair as I tried to swallow them.

"I'm so sorry. I never meant to hurt you."

I leant back and said nothing. *Please go*, I screamed inside my head.

As if reading my mind, he stood up. "We're not going to talk about this tonight, are we?"

I shook my head silently.

"You know you can't do without me looking after you. I only pushed you and look what happened. You're so clumsy." He continued stroking my hair.

I tried not to move. Tried to lie still on my back so that the huge ache that I'd become would fade for a while. For a minute, I wished for death. An oblivion where silence and darkness would swallow me up.

Michael stood up. There was a moment rustling as the sheets moved and then there was a pause. "I'll go home tonight so that I won't disturb you in the morning when I go to work."

Then the bedroom door closed, and he was gone.

In the silence, I thought of my friends who had slipped and faded away, confused by my distance. I thought of calling Sue and then stopped because it would only make me cry and the pain would return again. I remember vaguely hearing the rain outside, and slowly felt myself relaxing, the Panadol working. I was too tired to think anymore, too tired and sore to move. I wanted the world to fade away and let me sink into limbo where nothing hurt. If I lay very still, it didn't hurt as much. Nothing could touch me here. I melted into the darkness and heard my own breathing rising and falling sporadically.

I knew now how people went mad. They gave up fighting. They went mad because it was a hell of a lot easier. They went mad because they go to a far better place than where they are. You get tired of the constant battle with no victories and no ceasefires. You lose your grip on the world slowly and drift into the chasm of your own unhappiness and hopelessness. I was suspended above the chasm, hovering unsteadily, feeling my grip slipping. No hope, no relief, no reprieve. Ever.

I hate to admit that suicide even entered my head but of course, the children were always on my mind and I knew that it wasn't an option. How would they ever forgive me? The odd thing is, you can't see the light at the end of the tunnel.

Before I finally dropped off to sleep, I turned towards the phone. It was so tempting to call Sue but it was more than my life was worth.

ENOUGH

The next day was Saturday and Michael called me. Before he could begin talking, I took a deep breath and said, "You hit me for the last time, Michael."

Emboldened by my decision of the previous night and running my tongue over my swollen lip, I continued. "It's over. I don't want to see you again. I want you out of my life and I want my key back."

"It was just an argument," he laughed. "Why make more out of it than it was? Why exaggerate it all out of proportion? You always do that."

Once upon a time, I wouldn't have had the courage to argue but I didn't care anymore.

"It's over, Michael," I repeated.

"I'm not going to talk to you while you're in this mood," he continued.

"I don't want to talk to you ever again," I countered. Brave words when he wasn't standing in front of me with his fist raised.

"Fine. Let's not," he snapped. And before I could repeat that I wanted my key back, he'd put the phone down.

Despite his words, he kept calling back during the day, gradually getting more and more contrite while I tried explaining that I'd had enough.

Finally, I guess the realisation hit him when I asked him to leave the key behind that afternoon in the letter box, and then come and collect any of his things he'd left behind the next day when a friend of mine would be with me. Not before.

He turned wheedling and said, "I've changed, Trish. I know I had a problem, but I've sorted all that out."

Beneath his quiet manner, I could sense something not quite right. Like a painting sitting askew on a wall. I wonder now why I didn't see all of these things before.

"Michael, it's over. You've hit me more times than I care to remember but now it's over. You're not going to control me anymore. I am my own person."

I can remember saying those exact words and thinking it sounded like an emotional response, something I didn't want it to be.

"Haven't you been listening to me?" His voice was sharp, and I braced myself for the inevitable. "I said I was bloody sorry."

I took a deep breath and repeated, "You've hurt me too many times."

I felt so brave saying those simple words. Free from the hold he had over me.

"But I mean it this time."

I let that hang in the air for a second. "And you didn't mean it before?"

"Don't get smart with me, Trish. Give me a chance to explain."

I tasted my lip again with my tongue. It still tasted raw. Then for some reason, my mind wandered back to the orphanage, and the foster homes. To other days that were almost too painful to remember.

I'll never know if memory helps or hurts us. Perhaps both. In one respect you remember the helplessness and utter desolation, but you also know that it is something you've overcome, even though painfully. On the other hand, you hurt because what happened was so unfair and you were stupid enough, and gullible enough, to let it go on for so long.

I've often wondered at the human capacity for stupidity. Without even knowing it, I'd created my own private River Styx from Greek Mythology that I'd read about in school. My soul had crossed over from the land of the living to the realms of hell.

I ended the conversation by hanging up the phone while he was still telling me how much he'd changed.

THE CHERRY RED DOT

It had been a week since I'd last spoken to Michael. He'd collected his things the next day as Sue glared at him and left without saying a word to me.

There was a strangeness to the day when I woke that morning and I couldn't fathom out why. I'd woken with a sharp intake of breath and butterflies in my stomach and nothing I did could eradicate the trepidation and sense that something was going to happen. I just felt uneasy. It was a feeling in the pit of my stomach and I'd learnt to trust these feelings implicitly. They happened from time to time and usually there's nothing I can do about them except wait for the inevitable to happen. The day progressed normally however and by dusk, I had convinced myself I was putting more emphasis on these feelings than was necessary.

Trying to derail the residual feeling, I thought there is nothing like junk food on a Sunday night to calm the savage beasts, so I made hot chips and gooey toasted cheese sandwiches for the boys and me, a culinary delight they loved. Then we curled up in front of the television with a pile of CDs, Cheezels and coke – wine for me. Later, while they were having their showers and getting ready for bed, I put on a Dire Straits CD and poured another glass of wine.

Tony was sitting up in bed with his new Christopher Pike novel when

I walked in to his room. There were toys everywhere and I had to shuffle some of them out of the way to make a path to the bed through the action toys, small metal cars, picture books, Lego and Castle Grayskull.

I looked around with my hands on my hips. "Did a bomb just go off in here?"

"I'll clean it up tomorrow morning before I go to school, mum."

"Make sure you do, buster. Lights out in five minutes." He grunted softly but lifted his head for my soft kiss on his forehead before I walked into Mark's room.

Mark, then eleven years old, looked up at me and said, "Do we have to listen to that music?"

"Dire Straits?"

"Whoever it is."

If asked now if it were true, I know he would deny it, but at the time his favourite group was Bon Jovi, to be replaced (thankfully) by Eddie Vedder and Pearl Jam in later years.

"That's Mark Knopfler," I said, with a grin.

"He stinks."

Charming, I thought. With a smile, I said, "He's got a big nose but he can really play a guitar and you'll love him when you're older."

To that, he pulled the covers over his head and said, "If it doesn't send me mad before then."

Once the boys were settled, I began pacing nervously around the house.

Tiredness was beginning to take over and my attention was wandering towards the renovations I wanted to do, the impatiens budding in the garden and the coffee shop I was thinking of buying. The sales were good, and it was a Monday to Friday operation, which meant I could be with the boys at night and on weekends. It all looked promising.

The phone rang once before I quickly picked it up, hoping the boys wouldn't wake.

"Hello?"

"How're you feeling Trish?" Michael's voice was heavy with sarcasm.

"Go to hell!" I imagined him slipping from a foothold and pinwheeling face first into an abyss. After all I'd been through with Michael, it surprised me that he could still hurt me so much and that I could bruise so easily.

"I'm simply enquiring out of concern, Trish." I heard him chuckle. "Maybe you should see a counsellor."

I slammed the phone down and looked outside the kitchen window. The trouble with fear is it's everywhere, in every shadow. It wasn't only what I saw or heard that scared me. It's what I felt. A creeping sensation as if Michael was lurking in the darkness. But if he had been in the front yard, the outside light would have illuminated him. I pulled the curtains closed, feeling like a bug highlighted on a microscope slide.

It wasn't easy to put him out of my thoughts. The anger was still too fresh, and my mind continuously strayed to the events of the previous week. But I managed. I fingered the remote control and channel surfed through Fox finally sitting back in disgust. How can there be absolutely nothing decent on 34 channels? I stood up and opened the fridge surveying the contents. Nothing interested me.

Finally, I went around and checked the doors for the second time that night. I may as well have an early night tucked up in bed with a book I'd been meaning to start for over a week.

I did a last check through the curtains noticing all of the other houses were well lit, calm and peaceful when I spotted a bright red dot in the distance, at the entrance to my long driveway. It shone brightly but then disappeared.

I squinted at a grey shape but couldn't focus on it. If it was a man, why had he stopped right there? And what was the red spot?

Then suddenly it occurred to me. A cigarette! When you draw in, the end burns brightly.

I tiptoed outside and crept to the edge of the balcony and craned my head over the edge. I could hear the crickets and a far-off barking dog. There was the faint smell of some night blooming flower, probably jasmine, in the air and the rich damp smell of earth and things growing in it. Out in front of me, over the veranda railing, there was a section of darkness and a few stars. The air was moist enough to take on a glow of its own, like that of a streetlight through fog only softer, subtler, so that what little light there was at night from porches and streetlights disperses and reflects off everything. It was in that light I saw a man's shadow in the distance.

In an instant, I knew it was Michael. I saw him lift his cigarette to his mouth with exaggerated care and the angles of his face light up in the red cherry flare as he inhaled.

All at once I was terrified and I didn't really know what to do. Was he watching my house? Was he watching to see who came in and out or was he simply biding his time? All I could think was there was something indefinably menacing about the way he just stood there.

Sick with panic, I ran into the kitchen, my breath ragged in my throat.

Everything seemed in slow motion. Picking up the phone, dialling the police station number, waiting for someone to answer. Everything seemed to take an age.

While I waited, I turned and looked in the mirror and a stranger with hollow wild eyes stared back at me.

Finally, a male voice answered.

"Can I help you?"

It was the normal sort of question, but the voice sounded annoyed, as if I'd interrupted his favourite television program.

"Yes," I said quickly. "I need you to send someone out to my house right now."

I could feel myself beginning to jabber. I do that when I'm anxious. I talk and talk and I can't seem to stop. There's this little voice inside my head saying 'Shut up' but I never can. I just talk more and more.

"I broke up with my boyfriend a week ago and now he's stalking me. He's on the footpath, just standing there. He's out there watching my house!"

I felt my chin trembling, but I was determined not to cry because to the police it would look like weakness and what they'd call 'femaleness' instead of what it was: rage and panic. The last thing I wanted was for the police to think I was as close as I was to losing control.

In the silence, I swallowed and blinked. Then swallowed again.

"Has he threatened you in any way?" he finally asked.

I hesitated at the question. "Not tonight. But he has hit me quite often when we were seeing each other."

"But has he threatened you tonight?"

Immediately, I saw where this was going. "That's why I'm ringing you." I could hear the mixture of panic and anger in my own voice. "To stop it before it gets to that."

"He's on the footpath, you say?"

"That's right."

"Not on your property?"

"For goodness sake! I need your help here. Your job is to protect the public and I need that help right now!"

"Ma'am." His voice was so patronising, I felt like screaming. "Whoever is on your footpath, and we haven't even confirmed it is your ex-boyfriend, is on public property and not even in your yard. He has made no threats to you or your property, but you want me to waste taxpayer's money by sending out a patrol car to talk to someone who may very well be just walking his dog. I can't arrest someone for something you think he *might* do."

I heard him clear his throat. "With all due respect, the imagination can play strange tricks on a person when they're alone."

It sounded like something from a bad horror movie. The fact that he was patronising me made me all the more furious.

The hand not holding the phone clenched in a fist at my throat as I struggled to control my voice. "He's not walking his damn dog. It's *him* and he's stalking me."

In the distance, the red dot glowed again. I could hear the policemen on the other end of the line breathing loudly as if he found this all very tiresome.

I took a deep breath. "So what you're saying," I began again, a little slower, "is you have to wait until he enters my property and assaults me, or worse, before you can help me?"

"I'm sorry, ma'am. That's the law."

I slammed the receiver down, my hands sweaty and my heart pounding. I sank to the floor, my legs not able to support me anymore. After sounding so together on the phone, my mind had turned to slush.

Slowly, I pulled myself to my feet. The knife drawer lay right near my hand, so I opened it and took out the largest one I could find. If he came anywhere near me tonight, he'd soon know that he'd gone too far this time.

I put the knife down and dug around in a cupboard for a wine glass and a bottle of Merlot I knew was there. With a trembling hand, I managed to twist the cap off and pour a glass of the wine without spilling too much of the liquid on the bench. The first sip was delicious, and I closed my eyes, just to savour it. It was warm with a crisp flavour, fruity and mild. The second sip made me thirsty so I gulped the rest down in one go. The next glass of wine went down smoothly but my nerves were still frazzled.

"Terrific. That's what you need," I said out loud just so that I wouldn't feel alone. "Get completely drunk, like your mother, just because you're scared and then you'll never know what the hell is going on around you."

I twisted the cap back on the bottle and put it back in the cupboard.

That night, the knife slept on a pillow next to me, my hand closed over the handle. If there was a dragon coming into my castle, I was going to slay it.

Suddenly, I was looking up at the ceiling with no memory of dreams while I slept. A sleep of the dead they call it and that's how I felt. Dead inside, drained and exhausted. Still clutched in my hand was the knife and it's a wonder I hadn't stabbed myself with it.

I forced myself into a sitting position, my body feeling as though it wasn't even mine, unwilling to get out of bed. My limbs were as weak as if I'd gone fifteen rounds in a boxing ring with Mike Tyson. And lost.

The light outside was diffused and I remember thinking it must be early. On my side table the clock read 5.20am. I'd had all of four hours sleep. No wonder I felt disorientated.

I decided to have a shower to try and calm myself. I fiddled with the knobs trying to get the temperature right, veering between boiling hot to freezing cold. Eventually, I got it right and closed my eyes, savouring the warmth. As I leant back against the tiled wall, hot nettles pummelled on my shoulders leaving me feeling human again, soothing me like soft rain in the rainforest.

Finally, I forced myself to turn the taps off and I reached out to pull a towel from the towel rack. Condensation had covered the mirror and my eyes became riveted to what I saw.

HELLO

The words stood out starkly on the mirror, almost shimmering.

Terror clutched my heart and I quickly wrapped the towel around me as if hiding myself from a camera in a corner.

Michael had written the words. I knew! But when? While he was here the last time as he filled my bath? Or could I have slept through his movements in the night? It would mean he'd had a copy made of the key he'd handed back to me. Damn it! Now I'd have to change the locks!

I felt as if I was in a bad movie, shaking in a puddle of water pooling around my feet as I stared at the words, imagining Michael walking around my house in the dark hours of the night. Looking at my boys peacefully asleep in their beds. Watching me while I slept fitfully, clutching the knife. How could I have not heard him?

My first instinct was to check on my boys. Still with the towel around my body, I ran from the room, slipping and sliding in my haste to get to my children.

Through the thumping in my chest and the ringing in my ears, I watched them both sleeping quietly, Mark in his Donatello sheets and Tony in his Raphael ones. No sign of anxiety on their faces, just the sleep of the innocent except for the fact that my youngest had started sleeping with a baseball bat on the floor beside his bed. Toys were scattered around their rooms but no Michael.

My next instinct was to call the police again. But even as I rushed towards the phone in the kitchen, I knew it would be useless. They'd made it clear enough last night that they wouldn't come out to my house unless a definite threat had been made and even though those words were still evident on my mirror, there was no real threat in them. And how could I prove he was the one who'd written the words? Even *when* he'd written them?

I walked back into the bathroom and angrily wiped the words away. The squeak my hand made felt like a cleansing and my reflection stared back at me. Dark shadows had formed under my eyes and even to myself, I looked ten years older than I had six months ago. Michael had once said that I had an Olivia Newton-John look about me but if he could see me now, he would have denied ever saying that.

"He will never hurt you again," I said to myself in the mirror. I watched my lips form the words, watched each muscle in my face change as my mouth moved.

I finished dressing, feeling less than human but knowing I had to keep going, make the lunches for the boys and headed off to sign papers for the new coffee shop I was buying. When I looked at the clock, I was surprised to see it was 6 am, only forty minutes after I'd woken up.

An hour later, I had scribbled a quick note to the boys, locked the front door and walked down the steps towards my car. It was then I noticed the flat tyre.

I wonder how long it's possible to live in a world when nothing makes sense. There's a philosophy that says everything is pre-ordained. Fate, some people call it. My personal philosophy is that it's easy to believe this when things are going great. It's easy to look around when you're happy and say there's a meaning to everything, 'meant to be' even. But when your life is a nightmare and you can't see any way out, those words mean nothing. For instance, look at Biafra, Auschwitz, and Chernobyl. Are they a part of God's great plan?

The church says, *'God moves in mysterious ways.'* But why *does* he? Why *should* he? Is there a reason for torturing innocent people? Hard-working, well-meaning people?

I sighed and returned to the kitchen, turned the kettle on again and called RACQ to come out and change the tyre. I'd never changed a tyre in my life, and I wouldn't know where to start.

With a fresh cup of tea in my hands, I walked back downstairs and waited for them to arrive. The clouds looked like undulating sheets of tin in the sky. The sun had broken over the horizon and the wind had suddenly died leaving the sky as pale as bleached bone, as if the colour had been drained out of it.

Trying not to think of where my life was headed seemed hard. I could distract myself with TV or work but eventually thoughts and memories always creep back in as they did now. My wolf, sniffing at the door yet again, breathing over my shoulder, panting. Today a wolf, tomorrow something under the bed or in a closet, lurking under the dark surface of a cup of coffee.

I stood in the yard looking at the trees towards the front of the property, where I'd seen the tiny pinpoints of Michael's cigarette the night before. The tree trunks were a few yards back from the footpath and the morning sun was low on the horizon, sneaking under the foliage and veiled with mist. Standing on the driveway, I moved aside a branch of the Leopard tree and stared down at the dark soil and the sparse alyssum that was straining to survive in almost constant shade.

Then, through the dappled shade and the unraked leaves, I saw shoe prints less than a metre away. They startled me, my heart thumping good and hard as I looked. They were side by side, facing the steps, like someone had rested there and waited, or an invisible man standing there right now, offering his hand to shake. Or raising it in anger to strike me. Men's footprints. Big and fresh. Proof that Michael *had* been here last night, to me at least, but it wouldn't be enough for the police. The prints could have been made by anyone, they'd say: a salesman, a neighbour. Anyone. Even if they spoke to Michael, he'd smile that winning smile of his and laugh with them. After that, they would have no time for me and my suspicions, no matter how real they were.

The sound of tyres crunching on the driveway brought me back to the present. RACQ had arrived. A half hour later, as the boys waved goodbye to me from their bikes on their way to school, the repairman finished.

"All done," he said, wiping his hands on a towel. "Do you have an enemy?"

I could feel my heart plunge then catch on something, feeling as though it dangled lopsided by a single thread.

"What do you mean?" I croaked.

"This tyre of yours. That was no puncture."

"But it was. It was as flat as a tack."

"It was flat all right." As he was talking, he walked over to a tyre leaning up against a tree and rolled it over to me. He picked up a screwdriver as he continued talking.

"See this?" He pointed to a hole in my old tyre and pushed the screwdriver easily through. "That hole wasn't done by anything as small as a nail. If you ask me, someone deliberately wrecked your tyre and he, or she, used a screwdriver to do it."

I closed my eyes and rubbed my forehead. I had to try and think straight. Again, going to the police was useless. I had absolutely no proof that Michael had done this, but in my heart I knew. He'd watched my house last night, walked around my yard and put a screwdriver through my tyre before he left. What would he do next?

That afternoon on the way home from the estate agents office, every street I passed, every corner I took, every stop sign, I expected to see him standing there smiling his smug smile at me. I found myself scanning my rear vision, as I reached the vicinity of my home. I found myself caught between *hoping* I'd see him so I could contact the police to add to the growing list of my complaints and *scared* that I'd see him and I'd know for sure he was stalking me.

When I got home, I walked into a nightmare.

HE RETURNS

I told myself I wasn't seeing what I thought I was seeing as I stepped over smashed crockery, broken glass and pools of milk, juice and water in my kitchen. Everything I could see had been screwed up, stamped on or damaged beyond repair.

This can't be, I told myself again as I looked around in wide-eyed disbelief. I'd spent weeks speculating and re-speculating, my fears rising as the days progressed, whether Michael was still capable of hurting me now that he was no longer in my life. I'd played rehearsed scenarios over and over in my mind where I'd meet him somewhere and I'd treat him with contempt, prepared for whatever dangers he might throw at me. I had started to blithely believe that nothing bad could happen to me now. It hadn't occurred to me that he would do this sort of senseless damage.

As I stood in the kitchen, alert for any sound or movement in the house, I was uncomfortably aware that this could be the start of a new plan of attack from Michael. My surroundings seemed to recede, and I felt like I was being lifted up to the ceiling, staring down at myself. The only thing that kept me halfway sane was the thought *Is he out there right now, lurking in the late afternoon shadows, watching and laughing at my terror?* My eyes jerked to the window, imagining movement in every shadow. Worse still, would he come back tonight to finish what he'd started while I sat in scared silence waiting for his approach? Darkness is the most effective disguise.

I took a deep breath to slow the ones that were coming too fast. Even though I was close to the brink of hysteria, I felt a surge of anger surpassing all of my emotions.

Suddenly I heard the noise of shoes on the front stairs and I spun around in terror. Both boys stood at the door, their eyes popping with shock, and as I turned to hold them back with an outstretched arm, their looks of astonishment and uncertainty moved me into action.

Suddenly, my mind was sharp and clear, free of the emotional detritus of the past few weeks. I remember the sound and feel of glass and crockery cracking beneath my feet as I walked over to the phone to call the police.

Unlike yesterday (was it only yesterday?) when the indifferent reception I'd received from the police had sent me to the sanctuary of my bedroom with the knife in my hand, today's assault had motivated me to be positive and proactive. Even though I was still frightened, I had come to realise that I couldn't, and wouldn't, give in. If I cowered, I would be nothing but prey.

A male voice at the police station said, "Can I help you?"

Yes, you can. Give me energy. Give me answers. Give me peace, I wanted to scream. Instead I said, "Yes, I'd like you to send someone out to my house. My house has been broken into." I spoke the words calmly, disguising the panic surging through my body.

I looked back at the boys, still motionless at the front door. Trying to move them into action, I waved my hand at them in the direction of their bedrooms and mouthed 'Check out your rooms' as the voice over the phone said, "What's the address, ma'am?"

I told him, stopping short of mentioning the phone call from last night that had sent me to the dubious sanctuary of my bedroom. The last thing I needed was to get his back up before he'd even arrived.

Half an hour and a hundred angry circuits of the lounge room later, two policemen stood at my door surveying the damage.

"Have you had a look around to see if anything is missing?" one asked.

"This isn't a normal break and entry," I stated firmly. "My ex-boyfriend did this."

I waved my arms around to show them the extent of the damage done. Cups, plates and glasses had been taken out of the cupboards and smashed, the entire contents of the fridge was all over the floor and in my bedroom, the remains of the clothes Michael had bought for me in his attempt to change me into what he wanted me to be were shredded with a pair of scissors that had been left on top of the pile of clothes.

They both observed me politely. The one who was doing all the talking so far asked, "How can you be so sure?"

I waved my arms around at the damage again. "Look for yourself," I said with more assurance than I felt. "All of my things have either been smashed or ripped. The only things missing are *his* bits and pieces that belonged to *him*."

The two policemen exchanged a glance.

"He broke in and did this to my home and I want him arrested!"

"We're going to have a problem with that," the talkative one said.

"What do you mean, a problem?" I breathed deeply in and out, trying to calm myself. What I wanted to do was shout and scream. "He did it. I want him charged."

"That may be what you want but without evidence, there's not a lot we can do. For a start, he didn't break in. He used his key."

"It was *not* his key," I interrupted. "He gave *his* key back to me. Apparently, he had another one cut before he did so."

"That may be so. What I'm trying to say is he didn't break in. He used a key. Secondly, he took nothing that didn't belong to him, just his personal things."

"But what about the damage?" I was angry and frustrated and I wanted to snap at him for being so condescending.

"Not enough to charge him, I'm afraid. If we go to him with this, all he has to say is he was with some friends at the time, who will no doubt back him up, and then you've got nothing." His face was deadpan. "Have you spoken to the neighbours? Did anyone see him at all?"

"There aren't any neighbours on one side, just a vacant lot. The other ones both work during the day," I snapped.

The reality of my situation was setting in. Michael would escape from justice again.

"All I can suggest is to change the locks as soon as possible so he can't get in again," the talkative one continued.

Did he shrug or had I imagined it? I wasn't sure what astounded me more: his cavalier response or his lack of concern for my plight. In my present frame of mind, it was like throwing petrol onto an open flame. If this were a movie, the director would have had Will Robinson's robot in the background waving his arms and yelling *'Warning, Will Robinson. Warning.'*

"And what's to stop him from coming back again and again if he thinks he's left something else behind?" I asked angrily. "Is he allowed to just walk in here whenever he wants to because he thinks he's left a cigarette lighter behind? Or a biro? When will it all end and where is the safety I need for myself and my children?"

When he spoke, it was with a sigh. "We'll talk to him ma'am. But that's all we can do. As I said, have the locks changed and the next time it *will* be a break and entry."

For the second time today, I found myself trying to compose myself.

Next time? Next time!! I was flushed with rage at what I saw as the police fobbing me off again. I would like to say that I was contemptuous, but I was becoming too panicked at the thought of *next time* to carry it off. I could feel the anger rising and I was afraid if it bubbled up any further, I wouldn't be able to stop it.

Anger isn't sharp and clean like they say in books. It isn't cleansing. It's heavy and cumbersome as a wagon full of rocks and it weighs you down until you can't think straight.

What I needed to do was point my anger at someone else. Not at the policemen who stood so nonchalantly in front of me but at Michael's friend for damn well introducing me to him in the first place. At Michael for forcing his way into my life. At myself for being foolish enough to believe the lies he'd fed to me.

Nature's least likely fighter is the rabbit. This animal is made for defence with its camouflaging coat, ears that rotate to home in on any threatening sounds and eyes that see for 360 degrees. It's even a herbivore with chiselling teeth and claws that are intended to claw at leafy pants. But when it's cornered, where there's no chance of flight, it will attack its adversary with a shocking ferocity. That's what I would be. A gnarling, dangerous, ferocious animal. I was going to show Michael just what he was up against. There comes a time in your life when you know that you have to stand up and be counted.

At some point, I told myself I'd had enough. Consider a person without a sense of limit. Isn't that what it is to be a monster? Someone whose anger and pleasures have no restriction, no sense of limit?

I had reached my own limit. The way I saw it, awful things had happened to me and these awful things needed to stop. That was my moral voice speaking, my superego. Was I going to let him get the better of me once more? *I don't think so, Tim,* I thought; that oh-so-trite, smart-ass reply.

I could feel the saliva drying up in my mouth, more solid than liquid, and knew that this time my voice would emerge as a falsetto. Instead of saying anything else, I was silent as I watched them leave.

HIS LAST ATTEMPT

Both boys had basketball games on Saturday, so I dropped them off while I went down to the shops to do some grocery shopping. I returned half an hour later, rosy-cheeked and sweating under a cloudless sky and stopped to retrieve the mail from my letterbox.

I opened the flap and leant down to glance in. I never put my hand in anymore ever since a large hairy huntsman greeted me one day by running up my arm and disappeared inside my cleavage. This time however, it wasn't a spider I saw. Inches from my nose, a huge rat, gazed back at me, its eyes glassy and its fur patchy with blood, but most decidedly dead. A white piece of paper arranged on top of the body in a perfect upside-down V said, *'This could be you too.'*

I staggered backwards, a scream working its way up from my throat and I landed on my butt. I must have staggered back to the car but I don't remember doing so. Minutes later, I was down at the Police Station talking to the same policeman I'd seen only a day ago.

I refreshed his memory about what had happened, starting with the phone calls and the late-night visit, the punctured tyre and finished with the damage to my house he'd seen only too well with his own eyes. He breathed noisily through his nose as if he found this all very tiresome while I told him about the rat in my letterbox.

"What do you want us to do?"

"What do I....." I stopped, astounded. *What sort of stupid question was that?* "Well, I'd have thought for a start you would come back to the house and take the note and do whatever it is you people do with evidence. It's *his* writing and it's blatantly harassment. I want something done this time. How many times does he have to do something like this before you people help me?"

He listened without expression, then said, "Okay, okay," he said. "We'll send one of 'our people' down with you to check it out. Just wait a few minutes, please."

I threw my head back and squared my shoulders righteously. "Thank you, officer."

He seemed to be gone a long time during which time my mind raced without getting anywhere. I was just about to go back to the counter and ring the buzzer again when another policeman came through the door and asked, "Are you the lady who reported the dead body, ma'am?"

I tensed briefly, saying as tersely as I could, "My car is out front. You can follow me."

I turned abruptly and walked away listening to the sound of his shoes behind me, clicking in time to mine.

I parked my car on the grass and stayed in the car, allowing him to park in my driveway in full view of the letterbox. I watched him unfold himself from the police car and walk over to it, squatting on his haunches while he opened the lid and peered in.

As he stood up and walked towards me, I wound my window down but said nothing. He put his hand on the roof of my car and leaned down.

"This is where the body was, you say?"

Was? That wasn't what I'd expected him to say. "Well...yes." I stammered. "Why?"

He smiled laconically but because of his dark sunglasses, I couldn't see his eyes. "I've done a thorough search of the building," he said, grinning more as he continued, "and I've found nothing. Ma'am."

"But...but that's impossible." I stared at the open letterbox. "It *was* there before I went down to the station. I saw it clearly."

He turned away and made a remark, his voice too low for me to hear, then turned back with a grin on his face. "With all due respect ma'am, there's no body there now."

The fact that he was trying to patronise me only made me furious.

"I know what I saw," I stated firmly, not quite shouting but with a hint of anger. "I want to see for myself."

He stepped backwards as I jumped out of the car, pushing him aside in the process, and stormed over to the letterbox.

I stood looking down at the empty letterbox. "I know what I saw," I repeated lamely. "I didn't imagine it."

"Well, maybe so, but there's nothing we can do about it. I suggest you take your groceries upstairs and make yourself a cup of tea."

I was angry and mystified and I wanted to snap at him, but I bit my lip because to be honest, he was right. What *could* we do?

"He must have come back while I was at the station and taken it away," I explained lamely.

He watched me closely, trying to compose myself, his eyes travelling over my face, one eye to the other.

"I'll tell you what. We'll pay him a visit and have a talk to him. Let him know that you've put in a complaint. That's the best I can offer. If anything else turns up, phone us and we'll come down."

"Whatever," I said as I waved my hand in front of my face. I hated hearing his tone of forced tolerance. "Thanks," I said a little belatedly.

The wind was picking up and, on the horizon, dark clouds were gathering so I quickly took the groceries upstairs. Surprisingly, I drove steadily and calmly to pick up the boys. How long would it be before Michael realised I was out of his life forever? How long before he stopped scaring and degrading me?

After a series of deep breaths, I braced myself and walked inside the stadium to the sound of hundreds of boys bouncing their basketballs all at the same time.

NEVER AGAIN

I knew who it was without even looking. I knew the sound of the tyres crunching on the driveway. The drone of his car's engine. Everything.

I was terrified, doing my best to breathe. When I swallowed, my throat hurt. I thought I heard heavy footsteps tapping on the planks of the stairs.

Everything inside of me contracted. My heart was pounding and my insides felt like water. I was shaking so much, I could feel my limbs trembling as if from cold. I couldn't move. I just stood there staring at the door barely breathing so as not to make a noise while I waited for the door to open.

Then a figure materialised outside the window. Bulky and shapeless. It stood there for a few seconds. I heard a key in the lock before I saw the doorknob move and the door open. As the figure stood in the doorway, my eyes tried desperately to adjust to the sudden light. It surrounded him like a halo making his body a silhouette. The shape moved forward slowly and quietly. First the chest, then the body and then the head until the doorway filled. In the dim light, the hand on the doorknob looked monstrous.

I pressed the back of one of my shaking hands to my mouth to stop an involuntary gasp from escaping and I leaned, cold and sick, against the kitchen bench. The light he'd been blocking blurred and shifted and I saw Michael's face in the dim light.

Of course it was Michael! Who else had I thought it would be? In my mind I was hoping for someone else. An escapee from a prison, a burglar, a serial killer on the loose, but please God, not Michael.

I didn't move. I couldn't. My body felt cool from the cold shower I'd had, and my hair was still wet but I felt like I had a temperature or a fever making me sweat. My eyes blinked uncontrollably, and I looked around me for an escape, somewhere to run. When I looked at Michael again, when my heart had stopped beating so fast, his eyes were all screwed up as he smiled sardonically at me.

"Waiting for a bus, are we?"

When he spoke, terror swam inside my chest as though a hand had grabbed my heart. My heart began to pound again and I thought I was going to faint. Innocent enough words, *'Waiting for a bus,'* but I knew what was coming. I could see it in his eyes. Those black eyes that seemed to glisten darkly in the luminous whiteness surrounding them.

I managed to shake my head stupidly.

He smiled. Not a nice smile. Forced. Stretching his lips to expose his teeth. There was something in his expression that made me sharply conscious of the situation I was in: deeply in. I was alone. Any help I got now would only come from myself and I was well aware that I am not the stuff of which heroines are made.

"I'm...I'm expecting someone. You...you can't stay," I lied.

I'm not a good liar. I blush and stutter and look everywhere but at the person's face I'm talking to. He knew it was a lie straight away.

"Ah," he said. "The Cavalry comes."

I saw his jawbone flex. He stood looking at me like a teacher who'd caught me doing something I shouldn't and was trying to decide how I should be punished.

"You have to go," I repeated, my voice cracking. "The boys will be home soon." Another lie. The boys were with their father and he knew it.

"I'm not leaving yet." He took a step towards me and involuntarily, I took one backwards. Months ago, I would have been terrified by the sight of him and to tell the truth, my heart *was* hammering hard inside my chest. But my newfound resolve had taken over and deep down, I knew that he wouldn't go too far now that I'd gone to the police. I hoped anyway. You see, by now I knew he was a coward and he had crossed a boundary that he shouldn't have. All he could do now was to try and scare me to save what little dignity he thought he had left.

"Do you know why I'm here?" His eyes stared at me, not blinking, his voice soft and intense. Measured.

"No," I said as I shook my head. My voice was so quiet, even I could hardly hear it.

"I had a lovely visit from the police today," he said.

I blinked and managed to say, "I had to do it. You shouldn't have broken in to my house."

I said the words with a hell of a lot more confidence than I felt. Being reasonable is something I've learnt from my time with Michael. Explaining things in detail as if reasoning with a child: most of the time to no avail.

The atmosphere suddenly changed in the room from menacing to anger and as I backed away, Michael's response was immediate, as if I'd flicked a switch. He moved forward, panting, while I tried to control my own breathing. As I stared up at him, I was determined that whatever fear he'd instilled in me over the past twelve months would not be the overriding emotion tonight.

The tic in his eye was distracting me but it meant that I was getting to him.

He won't hit you. He won't hit you. He won't go that far. Not now.

"Where do you think you're going?" he growled as he grabbed my shoulder and shoved me hard against the breakfast bench. His eyes were as small as slits as he glared at me. He was trying not to sound angry, speaking through gritted teeth as if *I* was the one doing something wrong.

I pushed passed him, hating the feel of his body warmth as my arm brushed his chest, smelling the nicotine inground in his skin and the raw odour of perspiration that seemed pressed into his clothes. I expected him to grab my hair as I passed, was amazed when he didn't, and walked on jelly legs around the counter to the front door, holding it wide open as much to support myself as a safety move to make my point.

"I want you to leave. Now. Right now. And I want the key back."

As he stepped closer, I smelt a stale odour in his clothes as if he'd slept in them, that is, if he'd slept at all. But I stood my ground.

"You do, do you?" he sneered, a look of amused malice on his face. I closed my eyes to blot out the image.

"I want you to leave right now," I repeated.

"I haven't finished with you yet."

So damn sure of himself.

"I WANT YOU TO LEAVE NOW!" I yelled. My head was high, as noble as my patrician namesake, and I stared at him blatantly, straight in the eyes. I wanted him to know that my finger was on the pulse and the toe of my shoe was up his butt.

I left the door open and walked back to the bench, about to make a show of picking up the phone, when he stepped closer and took the phone out of my hand, placing it back on the wall.

He was so close now I could smell the pungent combination of sweat and aftershave.

"Why would you send the police to speak to me?"

His voice was soft but I recognised the threat underneath the words.

I stood there trying to hide my shaking hands, staring steadily at him as he stared back at me. I could see his pulse beating in his throat, but I tried to keep my eyes flat and my expression empty while inside my chest, my heart bounced against all of my ribs. *How could I have thought I loved this man?* I thought. When I looked at him now, I thought of baby rabbits being fed to reptiles. I had to stop myself from recoiling.

As I stared into his eyes, all my previous bravado left me. I was suddenly resigned to the fact that a fist would be appearing soon, and the horrible pain would begin again. Even as I thought those words, I saw him ball his right hand into a fist and I waited for it to connect again with my face.

When Michael flew into a rage he would use anything close at hand as a weapon. He once hit me continuously with a rolled-up newspaper until it fell apart in tatters on the floor. He once threw a tomato at me, which might sound funny but it wasn't at the time. It hit my mouth and split my lip and it was terribly difficult to eat for days afterwards. Nothing he did left disfiguring scars, but the emotional ones will always be there. That's all that's left after twelve months of fear and pain. Deep emotional scars. We began by smiling and we ended up – *I* ended up – terrified for my life.

"ANSWER ME!" he screamed in my face. I felt my eyes widening in shock.

It's funny the things that register when the unbelievable is happening. *Curry*, I remember thinking. *He's had curry for dinner.* I could see veins beginning to pop out on his forehead and if I'd wanted to, I could have traced a swollen one with my finger that led from an eyebrow into his hair.

I waited while he regarded me fiercely. Did he want me to answer him? I looked down at his hands, bracing myself for the attack. His hands were big with long fingers with thick knuckles. I didn't know how much I'd come to hate those hands.

I shrugged nonchalantly, trying to hide my fear of him, not wanting to give him even the slightest satisfaction of knowing that he scared the life out of me but I could feel myself becoming hysterical with fear. Tears were welling at the back of my eyes now and as much as I tried not to, I knew I was going to cry.

"Whores like you don't deserve men like me. They need to be punished."

A cold terrible fear sliced through me because I could see he meant it.

"Don't do this Michael," I whispered. My head was shaking of its own volition. I saw his eyes bulging and I remember cringing, sure a physical assault was going to replace the verbal one.

I felt his fist before I saw it. It went straight into my chest with a crunch. Tears were running down my cheeks by then as I lowered my head. Drawing in a breath, I placed a hand over my chest between my breasts. He hit me again, this time on my mouth, and I was propelled backwards, too quickly for my legs to cope, my arms flung out wide to balance myself.

I hit the side of my head on the bench as I went down and I heard a loud 'pop' in my left ear. I landed on my rump with pain shooting up my back and into my head. The coppery taste of blood filled my mouth once more and I gingerly felt the reopened cut on my lip with my tongue where my teeth had gone through. There was an enormous buzzing going on in my brain and millions of stars crossing my vision. I raised my hands to my face, and they came away wet with tears and blood. Feeling dizzy and sick, I touched my ear gently and felt blood running down my neck. Had my eardrum burst?

Everything had seemed in slow motion, almost unreal; only the sickness in my stomach and the pain in my chest were real. I was surprised at how much I hurt inside. As if I was made of glass and pieces of me had shattered and broken. Humpty Dumpty all over again. So broken that no one could put me back together.

Michael towered over me, shouting in my face and I realised that the bees in my head were so loud, they drowned out his words and I remember thinking that's just as well. I could see his mouth moving quite clearly but I couldn't hear what he was saying. Then he turned and walked away.

My mind took one of those wrong turns and I began to rationalise.

I know. This is a dream. I'll wake up and I'll be in bed alone. Michael won't be here and everything will be fine. Then I almost smiled and I felt the sharp pain in my lip and knew this wasn't a dream and Michael wasn't a ghost. Ghosts don't eat curry and they can't split your lips.

I could feel the tears coming again but I tried to fight them back. Funny thing. I'd never been a crier. I'd always kept my defiant and 'who cares' face showing even if I was screaming inside. I always made myself numb because I believed tears are nonsense.

But since meeting Michael, it was like I'd thrown the door open and let the pain in. And it hurt. Where had I gone wrong? This was supposed to be *my* time for finding myself and getting a fresh start. But again, I'd screwed up.

I don't know how long I sat there as the room spun around me. You lose track of time. It felt like half an hour but was probably no more than five minutes. I tried to breathe and gasped at the pain in my chest.

Stay calm. Be rational. Maybe I should just pack up my kids and run. Lock up the house and put it in the hands of a real estate agent. Run away and change my name.

I'd once played a game when I was young because my name was so strange. Patricia Gourgaud. Gourgaud. The way to pronounce it, it sounds like something a baby says. Go goo. So I'd played my game. Take my middle name, Therese, and make it my first name. Then use the name of the street where I was living as my surname. During my five years of fostering, I'd had a choice of about twenty different names. Changing my name had been my way of dealing with the anger and hurt at being so easily disposed of.

This time, the surname would be Garnet. Therese Garnet. I almost giggled, thinking it sounded like a bad porn name, but the pain in my chest stabbed at me again and I hunched over. Every muscle in my body felt weak and as the minutes ticked by, the terrible reality of what had happened reinforced itself on me.

They say it takes a while to comprehend a tragedy. You can't accept the reality of it or the finality of it. At first my mind refused to accept the truth, still clinging to the last vestige of hope that I was mistaken in the extent of Michael's cruelty. But as I sat on the floor, I couldn't deny it anymore.

I stood up slowly and began hobbling towards the phone gasping for breath, my mind fogged with pain and a terrible ringing in my ears. It's strange the things you notice when pain is the only sensation you feel. A crooked picture on the wall. A mirror where I saw a scarecrow looking back at me. A large dust bunny in a corner of the dining room. I passed a bookcase where some books had fallen and were now lying horizontally across the vertical ones. All I wanted to do was make it to the phone and call the police.

Ten minutes later, I heard the sirens blaring and the intermittent flashing of lights. Red. Blue. Red. Blue. Red. Blue.

Finally, I knew I'd be safe. This time, I would make sure he was gone forever.

Never again, I whispered.

DAD'S EYES

J was jerked back to reality by the flash of an oncoming car's high beam and realised I was going way too fast on autopilot. My thoughts had taken over and I hadn't been concentrating on my driving at all. Suddenly the turn-off was just ahead of me and I indicated and moved into the left lane.

I'd better slow down and get there in one piece, I thought. *I'm almost there.*

If it hadn't been for my boys, I would have run away to another state but because of them, I'd decided to stay in Brisbane. I'd lived here all my life. Be damned if I was going to let a violent man scare me away. I loved the beaches of the Gold Coast to the south and The Sunshine Coast beaches one hour north. I loved the mountains surrounding Brisbane; cool in the summer months with their picturesque waterfalls and bush tracks. I even loved the contradictions of the city, where busy commuters vied for better positions on the freeways and bridges while small boats floated lazily on the river that meandered through its heart. I loved it all.

And now I'd discovered that Sandra had always lived here too. All these years later, it looked like my prayers for a sister had been mysteriously answered.

Two minutes later, I pulled up in front of her house. As I walked up the path and knocked on the door, my hands were shaking and my stomach was doing somersaults.

Please, God I prayed. *If you're really up there, please make this be true.* It was the first time in twenty-five years I'd said a prayer of any sort. I'd become a closet Catholic. No longer a churchgoer but talking to a God I wasn't even sure existed.

A nervous-looking blonde woman greeted me at the door and all my doubts disappeared.

Those beautiful blue eyes! It was like looking at Dad's eyes! I just stood there staring at her. She was about my height and build with shoulder length hair and her high cheekbones accentuated the largeness of her blue eyes. Except for the eye colour, I could see the resemblance between us immediately. I felt choked with emotion as the reality of what was happening sank in.

We hugged a little bashfully, and she said, "Come in."

I followed her into the kitchen where a man was standing beside a table. "This is my partner, Farouk," she said to me with a shy smile.

He leant over and kissed me on the cheek and said, "I hope you don't mind having an Egyptian as a brother-in-law."

I smiled as I shook my head.

"Would you like a drink? Coffee? Beer?" he asked.

"A beer would be great," I said. My throat was dry and my tongue felt like it was stuck to the roof of my mouth.

I sat down and looked at the woman who was my little sister. I just couldn't take my eyes off her. She was absolutely gorgeous.

As I sat holding her hand, I tried to take in everything about her. Her eyes were large with long lashes, so like mine, only blue. Our hands were similar, and her way of speaking and mannerisms were all the same as mine. This was what I'd always wanted and more than I'd ever hoped for.

"Do you have any children?" I asked, trying to break the silence.

"Yes, four. Two girls and two boys. The boys live with their father, my ex-husband," she said as she looked at her hands in her lap.

As Farouk passed us our drinks, I made small talk to put her at ease. "How long have you lived here?" I asked.

"Almost three years in this house with Farouk, but I've lived around this area for almost ten." She looked up at me then back at her hands.

"I left home when I was really young," she began. "Sixteen. I was going to be a nurse but somehow things turned out differently. A boy I knew asked me if I wanted to go to Darwin and on the spur of the moment, I said yes."

She smiled and shrugged. "It probably was the worst decision I've ever made but at the time it seemed right. I'd already signed up at a hospital for nurse training but I let it all go and I went to Darwin. I worked as a waitress up there for a while but eventually, I hated it so much, I hitchhiked back."

Wistfully she said, "Sometimes I wish I could go back and do it right. I fell pregnant and had Linda before I married Tony, my first husband. After that, we had three kids of our own before things went bad and we got a divorce. Farouk was so good to me at that time. I really needed him and we've been together ever since."

While she talked, she kept glancing up at me then back down at her hands. I had a feeling something was bothering her but I wasn't sure. It was just a fleeting thought and then it was gone. Suddenly she looked up at me resolutely and said, "Don't you remember me at all? My adoption papers said that I was almost four months old before I was adopted and you were four years old."

Years ago, when Mr Anderson had mentioned a sister, I tried so hard to remember a baby. In the jumble of memories from those days at home with my parents, images flicked through my mind. The tiny flat with just two beds. The kitchen table with just three chairs. Nothing that ever hinted that a baby was a part of our lives.

I looked at her and shook my head sadly. That wasn't the answer she wanted and she looked back down at her hands again. I knew that for the rest of my life, I would never forget the desolate look on her face as I told her that I had no memory of her. I knew she didn't understand why. I didn't know why myself.

I leant forward, trying to change the subject. "Tell me about your childhood, before you left home at sixteen."

My eyes roamed her face, eagerly soaking up every twitch, every eye movement, every frown. I couldn't get enough of her.

Like a cloud crossing in front of the sun, a shadow passed over her face. I noticed a subtle change in her eyes, something indefinable as her face clouded and a small frown appeared between her eyebrows as if I'd trodden on forbidden land. I wondered what sadness had caused that reaction to my innocent question. It was an almost defensive attitude as if a barrier, firmly in place, had to be crossed in order to answer.

A small silence fell upon us before she continued haltingly.

"You know some of it," she began. "I was adopted when I was nearly four months old. My adoptive parents also adopted another girl who was older than me, called Jill. When I was four years old, our mother died."

Her unhappiness was evident in every gesture.

"Unfortunately, probably because we were so young, Dad couldn't look after both of us. Jill was at school and I was still in preschool, so Dad decided that Jill would go and live with our grandmother and I would go to a home for girls for a few years till he got back on his feet again. I know he didn't want to do it but our grandmother could only take one of us. So he sent me to a children's home called Nazareth House."

THE TRUTH

I stared at her dumbfounded and blinked a few times. Rapid little blinks of astonishment. *Had I heard wrong?*

She had dropped her head, staring at the glass in front of her as if she could read the future in the frothy surface. Through the kitchen window, I saw a flicker of lightning in the inky sky just as a car with a blown muffler roared past noisily on the street. Ten seconds later, the silence was broken by the rumble of distant thunder.

"Pardon?" I stuttered as my heart did little summersaults in my chest. I was barely breathing as I gaped at her. "Did you say Nazareth House? At Wynnum?"

She looked up and hesitated, seeing the intense look in my eyes.

"Yes." She cocked her head to the side questioningly. "Why?"

"Nazareth House." I was barely whispering, lost in the memory of the home so many years ago. "That's the orphanage *I* was in," I murmured.

Her eyes opened wide in surprise. "You were at Nazareth House? When?"

"Well, let me see." I dropped my eyes to the table and thought hard of the dates. "I went there when I was almost seven, so that would have been in 1962 and I left when I was twelve to go to my last foster home in 1967."

I glanced up as she inhaled sharply.

"I went in when I was four," she said, "so that would have been 1963. I left three years later in 1966."

A tingling sensation ran up and down my body and in the warm night arm, I shivered as my heart pounded.

Confused silence that followed slowly gave way to a growing understanding. I felt like I was in the twilight zone. The years and dates were racing through our minds as the dreadful realisation of what had happened started to dawn on us.

We had both been at Nazareth House at the same time! We had actually spent countless weeks and months together, with no one knowing we were sisters. She had been Sandra Stewart and I had been Patricia Gourgaud, and for three years we had lived with each other, eaten together and played together without even knowing who the other one was.

Had she been one of the little ones I dressed in the mornings or one of the ones I bathed at night? I wondered, amazed at the possibility.

All of a sudden, I saw myself with Dad at Nazareth House in the concrete playground, sitting around a makeshift table drawing with me. Occasionally he would lean over to help another little girl whose parents hadn't visited. To think, he may have helped his other daughter Sandra, without even knowing it.

I couldn't believe this.

"Do you remember Sister Philomena?" I asked, bewildered. I was finding it hard to accept. I could see Sister Philomena with her hands hidden inside her sleeves standing in the corridor on my first night at Nazareth while I stood with my hands on my hips demanding to go home.

"Oh yeah," she answered quickly. "Who could forget *her*? Do you remember Mr Pinky?" She leaned forward urgently as she shot the question straight back at me.

"Oh, I remember Mr Pinky." A noise erupted from my mouth, like a snort. "He and I had an intimate relationship." A vision came to me of Sister Philomena standing over me with the shabby old pink hairbrush in her hand after I'd coloured all my nails in with a lead pencil. The flippancy I felt just a few seconds ago suddenly disappeared and the words

Sister Philomena uttered danced unwanted into my memory. "*You are nothing but gutter trash.*"

So long ago, and yet the careless words spoken in disgust as she stared down at my grey nails still felt like a knife to my chest. When I spoke to her all those years ago, during one of the loneliest times of my life, she said to me, *Time heals all wounds*. But she was wrong. It doesn't. Those words are just fridge magnet philosophy. The pain bides its time in your heart, waiting patiently for just the right moment to poke its head up again and tear the scab off the wound to make you bleed once more.

And then, something amazing happened to me. While I watched Sandra raise the glass of beer to her mouth, shaking her head and smiling at the memory, something new began to worm its way to the top.

Visions of my boys popped into my head, both of them laughing and happy. Visions of my home that I had managed to scape enough money together to pay a deposit on, full of pictures, soft cushions, scented candles and books. Visions of my coffee shop, bustling and busy, full of smiling people greeting me warmly as they walked in. Visions of David, holding me and telling me he loved me more than anything else in the world. My life, now, full and immensely happy. Every morning, I woke up excited for what was to come, just as I'd always hoped. I was healthy and strong and satisfied with my life. I had friends who cared about me and who loved me for who I was. And now I had Sandra. Sitting there in front of me. My very own sister.

Suddenly, the ache in my heart began to subside and a sense of accomplishment took over. A sense of triumph and achievement. I was stronger now. I am focussed on my future, not obsessed with the past. I am who I am because I have begun to heal. I was broken but I am a survivor. I am ... worthy.

The relief I felt was staggering. It was as if I had suddenly stepped out of the darkness of a cave and into the sunlight, feeling the warmth of the sun on my face for the first time in thirty years. I felt as though a huge weight had been lifted off my shoulders as the tears welled in my eyes. Sister Philomena was right after all. Time *does* heal all wounds.

While I remembered those simple words she'd spoken to me, I suddenly realised that the human spirit is amazing in its ability to forge forward in order to survive. We are never given anything that we can't handle and the difficulties we experience are meant to make us better people, not bitter people. I read in a poem recently that mountains don't rise without earthquakes and the true meaning of the phrase made sense to me now.

I swallowed quickly to force down the lump in my throat and blinked rapidly. Blubbering like a fool was certainly not what I wanted to do tonight.

Sandra had been staring down at the beer in her hand, oblivious to my discomfort. Abruptly, she put the beer back onto the table with a clunk.

"God, do you remember dancing those Irish jigs in the playground?" she smiled.

Her rushed words brought me back from my memory and I mentally shook myself, forcing myself back to the present. "We had to keep our hands clenched and straight by our sides. Do you remember?" she asked quickly.

My eyes opened wide and I smiled at the memory. "Oh wow. Yes. To demonstrate the steps to us, she used to reach down and grab the hem of her skirt in each hand, holding her arms wide like Sister Maria in the Sound of Music and showing black stockinged legs up to her knees. She used to hop from foot to foot and spin around so nimbly for someone of her size."

My expression sobered as I remembered lying awake terrified that first night listening for the sounds of claws on the wooden floors which meant the black dogs were looking for little girl's hands to eat. The memory was so vivid, I could almost hear the sound of thunder and see the lightning flashes as the huge tree outside the dormitory glowed in the eerie light. It was so bare and skeletal in the winter months, devoid of leaves and flowers, that to an imaginative seven-year-old, alone and in a strange new place, it had seemed like it was reaching out to grab me.

I glanced outside the window again as another flash lit the sky. *Just like that night,* I thought.

"Did she ever tell you the story about the dogs coming in at night?" I asked.

When I had been very little with my parents, I couldn't sleep until I'd checked under my bed for monsters with tails swishing behind them. Then I went to Nazareth House and black dogs replaced those monsters.

"The ones that would eat you if you didn't keep your arms crossed over your chest every night?" Sandra asked. "Boy, do I remember those! She scared the hell out of me."

"And the concerts? The ones at Christmas? Do you remember them?" I asked, almost in a daze.

She nodded eagerly. "Marilyn used to take me out by the Poinciana tree. Do you remember that huge tree? She used to take me out by the tree and give me singing lessons when I joined the choir," she smiled. "She was the one who needed the singing lessons."

Memories of Marilyn jumped into my mind. I could almost hear her thin, quivery voice. She had tried to give all of us singing lessons. The eldest girls, myself included, had totally ignored her but the younger ones weren't so lucky. I could still see her long wavy hair when she first arrived and the uneven crew cut it had become on her first day. She had cried for days afterwards but the only comfort we could give her was that we all had the same style and we knew it would eventually grow back.

Both of us were leaning forward and talking quickly.

"You were in the choir, too?" I asked. There had only been about twelve girls in that choir. "We were *both* in it?"

All the girls in the choir stood in St Bernard's Hall day after day singing 'Puff the Magic Dragon' while a nun faced us, her back to the where the audience would be, silently mouthing the words and waving a baton in an attempt to keep our singing in time. I don't think any of us understood what it was she was trying to do.

"I was only little," she ran her hand through her hair, "so I had to stand in the front row. I hated it because everyone could see me."

"The front row," I gaped. *Surely this couldn't be happening.* "I was in the second row." I could see myself standing there, my hands resting softly on a tiny girl in front of me as we sang. The memory brought a gasp to my lips. "Do you remember singing, 'Puff the Magic Dragon'?"

She laughed as she nodded. "If Sister Philomena only knew what *that* song was really about!"

As the laughter died, we looked at each other in wonder.

"Can this really be true?" I asked.

"I think it is," she replied nodding, just as amazed.

As we stared at each other, a huge sadness came over me at the unfairness of it all. Neither of us would have been alone all those years – we would have had each other.

So many memories raced through my head. I felt like I was being drawn back into my past with the force of a whirlpool. I hadn't thought about those early years in such a long time. It hurt too much. I'd tried so hard to bury them deep in my subconscious. It wasn't that the years at the home were entirely bad. Sure, they had seemed that way to a little girl who had known freedom and then all of a sudden had it all taken away. What had hurt more was that my whole life had been taken away from me, along with my parents.

"Tell me about you," Sandra asked, her eyes glued to my face.

Haltingly, I began. I told her about the happy days with mum and dad in the Valley. I told her about the independent little girl who had skipped to the swimming pool on hot humid days and came home filthy after hours walking the streets. I told her about the ride in the police car to the orphanage and I explained that it wasn't Nazareth House that caused me the most pain. It was the dozens of foster homes I had visited over those years that had left scars. It had been all of those pious and 'holier than thou' hypocrites that had almost pushed me over the edge. The orphanage had been merely a stepping-stone to those dreadful years. As I talked, I let all the memories bubble to the surface.

I think in my mind, I'd reasoned that if I hadn't been at Nazareth House, I wouldn't have had to endure the bewildering pain that those foster homes had caused me along with my feelings of insecurity and lack of self-worth. To myself, I'd glorified those early, lonely years in Spring Hill because the next stage in my life was so horrifying.

Sometimes, in a strange way, I can be almost a little grateful for that past. Almost. It made me strong and very independent, the person I am today. I have been through so much and have come through it all and I know that no matter what happens in the future I will be able to cope. Nothing will ever again take me to the depths of despair that I had once endured at the Andersons. Still, even though the outcome has left me a stronger more self-reliant person, I silently wish God had thought about it a little longer and found another way to achieve this end. It was a hard lesson for a young girl to learn.

The one and only good thing that had happened while I stayed with the Andersons had been when Mr Anderson had mentioned a sister to me.

There was one thing I just couldn't fathom. Why didn't I remember a little baby at home with Mum and Dad? Even before that first visit to Nazareth House when I had been four years old, I just couldn't remember a baby at all.

Suddenly, I pulled myself up and said, "Hang on. I was at Nazareth House twice: once when I was four years old and again when I was seven. That first time, I was only there for a few months before starting school in January 1960. I was born in 1955, when were you born?"

"September 22nd, 1959," she replied.

The difference was four years!

"That's why I don't remember a baby! I was at Nazareth House when you were born. By the time I came out, you must have already been adopted."

Everything fell into place for me but Sandra's face dropped.

"Why did she give me up for adoption at four months old?" she asked tearfully. "They brought *you* back out of the home. Why couldn't they keep us both?"

She had a catch in her voice and I could tell this was going to be hard for both of us to understand. It looked like our mother had tried to keep her but something or someone had changed her mind. I had no answers for Sandra. No one alive did.

A change came over us both. This reunion was not a thing of gossamer dreams any more. Our own private memories had overshadowed our feelings of euphoria, leaving us confused and uncertain.

As I spoke, it was with a voice that sounded ill at ease.

"I guess I'd better go now." I'd noticed it had turned midnight. "I own a small coffee shop and I have an early start in the morning. You probably do too. Can I call you tomorrow? Will you be home?"

"Yeah, I'll be home. Do you like working in the coffee shop?" she asked as she stood up.

"It's hard work and the hours are long," I said instantly. "But the kids and I like to eat," I grinned.

I said goodbye to Farouk and on the way to the front door, I turned and said, "Are you sure it's all right to call you tomorrow?"

She nodded as she gave me a watery smile, the result of too many tears. It was just too much to take in on one night.

I could feel the knot of tension in my shoulders as I drove home and knew I would have trouble getting to sleep that night.

As the clock limped to 2 am, I stared at the ceiling with gritty eyes replaying the words of the night over and over inside my head. My mind was like a kaleidoscope, as I lay awake.

Eventually I fell asleep and the dreams began.

On many occasions over the years I've dreamt of my life at Nazareth House, but never have the dreams been as clear as the ones I had that night. I was standing at the gates to Nazareth, trying to enter but unable to because they were closed and padlocked. As I peered through the bars, no one could be seen on the other side and briefly I wondered why I even wanted to be here at all. The driveway wound away from me and as I fought to see the huge building in the distance, darkness slowly began to fall. Twisted limbs from trees hung low over the unkempt driveway, nothing like I remembered.

I had a sense of evil things crouched low and menacingly in the hidden recesses of the wildness waiting for me. My heart was beating fast in my chest and tears came easily to my eyes.

Somehow, miraculously, I was through the gate.

The concrete was cracked and choked with weeds, and the tree roots protruded across the driveway like skeletal hands reaching for my ankles as I passed. Trees crowded together, their branches mingling to form an arch above my head, and the dank smell of wet soil came to me. Smaller trees grew between the larger ones struggling to reach the diminishing sun. None of this was familiar to me.

Now and then, I caught sight of a flower, so pure and beautiful, hidden amongst the weeds and strangling shrubs. It receded into the dark ugliness that surrounded it, like the innocence of the children so many years ago, lost in the horror and pain, slowly becoming a part of the darkness themselves.

On and on I walked, sometimes thinking I was lost, pushing my way through the jungle growth. I hadn't thought the road was this long.

And then, there was Nazareth House, silent and towering above me in the moonlight, just as I remembered it. Turning to my right, I could see the silvery moonlit water in the distance, so quiet and peaceful, not even a ripple to mar its beauty.

I turned back to the orphanage and as I did, I glanced towards the nun's cemetery, now overgrown with weeds crawling across the graves on their way to take over the main house. In my dream, I floated across the weeds, being drawn inextricably, toward lights that shone weakly in the windows.

As I hovered silently in the empty hallway, I had a feeling that I wasn't alone. The house lived and breathed all around me. Doors stood ajar and I could hear the faint lilt of an Irish ballad playing softly in the distance amidst the whispering voices of young children.

A breath of wind came up and just as suddenly all lights were extinguished, leaving me terrified and alone in the darkness.

My fear, so long buried, was threatening my sanity and a scream was making its way up into my throat.

Suddenly, I was awake bathed in sweat with tears rolling down my face. To anyone watching, my eyes would have looked wild.

Eventually, the pounding of my heart slowed as the comfort of my room fought its way through my terror.

GROUNDHOG DAY

My alarm was set to go off at 5am but I was awake and up out of bed well before that.

As I opened my car door at 5.30 am, birds twittered their disapproval for disturbing their morning rituals. *Oh, be quiet*, I thought. *I was up earlier than you.* It was then the kookaburras started to laugh.

The sun was moving slowly up over the horizon and the trees were casting long shadows but this morning I had absolutely no urge to go to work. Especially to Wynnum where my coffee shop was situated.

It's funny how certain places keep drawing you back to them. Wynnum was my magnet. It seemed I always ended up back there. When I'd finally passed my management exams, the company sent me to Wynnum. When I was looking at coffee shops to buy, I'd finally bought one, at Wynnum.

Every morning for the past three years, I'd done the same thing, five days a week, fifty weeks a year. I left home and drove down Old Cleveland Road, turned left into Ricketts Road and then right into Greencamp Road. I drove past Tilley Road on my left, surprised this morning that there were fewer roadworks holding up the traffic as they did every other morning. I then turned right onto Manly Road until I reached Tingal Road.

Every morning as I crested the hill and started the final decent to the shop, Nazareth House loomed high on the horizon just a few miles ahead, unchanging and judgemental, grey against the blue clarity of the sky, and dominating the skyline. Like a ghost haunting me. Almost like Groundhog Day.

I'd often thought God might be a sadist. I'd tried for so long to tuck my past away in the dim recesses of my mind, but He kept on bringing it back in to view, rubbing my nose in it, never letting me forget. Enforced therapy, you could call it.

As I looked out at the streetscape from the front door of my shop, I felt like a time traveller fresh from his Tardis. To my right, I could see the railway station I'd stood on thirty odd years ago as a ten-year-old and to my left was Edith Street where Crazy Clark's now stood replacing the Woolworths store.

Wynnum hadn't grown much since my childhood. There's been no nip and tucking here. The town of my youth has not transformed much. There's been no facelift, no exfoliation of its patchy exterior and no tarting it up for tourists. It still had only two main streets with little shops and offices facing each other across the washed-out pedestrian crossing on the main thoroughfare dotted with discarded cigarette butts and gum. The barbershop was still there, as was one of the jewellery stores, and the fish and chip shop with its fading Coke sign and hand-written menu offering a free potato scallop with every meal over $20. Replacing a few of the smaller clothing stores was a take-away chicken shop, an op shop and a Chinese takeaway. A few keen shop owners were making an attempt at providing alfresco dining with A-framed chalkboard menus, emblazoned with Italian coffee brands, standing unsteadily on the uneven bitumen sidewalks. But most residents were retirees and the effect was lost on them. There was no protection from the sun or rain and the pensioners much preferred to sit in air-conditioned comfort out of the weather.

Once, vacant blocks had dotted the streets like missing teeth but now there were fewer and fewer lots visible with steel and concrete commerce buildings emerging optimistically, blocking out the view to the beach. It was as if two towns were superimposed: the retirement village it had once been and the tough-working class community it was trying to become.

Some fairy godmother had visited, sprinkling silver pixie dust in the form of family trusts, self-managed funds and negative gearing, but she'd sprinkled it unevenly.

As I looked around, it looked like the youth had been ripped out of it. In the distance, an old man meandered unhurriedly, unburdened by unemployment, dressed in shorts and an unironed Hawaiian shirt. He ignored one of his contemporaries, unshaven and bleary-eyed, talking earnestly to himself, a brown paper bag clutched in his hand. A young girl shuffled past both of them, happy in her dreadlocks and dirty hippy-style dress and scuffed sandals, as a lycra-clad biker whizzed past on his carbon-fibre bike.

I was attempting to lure them all over to my shop. I had a good location, right near the railway station, and everyone had to pass my shop to go to the main shopping area. Unfortunately, that's exactly what they did some days. Walk right past. But, like everyone else, I had good days and bad days.

This day, I opened my shop at 6.30am after putting pies, a lamb and pork roast, a couple of quiches and a meatloaf in the big industrial gas oven. I cut up the salads for sandwiches, fried some dim sims and chiko rolls and made burger patties like a robot without even thinking about what I was doing. I had too much on my mind.

A group of roadworkers, dressed in hi-vis, came in and wolfed down their egg and bacon rolls at one of my outside tables as another group from the local hardware store streamed in, eyeing off the contents of my bain-marie. A steady flow of customers from the trains came and went but my mind was not on my work. I filled the drink fridges, put more pies in the oven, made a Lasagne and a teacake as well as an apple shortcake, another quiche and a chocolate cake. But my thoughts were with Sandra.

Margaret, my part-time helper, bustled in just before 10am in time for the morning tea crowd, so I couldn't tell her what had happened until our break at 11am, but she knew something had taken place. I couldn't stop smiling.

As I talked, I fiddled with a toasted cheese and tomato sandwich and a cup of tea that would be my lunch. I could barely form a coherent thought much less have a conversation with someone.

"What are the odds on something like this happening, Margaret?"

Her elbows were on the table as she looked at me over the top of her teacup. "It's certainly amazing. I can't wait to see a photo of her. Does she look anything like you?"

"Yes, I think so. When I first saw her, I thought *'I know you from somewhere'*. But you know what it was that was familiar? I could see myself in her face. She looks like me, particularly around the eyes and mouth. And definitely her hands. I only noticed just how much when I looked in the mirror this morning. You can definitely tell we're sisters. There's no doubt about that."

As I talked, a warm feeling ran through me, a sense of belonging at last. I'd never had a feeling so strong before. I wanted so much to be a part of my sister's life, it hurt.

I jumped up and said, "I'm going to call her."

"What are you going to say?" Margaret asked.

"I don't know. Just hello."

When Sandra answered, I felt a familiar lump in my throat.

"Hi." I said timidly. "I just wanted to say hello. I don't have much to say. I really just wanted to hear your voice again." I was beginning to sound and feel foolish.

"I was just thinking about you," she said almost shyly. "I rang Paula this morning and she wants us to go and see her on Sunday morning. Are you doing anything?"

"Not a thing," I said happily. With the shop closed on weekends, my time was spent with the boys, driving them to various basketball games. But miraculously, this weekend was a basketball free weekend. David would be home from a trip tomorrow but away again the next day, so Sunday was perfect. It didn't matter anyway. I would have changed any plans I had. I wanted to see her again.

David was the orderly who had married my friend at Greenslopes Hospital, the same one who'd left to join the Air Force all those years ago. I'd kept in touch with them both and over the years and they had two boys, whose ages were in between those of my two boys. They had moved around wherever the Air Force had sent them and had ended up living in Malaysia.

I lost contact with them around that time for many years but six months ago, I'd noticed David at a basketball game and our friendship revived again. He and his wife had divorced a few years ago around the same time as mine but it had taken five years for fate to work things out for us. A year ago, his work base changed from Melbourne to Brisbane and here we were, a couple. I never thought I'd fall in love with my best friend. Someone who had known me when I was young and could touch my face and trace the lines around my eyes with love and familiarity.

Sandra's voice brought me back to the present.

"I was thinking last night after you went home. I'm going to write back to Children's Services and get what they call Unidentifying Information," she said. "That's supposed to give you more information about your adoption and parents that's not included in the first lot of papers. Maybe it will tell us some more things that happened. I really need to know. I keep looking at my birth certificate. Open, close, open, close, to see if it's really true. I can't help feeling that it's just not fair. All these wasted years, you know?"

"I know exactly what you mean. I feel the same way."

I could hear voices filtering into the shop and I knew Margaret would have her hands full soon so, as much as I hated to, I had to go.

"Look, I'm sorry, I'm not brushing you off or being rude, but I have to go. It's starting to get busy here. I'll ring you later, okay?"

"You don't have to do that." I could hear the smile in her voice. "I'm all right. Really, I am. If you like, just meet me at my house on Sunday at about 10am and we'll go to Paula's together. She doesn't live very far from my house. Isn't that amazing?"

"I'm learning to expect the unexpected these days," I smiled. I could hear more voices coming into the shop. "I've really got to go but I'll see you on Sunday at ten. I'm really looking forward to it. Bye".

"Bye," she almost whispered, and hung up.

MEMORIES SURFACE

Saturday morning dawned clear and warm with only a few stray clouds in the sky. The boys had dashed out after breakfast with plans to meet friends at the PCYC, promising to be home by lunchtime. It meant I had the morning free to myself although I knew David would be dropping in before heading home after his three-day trip.

As I finished up the last of the breakfast dishes, my thoughts were with Paula and our meeting on Sunday morning. I looked forward to meeting her, but I was also feeling more than a little nervous. I also had an ulterior motive. I was desperate for any information about my father, no matter how inconsequential it may seem to her. I wanted it all. I needed to know everything about him. When had Paula last seen him? Did she have photos? How had he died? Where was he buried?

As I put the last of the dishes in the drainer, I dug desperately through my memories, but I just couldn't picture him.

How could I forget something so important? I asked myself. *His face, for goodness sake!*

My thoughts drifted back and I remembered occasions we'd spent together as if they were yesterday, but it was as though his face was in the shadows just out of reach, out of focus.

I remembered the time walking hand in hand with Dad down the hill to busy Wickham Terrace when the Queen visited. He perched me on top of his shoulders to catch a glimpse of 'Her Majesty' waving as her car drove past us. I remembered how my father had led me by the hand on Anzac Day as we marched proudly in the parade with the men of the 9th Division on our way to Anzac Square. I remembered the hat he always wore, the gentle smiles and the tender hugs. I could even feel his touch, smell the cigarette smoke on his fingers and feel his whiskery kiss.

I just couldn't *see* him.

I had just switched the coffee pot on when the front door opened, and a male voice called out.

"Hello? Anybody home?"

Stepping through the front door was David, still carrying his overnight bag and wearing his Qantas uniform. The boys would be spending the night with their father and I was looking forward to spending a quiet evening with him and catching up on all my news. Last night as I lay in bed, trying to go to sleep, I'd sent texts and voice messages to him, outlining what had happened so there were lots to talk about.

I wiped my hands on a tea towel and tossed it onto the kitchen bench before walking around to greet him with a smile and a hug. His blue eyes twinkled back at me as he put his overnight bag on the ground near the lounge chair and leaned in to hug and kiss me in return.

"Mmmm. I needed that," he smiled down at me, finally releasing me from his bear hug.

"Did you get my voicemails and texts last night?" I asked, eager to fill him in on everything. "I had to send three because they kept timing out," I laughed.

He beamed at me. "I listened to them all! That's why I wanted to come here first before I went home to shower and change." He held me at arm's length and grinned. "Wow!"

"I know! I still can't believe it! I have a sister and she's absolutely gorgeous," I gushed.

He pushed a stray hair back from my forehead and his eyes roamed my face. "Must run in the family."

I punched his arm playfully. "Seriously. The funny thing is, she *does* look familiar somehow. I couldn't place it for a second where I'd seen her before. Then it suddenly clicked. She looks a little like me! Can you believe that?"

"I'm so happy for you, honey," he said, taking his tie off as he spoke and throwing it over the lounge. "Did you have a late night?"

"Latish." I jiggled my head from side to side. "It was probably about 12pm when I left her house on Thursday night so Friday is a bit foggy. It's lucky today is Saturday. I don't think I could face another day of work. My mind is just not on the job. I need time to process all of this."

As I spoke, I was making coffee for us and he had perched himself on a stool on the other side of the bench, listening. I'd taken two cups from an overhead cupboard just as the coffee pot gurgled, announcing the coffee was ready.

Neither of us put sugar in our coffees, so I put a dollop of honey in each and gave it a quick stir before pushing the cup over to him. He smiled his thanks but left it sitting on the bench while he listened.

He knew me well. He knew every nuance, every frown and every tone of my voice. I was happy, no...ecstatic, to finally have a sister, but there were other issues involved here as well.

"We've made plans to see each other tomorrow as well." I'd been staring at my cup but not drinking either. I glanced up at him. "And to meet Paula."

"Ah," he said, nodding. "The half-sister."

He stood up and walked around to stand in front of me. He took the coffee cup from my hands and placed it on the bench before turning me to face him.

"I wish I could be there with you tomorrow honey but I'm off on another 2-day trip tomorrow afternoon. I'll be back on Tuesday though and you can tell me all about it." When I didn't answer he continued, searching my eyes. "It's probably best I'm not there anyway. It'll give you girls time to get to know each other a little more."

I was silent and he leaned down to look into my eyes. "Are you okay?"

I nodded. In the past two days, my emotions were in free fall. I went from happy to sad to nervous to angry, all in the space of an hour. I was having trouble controlling them all.

"So many wasted years, Dave. Thirty of them." I was beginning to tremble with anger. "We should have been allowed to grow up together. Or at least know that we all existed." I took a few shaky breaths. "I truly believe Sister Philomena knew. She had to. She had the paperwork from Children's Service for all the kids in the orphanage, so she'd have had ours. I even rang her years ago asking if she knew if I had a sister and she said no. A definite no. But she had to have known. Why did she say there was nothing?"

My voice had risen as I spoke. I was angry and hurt at the same time and full of pent-up resentment. Although I knew it was a futile thought, I felt like hitting out at the unfairness of the system.

"That was her big chance to make things right," I continued, as I searched his eyes for answers. "And still she didn't do it. Things could have been so different if she hadn't lied to me."

Emotion poured from David's eyes as he watched me.

"I know, honey. But don't concentrate on that. You know each other now. Be happy for that."

He stepped closer to pull me into a hug, but I stepped back out of his reach, crossing my arms over my chest in a defence motion.

I have no idea why I did it. I wanted him to hold me, to wash all the pain away. I *longed* for it. But something held me back. Something made me hesitate to open myself up to him.

He looked taken aback.

"What was that for?" he asked, a little shocked.

I glanced up at the hurt in his eyes and dropped mine to the floor.

"What was what for?" I asked.

Why did I just do that, I asked myself.

He stepped back. "That!" He waved at my crossed arms. "And pulling away from me!"

All I could do was shrug. It must have looked petulant but I had no answer for why I was doing this. One minute ago, I'd been laughing and now, I was withdrawing from the only person who has supported me and comforted me. There were so many emotions rampaging around in my head, each one was fighting its way to the surface.

"Come on," he urged. "What's up?"

A shuddering breath escaped as I whispered. "I'm afraid."

"Afraid?" His blue eyes opened wide. "Of what?"

The dreaded tears I'd been holding back now threatened to overflow and I angrily brushed them away. "I'm just afraid, okay! I'm afraid of losing her. I'm afraid of us. Me. You." A sob escaped. "Everything!"

He stepped forward but held himself back from touching me. Somehow, he knew not to go that one step further.

"Whoa! Where did all this come from?" He was shaking his head. "Afraid of *us*? *US?*" His voice softened. "I thought we were doing great."

He held his hand out tentatively. When I didn't pull back, he lifted it to cup my chin. Still I couldn't stop myself. I pulled my head back from his hand as the tears filled my eyes.

"Honey?" he said softly. "This is me." His eyes raked mine, waiting for me to reply. In the silence, I could hear his raged breath. "Tell me what's up. Please."

I gulped the tears back. "You *knew* it was going to be hard when we first started dating."

I had no idea where this anger was coming from. I knew he didn't deserve this but somewhere inside, a dam had broken and all the pain and hurt buried deep inside was rushing to the surface.

"If you only knew how hard it's been and how long it took me to rebuild my little universe, you would understand why I'm so careful about who I let in," I gulped. "I told you I have to learn to trust again. And it's hard! I'm so tired of hurting. And being hurt." I turned and grabbed a tissue from a box on the bench, dabbing angrily at my eyes. "I told you! I'm never going to let *that* happen to me again."

I blew my nose before continuing. I wanted to stop but I couldn't. "So if it's too hard for you, you can go." I looked up at him angrily. "In fact, why don't you just go now!"

In the first year after Michael's departure from my life, I would call up his face when I felt lost and hopeless. Whenever I would sit, my mind would wander and I would soon think of him. Even when I hated doing it. Even when I tried to make my life go forward, the horrible memories tugged at me. Then, I reminded myself of how low I'd been, and I used his memory as a prod to rise above my misery. To realise how lucky I was to have survived *that*. I'd been to the bottom. Now I was ready for the top.

It had been five years since then and my life has changed. And I've changed with it. Or so I thought. What the hell was happening to me now? Why was I raging like a maniac at David when he'd done nothing to deserve it?

David's hands were up in a defence pose, and I could see the confusion in his eyes.

"Hey! Trish! Stop this! This is *me*! You know I'd never hurt you."

I gave a little snort. "If I had a dollar for every time I heard *that* one…"

"But not from me!" The hurt in his voice almost broke me. "You *know* that's not me. YOU KNOW THAT. You've known me for 25 years! I'd NEVER hurt you."

I hated myself at that moment as I stared at the tears swimming in his eyes. I'd let my pain take over and I'd lashed out at the one person who I knew beyond a doubt would never hurt me.

Just as suddenly as the tension had crackled in the air, it subsided. He lifted my face with his hands.

"And I will never abandon you, honey."

His voice was so soft it was almost a whisper. But the words, the words! All of a sudden, my shoulders began to shake, and the sobs rose unconstrained. I put my hands over my eyes and let the tears fall. Through the sobs, I could hear his voice, tender with emotion.

"You're pushing me away because you think I'll do the same as everyone else. Your parents. The foster parents you went to. The nuns. Everyone." There was a second of silence. "But *I* won't. And that's a fact."

I dropped my hands and looked up at him through the tears.

"I'm not going anywhere." He did a little jiggle with his head. "Well, I have to go to work but…"

We both smiled at the attempt of a joke, and it was all I needed. How could I do this to him? How could I wound him so terribly when I knew he didn't deserve it?

"There's something else, too, isn't there?" he asked softly.

I nodded. "I don't know what to do," I whispered. "How am I supposed to act around her, Dave? What do I say? She's hurting. I'm hurting. And I have no idea what to say to her." My voice was beginning to sound panicked, even to my own ears. "All my life I've been able to change myself into someone else. Someone that people wanted me to be. As a kid, I'd watch all the other kids and I'd smile if I had to. And I'd laugh if I had to. Even if I felt like the world was crashing down around me, I smiled and laughed and never let anyone know how I was really feeling. That my heart was breaking."

My breath was still shuddering as I spoke.

"I never let anyone know there was this pain, right here in my heart," I held a hand over my heart, "that never went away. *Changing* myself was the only way I knew how to survive. I had to change myself into someone I thought was lovable, just to bloody survive! But at least I knew what I had to do! But now," I clenched my hands together momentarily in front of my mouth to stop the gulps, "what the hell am I supposed to do *now*? How do I act around her? What do I even *say*?"

I dropped my hands and looked into his pained eyes. "I just don't know, Dave. I hardly even know who *I* am. How do I help *her*? I've tried so hard to forget everything and here it is, all over again."

He brushed my hair away lovingly from my tear-stained face. "Honey. That's just the little girl in you. You were abandoned as a child but not because you weren't lovable. It was just circumstances beyond your control. Beyond your parent's control. You were just a kid. It wasn't your fault or anything you did."

He smiled softly at me and I could see the love flowing out from those beautiful eyes of his. The love was swallowing me whole and a calmness was beginning to take over.

"You never act around me," he smiled softly. "Do you?"

I shook my head.

"And I've never seen a more lovable person."

I bit my lips before asking, "What if I lose her, Dave? I couldn't bear it."

"You won't lose her, honey. She wants you as much as you want her."

"But what if she doesn't like me," I persisted. "What if she suddenly thinks she's made a terrible mistake and doesn't want to see me anymore? And what about Paula? She has every right to hate me. My mother stole her father from her. I'm so scared Sandra will walk away from me and I'll be alone again." I was shaking my head. "I can't do that again. I just can't!"

David took me in his arms. "Come on, sweetheart. Paula won't hate you. You've done nothing wrong. And Sandra is not going anywhere. You know I'm right."

I looked up at him. "This has brought back so many memories, Dave. Don't get me wrong," I said quickly. "I'm so happy she found me. But it's also brought back so much sadness. It's brought back memories of all those years in the orphanage and foster homes. Years of feeling like I wasn't good enough. Years and years of hurt and pain. It hurts so damn much! What if Sister Philomena was right all along? What if I'll never amount to anything? She used to call me gutter trash."

David snorted. "You've already proven her wrong! You're a wonderful strong woman. You almost own your own house. You've raised two wonderful boys and you're a successful, beautiful businesswoman.

I chuckled weakly. "I own a small coffee shop. A VERY small coffee shop. I barely make ends meet at the end of the month."

He shrugged. "That's beside the point. You were determined to make a go of it, and you did. You've gone through more shit in your life than most of us, and you've survived it all. You could have just given up, but you didn't. You pushed on and you succeeded. You should be proud of yourself, girl, not doubting yourself."

The tears had subsided at his words and I could feel the panic leaving me.

"She's going to love you as much as I do," he continued. "I've loved you from the first moment I saw your beautiful legs in that obscenely short dress at Greenslopes Hospital. And I've loved you every day since. I've always loved you and I'll never stop loving you. Come on." He pulled me close. "Be happy. You have a sister. And you have me. You're a very lucky girl. Now come here and give me a decent kiss."

Suddenly, all the pain melted away.

OUT OF THE SHADOWS

Sunday was a typically beautiful March day with clear blue skies and a few clouds that looked like they'd been shot out of a whipped cream can.

I picked up Sandra and Farouk at their house and as we drove to Paula's, the car was filled with a heavy silence with none of us knowing what we might be walking into. Neither Sandra nor I had anticipated the nerves we both felt as we approached the house.

Paula was now a woman of fifty, thirteen years older than Sandra and nine years older than me, but still I felt very tentative about meeting her. In her shoes, I'm not sure how I would have reacted. She was, after all, meeting two children from the relationship of her father and his mistress: the same woman who took her father away from her mother when she was nine. The best we could hope for was that she didn't treat us with animosity.

As we passed through the front gate, we heard a buzzer sound inside the house, obviously from a sensor set up in the garden alerting Paula that we had arrived. The path to her house ran alongside a forest of a garden that let in sparse light to the ferns massed around the trees. Before we could knock, Paula was standing at the open door.

She was taller than both of us, slim, with hair as dark as Dad's had been. Her large eyes were the same size as ours but they were a soft blue, much the same as Sandra's. She had an air of self-confidence as she greeted us with a smile.

We needn't have worried how she would react to us. She was obviously pleased to see us both.

After she gave us all a hug and introductions were quickly made, she said, "Come on in," and we trooped single file through her lounge room to a cosy kitchen where a middle-aged man stood beside a table that was laden with enough food for an army. She said, "This is Barry, my husband."

I looked at Barry, trying to recognise the man I had met at the Exhibition. I barely remembered his face from so many years ago, so I had no chance of recognising him now. He was in his early fifties with a full head of grey hair and a quick smile.

"Please, sit down," he said, pulling out a few chairs.

Paula looked at me, smiled and said, "Promise me you won't throw up on my carpet."

"Excuse me?" I was totally confused and just a little insulted. What on earth did she mean by that?

"Didn't Sandra tell you that I remembered you from when we went to the Exhibition?" she asked with a smile on her face.

"Yes, she did," I replied, still not knowing where this conversation was going.

"Don't you remember what happened when we left? In the taxi? Surely you couldn't forget *that*."

"Oh, God. I *do* remember!" Suddenly it all came back to me. "The taxi. I threw up in the back of it. Now I remember." I could feel myself blushing as I remembered the end of that day came back to me. "After all that rubbish I ate, and a strawberry milkshake, I went on a ride in side show alley. The Beatle Bug, wasn't it?"

"That's right. I can still see the look on the taxi driver's face when he glanced over his shoulder at his new décor in the back seat. What a spectacular colour it was. I doubt that the extra money Dad gave him made up for the time spent cleaning and airing his cab for the rest of the night."

I was feeling very embarrassed as I said, "I hope I make a better impression this time. I had no idea who you were, or that you were my sister."

She was nodding as I spoke and finally said, "Yep, that was me. You stayed with Barry and me for that weekend."

"God, you were a quiet kid," he said shaking his head. "You hardly said a word the whole time."

"I must admit," Paula continued with a half-smile "I was very dubious about this meeting today. Mr Anderson rang me years ago looking for you when you ran away. After he told me you had gone wild, I had visions of someone with tattoos and multiple body-piercings turning up on my doorstep in leather after stepping off a motorbike."

Unwanted thoughts of that bastard jumped into my mind. All the sleepless nights I'd spent listening for the creaks outside my door. The many nights sitting on his lap while his hands ran up and down my legs as I gritted my teeth and tried to think of anything but what was happening. I remembered sitting in the corner of my room feeling sick to my stomach and sobbing quietly, praying God would take me and put me anywhere else but where I was. I'm sure Mr Anderson didn't tell Paula all the hideous things he'd made me endure over those three years.

I could barely keep the bitterness from my voice as I muttered, "Don't believe everything you hear, Paula."

As we sat and drank cup after cup of coffee, reminiscing came easily.

"You know," she said with a little barb in her voice, "You probably have as many memories of Dad as I do."

The words were not really aimed at me but aimed at circumstances as they were. I realised then that I wasn't the only one who adored and missed him. It was only then I realised the hurt had not stopped with me. Paula and her family had been affected as well. I'd been so engrossed in how *I* felt, I hadn't looked past my own feelings.

"When Dad left us, he only came back every now and then to see us, sometimes with Pop. You remember Pop, don't you?"

I nodded. I remembered the white-haired magician who produced coins from behind my ears.

"He adored kids," Paula said. Then, "Do you remember they both loved horse racing?" she mused. "One Saturday, Dad and Pop had been to the races, and as I stood in the front yard expecting them at any moment, I saw them both coming down the road, but on opposite sides of the street. Neither of them were talking or looking at each other and the expressions on their faces were as black as thunder. It looked so funny, but it was obvious they'd lost their money."

She stood up abruptly, walked into the lounge room and brought back some photos. Silently she handed one to me.

And there he was! Finally. Out of the shadows, and back in focus. DAD.

I gasped and tears rolled down my face as I stared at the photo.

"Oh God," I spluttered. "That's him!"

He was smiling that wonderful smile I remembered, as though he was pleased to see me again after all these years. It was a black and white photo taken when he was in Egypt during World War 2, standing in his uniform, hands behind his back and legs slightly apart, looking so handsome and happy. I wanted to hold that photo close to my heart and pretend it was Dad I was holding.

Through all of this, Sandra sat and listened silently, not able to participate, not knowing anything about this man we were discussing. Fragmented as our memories were, she had nothing like we had, no memories at all. All she had was this black and white photo of a stranger while Paula, yet another stranger, told her that this man was her father.

It didn't occur to me at the time that the coming years of adjustment would be hard for us all as we learnt about each other, becoming not only friends but sisters as well. I was totally oblivious to all this at the time. All I knew was that I was happy. I had a sister, plus a half-sister, photos and loads of memories.

"I would have taken you when Dad died, you know," Paula mumbled as she looked down at her hands. She lifted her head and said, "But I had kids of my own by then. A two-year-old and a new set of twins. I just couldn't."

"Oh Paula, I don't feel bad about all that. Don't even think that." I was sad to see her distressed.

On my way home, I decided the afternoon had turned out better than I could have expected.

BUT WAIT...THERE'S MORE

Sandra and I started to settle into our new roles. One weekend, she came over for afternoon tea. We were still a little nervous, each of us trying to please the other one, on our best behaviour.

While I made the coffee, she walked outside to sit at the table and chairs under the pergola. I loved this area with all its hanging plants and ferns everywhere. I called it 'my jungle'.

My dog, a lovable Doberman by the name of Zoe, came bounding over to Sandra, waiting patiently for the pat she hoped was coming. Zoe was a legacy of David's. He had moved in with me several weeks ago and had brought her with him. She was wonderful company for me when he was away and both my boys were doing their own thing.

"How can you stand to have a black dog around?" Sandra asked, looking down at Zoe.

I knew exactly what she meant. It had taken me many years to overcome my phobia about black dogs.

"I couldn't for years," I smiled. "But as I grew older I realised just how stupid I was being. Sister Philomena's story about the black dogs couldn't possibly be true. It was just a story to keep all the children in their beds at night."

I could see her staring at Zoe.

"Do you remember the long walks the nuns used to take us on?" She looked up at me. "We used to walk hand in hand down to the front gate and back again through the paddocks. Mostly Saturdays after hair washing, I think it was."

I nodded, remembering only too well the cowpats we had to avoid.

"I remember one Saturday when Sister Philomena took us for a walk. We had almost reached the gate when we all saw a large black dog on the outside of the gate, sitting and watching us while saliva dripped off its tongue. We all stopped and gasped as we turned to look at Sister Philomena. I remember being so scared."

Sandra was looking down at her hands again. She had a habit of doing that when she was thinking about things that were painful for her. She looked up at me and continued.

"She said to all of us, *'Children, make a sign of the cross and say Jesus Mary and Joseph protect me'*. Everyone remembered vividly the stories of devils and black dogs so we hurriedly crossed ourselves. When we turned back to look at the gate, the dog had gone!" She laughed, "I suppose the sight of fifty noisy children bearing down on you is enough to make any sane person, let alone a dog, turn tail and run. At the time, that never occurred to any of us. We thought this was the best magic we had ever seen and we all walked back quickly, thanking Jesus, Mary and Joseph for protecting us and knowing that our hands would definitely be staying in bed crossed over our chests that night."

I sat there staring at her with my mouth agape. Sometimes, I felt the world tilting crazily. I remembered that day. I'd been there at the gate as well.

As I looked at her, the resemblance between us was striking. How could the nuns not have seen it as well? We didn't remember each other but we had been children. Surely the obvious resemblance that existed between us now, existed then. I wished to God that it had been noticed.

The hours passed by quickly and soon she rose to leave.

"Why don't you ring Farouk and see if he wants to come over for dinner?" I asked. I didn't want to let her go.

"Depends on what's for dinner," she replied playfully.

I grinned as I said, "Your choice. Tripe or Haddock?"

"Oh, God. You just lost me. Never again in my life will I eat Tripe or Haddock. I can't even stand the smell of either of them. Three years of eating that stuff in the home is enough to last me a lifetime. No, I'm going home for a pizza."

* * *

ONE WEEK LATER, Sandra rang while I was standing in the shower. She did this so often, it seemed as if she knew when to ring.

I grabbed the towel from the rack and threw it on the carpet before standing on it to answer the bedroom phone.

"Hello," I said breathlessly.

"It's me," she said simply. "Can you come and see me? I've received my bits in the mail from Children's Services and you're just not going to believe what it says."

"Can't you tell me over the phone? You've done it again. I'm in the shower," I laughingly replied.

"Oh, no. You've got to see this to believe it." She was serious.

"Okay. I'll probably be an hour by the time I get dressed and dry my hair. Is that alright?" I asked. My curiosity was getting the better of me.

"Sure," she said. "See you soon."

An hour later, we were sitting at Sandra's dining table with paperwork spread out on the table.

Sandra reached across and picked up one individual piece of paper. "Merle's birth certificate is here as well," she said. She couldn't bring herself to call our mother *Mum*. "I went back to the Registry Office with mine and bought a copy of hers. I made a copy for you too."

I took the certificate from her and mumbled my thanks.

"I never thought to do this," I said, looking down at the certificate. "I guess if I'm honest, I never wanted to. I was hurting too much. I never believed she loved me. Not even a little bit."

Tears were welling up in my eyes as I looked down at the certificate. "I don't even remember much about her. She was always this *vague* person. Just this wispy person in the shadows. After I ran away from my last foster home, I used to walk through Queen Street Mall hoping to catch a glimpse of her. I imagined walking up to her and saying, 'Remember me? I'm doing great without you, thanks very much.' Not that I remembered what she even looked like."

I tore my eyes away from the certificate. "She never even visited me in the home, you know. Not even once. I know it's sad for you because you never knew her. And I know you wish you had. But I was with her until I was seven. I was this little girl with a personality and all I wanted from her was love." I sniffled. "But I don't think she really ever loved me. I was always this dirty urchin who broke things and spilt things. But all I wanted was for her to love me and take me home. But she never came to visit and I finally stopped asking for her."

It felt so natural talking to her and she was such a good listener.

"Dad came every now and then," I continued. "But he eventually gave up on me too. He couldn't even bother to visit me when I was thirteen at the last foster home. That was my big chance to escape and he couldn't even drag himself away from the pub to see me. Not even for half an hour."

The pent-up emotion was spilling out of me now, taking over, but still she listened.

"I gave up on both of them after that. I learnt to despise both of them for not wanting me. It was just my way of protecting myself, I guess."

She touched my arm softly and took the certificate out of my hand and placed another sheet of paper in my hand. "Read this instead. I'll make us a cup of tea."

She stood and walked to the kitchen bench and busied herself as I read the paperwork.

"Read it out loud," she called out. "I want to hear it again."

The letterhead read 'State Children's Department'.

"*At the time of adoption,*" I read, "*it was not departmental practice to obtain detailed background information from birth parents as is the case today. As such, there is no record of any physical descriptions, special interests, hereditary traits or medical information. It appears that at the time of your birth on September 22nd, 1959, your birth mother was living as man and wife with your birth father. He was listed as 'married with children from a previous marriage'. It was her intention to care for you herself and she said that your birth father* *was willing to support you both. However, your birth mother signed a consent for your adoption in January 1960. No reason is recorded for her change of intention'"*

I stopped reading as Sandra walked over with two teas in her hand, not sure if she wanted me to continue. The words must be painful for her to hear.

She placed a cup in front of me and took a seat beside me. "Keep going," she urged softly.

I took a sip of the tea before continuing. '*Your birth mother had two daughters born 1952 and 1955 who were also adopted.*" My eyes opened wide. "*Your sister born on 16th March 1952 was named Annette Maud Miner and your sister born on 21st May 1955 was named Patricia Therese Gourgaud.*'

I dropped the letter on the table and raised my eyes in shock to look at Sandra as goosebumps ran up and down my legs and arms.

"Another one! Before me?" I asked, stunned.

"Looks like it," she said with a catch in her voice. I could hear something different in her voice now. A hesitation almost. I tried to see what it was but it was like the shutters had come down.

My eyes dropped to the letter again. "Hang on a second. Look at this."

I pointed at the section that said, 'Living Issue' of Esmond Terence MOONEY, Merle's father, at the time of her birth. There were two names: Terence Ronald aged 4 and Kevin James aged 2.

"She had two brothers," I exclaimed. "Terence and Kevin. Both older."

"One problem at a time," she put her hands up in surrender. "First, let's think about this other sister." She picked up the letter and began reading again.

"Shall we ring Paula?" I asked. "She may know something. What do you think?" I was in a daze.

Sandra was just sitting, holding the letter but not saying word.

"Sandra? What do you think?" I repeated.

"Huh? Oh. I guess so. I don't know what to think any more."

I dug around in my bag for my address book. Even though she was now married and had a different surname, she was still very proud of her maiden name and we had a standing joke between us, calling each other Ms P Gourgaud.

Paula answered the phone after only a couple of rings.

"Hi, Paula. It's Trisha here. Have you got a couple of minutes to spare?"

"Sure," she said. "What's up?"

I glanced over at Sandra. She was still sitting at the table looking at the letter. Both our cups were empty now and I mouthed, *Shall I make another cup of tea?* She nodded absently.

As I talked, I put the phone between my shoulder and ear and filled the jug before switching it on. "Sandra received her papers in the mail today from Children's Services and you'll never guess in a million years what they say."

"Okay. What?"

"They say that we also have another sister four years older than me who was adopted at birth. I thought you might know something about this. My first thought was to call you."

After a slight hesitation, she said, "Was she one of the twins?"

"Twins?" I asked dumbfounded. "What twins?"

Sandra's head snapped up and her mouth opened in amazement.

For goodness sake, what next? I thought. I felt like Alice in Wonderland, falling down a hole and finding myself in another where everything was different and weird. I'd studied chemistry at school, but I hadn't learnt too much, apart from discovering that you could throw something extra into a test tube and it could blow up with a bang. We'd just found that something extra. That's how I felt.

"I'm not sure of the details," Paula started, "but I remember Dad coming home to visit us one day saying that there had been a set of twins. I haven't any idea what age I was."

This was getting out of control.

"Paula, are you sure he said that? There wasn't any mention of twins in Sandra's letter. Do you think you could have been mistaken? God, how many kids did they have?" I asked dumbfounded.

The kettle was boiling softly, so I put the phone back between my shoulder and ear again, turned it off and started pouring water into each of the mugs holding a tea bag each. Still balancing the phone, I opened the fridge and found the milk. I glanced at Sandra to see if she minded me rummaging around in her kitchen. Although sisters, we were still strangers to each other in many ways, and a woman's kitchen is her own private domain. She hadn't even looked up from the letter.

"I suppose I could be mistaken," Paula said hesitantly, "but I can almost hear his words. Maybe he was talking about someone else. I just don't know. I was very young."

She had sounded so sure to start with but was gradually getting more and more doubtful as she continued. "I wish I could help, but I don't really know anything."

I hung up feeling more confused than I had before the phone call.

"You know what I'm going to do?" I said as I jiggled the tea bags. "I'm going to request my papers as well from Children's Services. I'd like to get my own original birth certificate anyway, and maybe there'll be something in my papers that isn't in yours."

"Sure," she said, sounding distracted.

I walked over to her with the mugs in each hand and handed one to her. "Here. Drink this." It came out sounding more like an order. "It'll do you good." My voice was low, barely a whisper. "Everyone knows that tea is the remedy for any shock. You're half Irish so you must know that. It's bred into us."

I knew she was having a hard time with everything. I, at least, had some hint that she existed. This was all so overwhelming for her. As she had once said to me, she had only started all of this to find a mother.

As we sipped our tea, I didn't come up with any solutions or theories. I was just there. I just wanted to wait for her lead.

BUTTERFLIES IN MY STOMACH

I was watching the clock on Monday morning and as soon as Margaret arrived, I rang Children's Services and asked them to fax me the appropriate forms. Following all the guidelines, I filled them out and by the end of the week I'd posted them back. In the meantime, while I waited for the papers to arrive, we had a sister to find.

The next Saturday evening, after spending the entire week wishing for it to end, we were sitting together making plans.

"Okay," I said to Sandra, "let's start in the phone book again. That's where you started when you were looking for me." I looked around. "Where's your phone book? She'll probably be married but we may be lucky and find a brother or parents or some relative."

Sandra walked over to the phone table and brought back the White Pages and opened it at the 'M' section.

"There's a full column of Miners. This'll take all night," she grumbled.

"Well, I guess we can start tonight and see how far we get. Tomorrow, we split the rest and you ring half and I'll ring the other half. All right?"

"Okay," she said. "You start first."

It took only three calls before an elderly sounding woman said, "Yes, I have a daughter called Annette."

She listened quietly as I innocently, and perhaps naively, told her my story of a newly found sister and how I hoped I'd traced Annette to this number.

There was a long silence and I almost thought the connection had been broken. Then I heard her take a deep breath before speaking.

"I've been dreading this day all of Annette's life. My husband and I adopted Annette at birth as well as a boy seven years before her. Neither of them knows they're adopted. And I'm not going to tell them," she stated with growing agitation. "I'll lose her. She won't love me anymore and I can't risk that. Does your mother want to meet her too?"

"Our mother is dead, Mrs Miner," I told her. "It's just Sandra and me, now."

"Oh," was all she said. I thought she sounded a little relieved.

Her pain touched me as I tried desperately to reassure her.

"We're not taking her away from you, Mrs Miner. We just want to share her." I had an overwhelming urge to make her understand. "No one can take Annette away from you. You will always be her mother. You were the one who tucked Annette into bed when she was little. It was you who bandaged the scraped knees and who was there on the first day of school and marriage. It's not just having a baby that creates a bond; it's the day-to-day living and caring that makes a relationship. You're more her mother than the woman who gave birth to Annette. It's only a myth that the act of giving birth immediately makes you maternal or gives you the ability to be a mother. She will always love you. You *are* her mother."

Still, no matter what I said, she would not change her mind. She flatly refused to give me Annette's married name or her phone number.

We ended our conversation with my vow to her, "I'm not giving up, you know. No matter what you say, I'm not giving up." I was angry at what I saw as selfishness in the woman. "You've had her to yourself all of her life." I knew I sounded desperate but I couldn't help it. "Sandra and I have spent our whole lives not knowing her, and now it's our turn."

"You'll end up killing my husband," she said as she started to cry. "He's not well. This will be on your head. This will kill him."

"I'm sorry for all of this. I really am. But you have to see it from our side as well. It's not fair what you're asking me to do. Surely, you see that, don't you?"

"Please don't do this," she begged.

I took a deep breath. "I have to. The best I can do is to call you when I find her married name and address. I will keep looking, you know. But I promise I'll think seriously about what you've said before I do anything. That's the best I can offer."

"Thank you," she said meekly before she hung up.

In hindsight, this pretty speech was probably just as selfish of me. I was possibly too eager to get on with this next phase of my life and it hadn't occurred to me yet that maybe some things are best left alone.

But I was unstoppable and unrelenting. I had been given a challenge and I was oblivious to the possible distress that the outcome could cause. All I knew was I had been deprived of my family for thirty-five years and the fighting Irish in me was not about to give up and stop looking now. The possibility of failure never entered my mind.

Sandra listened to every word of the conversation. "What do we do now?" she asked.

"We keep looking," was all I said.

Mrs Miner had unwittingly given us the key to finding Annette by telling us she also had an adopted son. With renewed determination, Sandra and I went back to the phone book once more looking for Annette's brother, knowing this would be easier since his name would still be Miner.

Again, after only a few calls, a woman answered the phone and said, "Yes. I know Annette Miner. She's my sister-in-law but she's not Miner anymore. She's married. Her name is Sullivan now. Who did you say was speaking?"

I looked at Sandra and put my index finger and thumb together in the universal gesture of 'okay' as I continued.

Having been bitten once, I knew I would have to change my story. This time, I made no mistake.

"I'm an old school friend and I'm organising a school reunion," I lied as I crossed my fingers. "Do you think you could give me her phone number and address so we can contact her?"

"Sure. But I doubt if she would be able to come. She lives in Cairns now and has since her husband died. She remarried and went to live there about thirteen years ago." I could hear papers rustling. "Here it is", she said. "Do you have a pen?"

I wrote the number down and thanked her, marvelling at the ease with which this white lie had succeeded. I hung up feeling very pleased with myself, although a little guilty at the deception.

"You call her," Sandra stated.

"Not right now. Let's think about it. You heard what Mrs Miner said. She doesn't even know she's adopted. Do we have the right to do this? You know, she may not even be the right Annette Miner. Stranger things have happened before. We may have the wrong one. Have you thought about that?" My conscience was telling me to stop. "I even promised Mrs Miner that I would ring her first," I continued, stalling.

"We'll ring her from the airport," Sandra said determinedly.

"No, Sandra. Come on, let's think about it tonight."

"One night," Sandra said holding up a finger.

* * *

THAT NIGHT, I lay awake for hours thinking about whether what we were doing was right. My mind was running in circles and I could feel a headache coming on behind my eyes. A tension headache.

A lot depended on this decision. People's lives would change because of it. But if we didn't call Annette, we would forever wonder if that had been the right decision. Didn't she have a right to know the truth? I was convinced Mrs Miner had been wrong not to tell her about the adoption. Perhaps I was being selfish again, but the thought lodged firmly in my mind. She should have been the one to tell her, not me, I thought. If Annette had decided not to contact her birth family, that would have been Annette's decision. But instead, she had never been given that choice. I know it had been done out of love, but it had still been wrong. It was Annette's right to know the truth. Wasn't it?

It may not even be her, I thought. The clincher would be the birth date given in the letter from Children's Services. If it matched with hers, then we had the right person.

With butterflies in my stomach, I made the call the next morning.

She answered the phone with a bright, "Hello".

"Annette Sullivan?" I asked.

"Yes," she replied.

"I'm sorry to bother you," I haltingly started, "but could you tell me if your maiden name was Annette Miner?"

"Yes, it was," she answered with a slight question in her voice.

"Annette Maud Miner?"

"Yes."

"And is your birth date the 16th March 1952?"

"Yes." I could hear her wariness growing. "Why are you asking?"

We'd actually found her. But once again, not having thought first about what I was going to say, I'd walked into a situation like I was John Wayne with all my guns blazing.

"I'm sorry," I started. "I can't tell you right now, but I promise I'll ring you back tonight."

"Wait! Did somebody die?" she quickly asked before I hung up.

"No, no, nothing like that," I replied as reassuringly as I could. "I really am sorry, but I'll explain it all tonight." And then I hung up.

If someone had left me high and dry like that, I would have gone mental, but I felt I had no other choice. I needed to think this through. I was again starting to have doubts about what we were doing.

Annette was forty-four now and so many people's lives could be affected by this next call to her. Did I have the right to make it? On the other hand, I was ecstatic at having not one sister, but two! Three if you counted Paula. And then I remembered that Paula had a sister, which meant she was my half-sister as well. Four! And a half-brother! My head was swimming.

All my thoughts from the night before ran through my head again, but my doubts were quickly overridden by the prospect of future happiness and I could hardly contain myself. I knew that deep down, I desperately wanted to make that call. The lure of my elusive family was too much for me to ignore.

That night after telling Sandra what I was going to do, I rang Annette. She answered after only one ring, obviously waiting for the call.

I took a deep breath and launched into the story.

"I'm sorry about this morning, but I had some things to think over." I was so nervous my hands were shaking as I held the phone. "My name is Patricia, Trisha, and I was adopted when I was quite young. About six weeks ago, I had a phone call from a woman by the name of Sandra who has also been adopted and who has recently discovered that she has a sister. Through a long process, she discovered that sister was me. She sent away for more information from Children's Services and they sent a letter back saying that we also had an older sister. They gave us the name and birth date."

"But what has this got to do with me?" she asked.

"It says you're our older sister," I stated bluntly.

There was complete silence at the other end of the phone. Then, "But that can't be true," she said. "I already have a mother and father."

"Yes, I know," I haltingly started. "I spoke to your mother yesterday and told her the story and she eventually admitted to me that you and your brother were both adopted. She said she didn't tell you then and won't tell you now because she's scared of losing you."

"I...I...I can't believe it. Mum said that? How is she? Is she upset you called me?"

"I haven't told her yet. I wanted to talk to you about that."

"There has to be some other explanation. I just can't believe this. This is all too much for me to take in."

She was denying everything. What else had I expected?

"I've got to think about all this. Does Paul know, too?"

"If Paul is your brother, then no, I haven't told him anything. That's up to you if you want to tell him."

"I've got to find out for myself if this is true. I can't think right now. I'll have to call you back after I sort this out."

I gave her my number and sat back, praying I'd done the right thing.

I don't know what I expected but this wasn't it. I thought we'd both be happy. Instead I felt empty. Had I expected her to open her arms to me straight away? It had been very unrealistic of me to think that would happen. Of course she would be upset. Of course she would be doubtful. How stupid of me to think that she wouldn't be. I tried to put myself in her shoes but I couldn't. I'd never had a normal family life and I couldn't imagine what it would feel like.

Oh, God, I hope I've done the right thing.

* * *

As promised, she called back a few days later with endless questions.

"I've written to Children's Services and requested my own papers," she said determinedly. "I have to see it for myself in black and white. In the meantime, could you ring my mother back and tell her that you decided not to contact me? Both my parents are in their seventies now and I don't want anything to upset them. Besides, Dad's not well. If it turns out that we are sisters, I probably won't tell them anyway. I'd rather their last few years are happy ones."

With this sentiment in mind, I was able to make that call to Mrs Miner after all.

FOR SHE MEANS THE WORLD...

The ensuing weeks of occasional phone calls between Annette, Sandra and me brought an acceptance by her that we probably were her sisters, and during this time, we learnt about each other's backgrounds.

"I've always lived in Brisbane," she started. "Until about twenty years ago when my husband and I moved to Townsville. Allan was my second husband. I married way too young the first time and got a divorce a couple of years later."

I could hear her take a deep breath before she continued. "Allan and I had three children before we moved up there. We bought a house and were trying to do it up ourselves. One day, he was standing on a stool fixing a light fitting and something went wrong. All he could say was, "Turn the electricity off, Annette." By the time I got back inside the house, he was dead. He'd been electrocuted. I felt so empty for ages. I couldn't even cry for a while. Shock, I guess."

"Do you want to talk about this? You don't have to, you know," I said hearing the sorrow in her voice.

"No, it's fine. That was thirteen years ago. You never really get over something like that but you have to keep going. After all, I had three little girls to look after. Anyway, Don was a close friend of ours and he helped me when he could. After a while, we fell in love and moved to Cairns, and then Mary came along."

"You've got four girls?" I asked.

"Yes. Mary is the last one."

"You're very lucky," I said, laughing. "I would have given my eye teeth to have a girl."

"It's not all fun and games. Four girls are a lot of work." There was silence for a few seconds before she said, "I've been thinking. Last week, you told me Merle had two brothers. The names were Terence and Kevin, weren't they?" She was hungry for any information I could give her and she had honed in on one of my age four memories. "Do you know where they are?"

I hadn't even thought of contacting them, but she was right.

"Hang on. You're right. Let me have a look." I grabbed the phone book and found to my amazement, a Terrence Mooney living only twenty minutes from me and only ten minutes from Sandra.

"You know, there's a Terrence Mooney in the phone book living at Waterford. Surely, it can't be this easy to find him?" I said shaking my head.

"Why not," she said. "You found me quite easily."

All these years, I thought, *and he was right here!*

I could hear the enthusiasm in Annette's voice. "I know he won't know me, but I want to call him. Do you mind?"

"No, I guess not." I wasn't sure if that was the best way to go about it, but she sounded definite. "If you're sure you want to."

"Yes, I am. Sandra called you and you called me. Now it's my turn to call him."

"Okay," I said dubiously. "Ring me back after you've spoken to him. And don't forget it's an STD phone call. It'll cost you a fortune," I reminded her.

"I'll call tonight. The rates are cheaper after seven. I'll ring you back tomorrow and let you know what happens. Wish me luck."

* * *

THE NEXT DAY, Annette rang to say that she had talked to Uncle Terry for almost an hour, while she gave him a sketchy rendition of the past few weeks.

To my amazement, Annette said he remembered me instantly. As expected, he didn't remember anything about Annette and I could hear the disappointment in her voice. As much as she would have liked to know more details, he was unable to remember any. He hadn't been able to tell her much at all.

Now it was Sandra's and my turn to meet him. After ringing him to introduce myself, we arrived at his house at the pre-arranged time, me all smiles and Sandra quiet as a church mouse.

I had the feeling that everything was taking its toll on her and she felt out of her depth. She had started all this by trying to find her mother and it was all snowballing for her. But I loved this role of 'big sister'. I had wanted it for as long as I could remember. I also knew that meeting Uncle Terry must have seemed like meeting a ghost connected to another ghost for her.

We pulled up outside a low brick house with a tidy garden and a trellis of flowers covering a walkway to the front door.

I patted Sandra on the knee reassuringly. "Everything will be fine. Trust me. How many times have I lied to you in your life?"

She gave me a *'you've got to be kidding'* look and said with a smirk, "Ha! Ha! Very funny!"

A tall, slightly stooped, wiry, seventy-five-year-old man greeted us at the door. I had no recollection of this grey-haired man with his strong square jaw and pale, watery hazel eyes, and since he hadn't seen me before, he wouldn't have recognised me either. But he still smiled at me as I hugged him. He gestured us in like a friendly old butler ushering us into a room that was small but well kept and loved. It was like I'd stepped into a picture gallery. There were photos of children everywhere: over the walls, on a side table, on a bureau. Everywhere.

"They're here," Uncle Terry called out over his shoulder.

A tiny frail woman walked slowly out from the kitchen. When she smiled at us, it was like the sun coming out from behind clouds. She was so thin and fragile; hugging her was like hugging a bundle of sticks. But she smelt wonderful: like lavender flowers. Following behind her were two women and a man.

"This is my wife, Laurel," Uncle Terry introduced. "And these are three of our children, Donna, Roslyn and Brian."

I couldn't help but recognise them from some of the pictures on the walls. We hadn't expected to see anyone one else and I could feel Sandra's tension increase. Brian had black hair and looked so much like his father that I could imagine that was how Uncle Terry would have looked when he was young. You could also tell both women were sisters although Roslyn had dark hair and Donna had long fair hair that fell in waves down her back. As I looked around at the photos on the wall, I saw where my fair hair had come from. So many times, I'd looked in the mirror and wondered. Four of their seven children had fair hair. I truly *did* belong in this family.

"Can I make you both a cup of tea?" Aunt Laurel asked us in a low, breathy voice.

"That would be wonderful. Thank you." Beside me, I could feel Sandra nervousness. She nodded but said nothing.

Uncle Terry told us to sit down as he started to tell us about himself. He had been the elder of two brothers my mother had, and together with his wife Laurel, they'd raised seven children right here in Brisbane. He had lost contact with his sister many years ago, after I went to Nazareth House. The last he heard of her had been when a man she had been living with rang to say that Merle had died.

"I don't remember a baby being born before you," he said to me. "I do know Merle had a baby when you were just a little tyke, Patricia. I think the baby was about three months old when she came home one day without the child and wouldn't talk about it. She was living with our mother at the time and all she said to her was that she had put the baby up for adoption. No one knew what was going through her mind at the time or why she did it."

He looked at Laurel as he said sadly, "It wasn't the same for unmarried mothers then as it is now, was it Laurel?"

She shook her head, as she said, "No. There were no pensions or social service groups in those days. You just had to cope any way you could. I guess that was her way."

Donna had disappeared into a back room while we were talking and came out with some old photo albums to show us.

We all sat close together, gathered around Uncle Terry as he turned the pages of the albums.

Sandra and I watched transfixed as page after page of photos showed our mother at different times of her life. My heart did a little skip knowing this was actually *her*. Up until then, she had been a vague outline to me, a silhouette almost. What shocked me a little was that I felt nothing for her. No love. No emotion. Not even anger anymore. Nothing. It surprised me because I'd been angry at her for so long, I'd expected to feel ... *something*. Had my heart hardened so much towards her? Or was it the long absences in my youth that made my mother as much a stranger to me as she was to Sandra.

In my youth, I'd seen her in my dreams every night. I remembered the dreams so clearly and the overwhelming feeling of loss that resulted. No matter how fast I ran towards her in my dreams, my arms out beseeching her to hold me, the gap never lessened. She always turned her back on me and walked away. Now, I felt nothing. And it saddened me.

"She wanted to be called Esme," Uncle Terry said, pulling me out of my reverie as he came across a photo of Mum when she had been his and Aunt Laurel's bridesmaid. "Our father's name was Esmond and she insisted on being called Esme. She hated the name Merle."

He looked at us and then down at the photos and said, "You've both got her high cheekbones but Sandra looks more like her." He looked at me. "You look more like your father. Except you've got her eye colour, Patricia."

We flipped through the pages and Nana Mooney's stern face stared back at me in several of them. Then Uncle Terry pulled out a photo with a tear at the bottom and a hole near the centre. It was a worn photo of Mum holding a happy white-haired baby both smiled into the camera. She looked so happy and I had to bite my lip to stop the unwanted tears from brimming in my eyes. He turned it over and tried to read the writing on the back that had been faded by age. The hole replaced some of the words, leaving incomplete sentences.

He put his glasses on and said, "It looks like it says, *'This is a good snap of me and the baby only...'* this is where the small hole starts, but then it says *'....for she means the world....'* there's the hole again and then she says *'...not a bad look. What say you? I think she will be tall like you.'*" He looked up at me. "I think this is a photo of Esme and you, Trish. You can have it if you want," he said as he held it out to me.

That had been enough to open the floodgates. To my horror, I felt the sobs rising. My throat contracted and no matter how much I gulped them back, I couldn't stop the tears. The sobs rose suddenly and embarrassingly and I began to tremble. I felt someone's hands on my shoulders comforting me, but I couldn't stop myself. My eyes were riveted on the photo.

What had been the missing words? She'd written, *'for she means the world...'*. I was almost too scared to ask myself the next question. Had the hole replaced the words *'to me'* on the back of the photo? Could this be true? I cried harder. *Had* I meant the world to her? *Had* she really loved me all along? All my life I'd desperately wanted her love; wondering why she hadn't, wishing she had. But here she'd written that I'd meant the world to her. I was almost too afraid to believe it. But *not* to believe it would be as painful as losing her all over again. For most of my life, I'd resigned myself to the fact that I hadn't measured up to her expectations. It was a part of my life. I'd accepted it. This photo changed everything. God, how I wanted to believe those words.

I stared at the photo, taking in everything about her this time. Her hair looked different from how I remembered it. By the time I was six years old she was getting it permed. In this photo, her hair was in a fashionable style I'd seen in old movies. It was still dark but rolled back off her forehead, tucked behind her ears and rolled under to her shoulders.

Uncle Terry was caught up with all the memories as well. "I remember the first time I met your father."

I looked up at him and swallowed as he continued. "It was my father's funeral and for some reason, no women where allowed at the cemetery," he said. "Your father turned up to pay his last respects and he was asked to leave. I don't remember why." A shadow passed over his face. "Perhaps because he was married. Our parents never approved of Esme's relationship with him. I do remember it was a couple of years before you were born, Patricia. That was in 1953, I think. After you were born, he often came with you to visit me at the Post Office in Roma Street where I worked."

He looked over at Laurel and said, "I remember the first day I met Laurel. It was at a dance and I walked up to her and asked her to dance. She smiled at me as if she was very happy. We were married three months later."

They looked at each other and smiled, obviously still in love after all these years.

"We didn't see too much of anybody in those days. We bought this block of land and lived in a shed for a while until I built the house we now live in. The children started coming along and then we moved into the house. I felt so proud that I'd built it by myself. It was only small but it was ours. We lived a long way from anyone and to get to work I had to walk quite a long way to catch a train. We didn't have a car and we didn't have a phone. We were pretty much cut off from the family and had no idea of what was happening outside of our little house. We had our hands full, didn't we Laurel?"

She smiled and nodded. "And I loved every minute of it."

"What was Mum like, Uncle Terry?" I asked, leaning forward eagerly.

Staring off into the distance while Laurel and our cousins brought us more cups of tea and slices of homemade teacake, he shook his head sadly. "She was a beautiful girl, Trisha. A little bandy and pigeon-toed," he smiled, "but that was all." He looked up at us with moisture in his eyes. "She was beautiful."

That was her legacy to me: green eyes and bandy legs.

"She had everything going for her," he continued. "But she liked lairy things. I suppose, the grass was always greener someplace else. I don't think she really knew what she wanted."

I had the feeling that our mother was on the outer limits of Uncle Terry's ideas of acceptability, that perhaps he was a little ashamed of the mistakes his sister had made all those years ago and was more than willing to put those years behind him.

As we left, I hoped his sister's children had earned his tick of approval.

As much as I'd loved listening to Uncle Terry talking, I was glad to be on my way home. I dropped Sandra at her house and drove home with my head spinning. I had so much to think about. My whole outlook towards her had changed. It frightened me that for so long, all I could remember was the bad times. I was forty-one now. I didn't *want* to remember old hurts that lurked in the background ready to spring forward when I least expected them. I remember reading somewhere years ago that for every happy childhood there are ten unhappy ones. I was not the only one who had had an unhappy childhood. There were plenty of others who had suffered as well.

Somewhere through the generations, a thread of weakness had appeared in our family in the form of alcoholism. I knew it then. I know it now. My mother sometimes didn't get up in the mornings after she'd come home stumbling in with and shushing yet another stranger. She'd never even been aware that I'd heard her.

But who was I to judge? I'd made some dreadful decisions as well in my life, decisions that had affected my children's well being. I hadn't meant for things to happen, but they had, and my boys will have those memories for the rest of their lives. We all do the best we can at the time, but sometimes circumstances out of our control happen.

If put in her situation, in those difficult times, I'm not sure how I would have reacted. I sometimes think she did me a favour. She spared me from continually seeing her unconscious till mid-afternoon. She spared me the sight of seeing her too sick to get up so all she could do was just turn her head to one side and be sick beside her bed and she spared me the embarrassment of seeing her fall over drunk in public. For a child, to see this just once was enough.

There was the reason she had sent us away, staring me in the face. Mum had done the only thing she could do. She had given us to someone else who could raise us and look after us, because she couldn't. Instead, I was left with the memory of a beautiful woman with black hair and green eyes who had written *'for she means the world to me'*.

* * *

M<small>Y TRIP HOME</small> was one of those trips when you arrive at your destination without remembering any of the drive there. I pulled in to the driveway and sent a silent 'thank you' to the heavens that I'd arrived home in one piece.

I locked the car with my remote and walked to the letterbox. Pieces of junk mail poked through the slot and I pulled them out, tucking them under my free arm to throw in the recycle bin. I lifted the front latch and inside was two large A4 manila envelopes. I took them out and turned them over to see the return address and my eyes opened wide when I saw DEFENCE SERVICE RECORDS typed on the back of the first one. I did the same for the second one and saw CHILDREN'S SERVICES typed on the back.

I did a little whoop of joy and almost ran to the front door, fumbling with the key in my haste to open it. Once inside, I tossed the keys in the bowl on the sideboard, flung my bag on the lounge and shoved the junk mail into the bin.

My heart was beating fast as I settled into a dining chair and slit open the top of the envelope marked DEFENCE SERVICE RECORDS. Inside was a folder marked NATIONAL ARCHIVES OF AUSTRALIA and I took a deep breath before opening it.

Sitting on top of the paperwork was the photo of Dad in his full uniform in Egypt, the same one from Paula, and it had the same effect as the first time I saw it. My hands flew to my mouth and I let out a whimper as tears welled up. A minute ticked by as I took in everything about him. He was standing so straight and tall, so happy, and it was obvious this photo had been taken before he'd contracted tuberculosis, before his health deteriorated. I took a deep breath and turned to the next photo. His enlistment photos appeared, almost like mug shots: one looking at the camera and the other in profile. I sat transfixed as my eyes went from one photo to the other and back again, desperate for more. The feeling was so surreal, it was as if he had jumped through time and was standing in front of me.

Hungry for more information, I checked the typed notes underneath. He had been twenty-two years old when they were taken and even though they were black and white, it was obvious his eyes were pale in colour.

Suddenly, he was there in the room with me as memory after memory surfaced.

Dad and me walking down a street, him pointing his index finger at the ground and me holding on to it tightly, both of us smiling.

Me sitting high on her father's shoulders as we both walked down busy Boundary Street, with me leaning over, laughing wildly and holding on to him tightly.

Me sitting in the Alliance Hotel with my peg family on the table, a glass of sarsaparilla and a bag of crisps sitting beside me, and Dad smiling down at me as he taps the ash from a cigarette with fingers heavily stained with nicotine.

Both of us standing in front of the Children's Services office. Over his arm is his suit jacket and his left shoulder dips when he turns to face me, his back slightly concaved.

Dad and Pop walking across Wickham Terrace after having stepped off a tram. I am in the middle and both are holding each of my hands. Both are wearing suits and hats and I am dressed in baggy pants, a loose shirt and a floppy hat.

Finally, I put the photos aside and picked up his discharge papers. Enlistment date: 4th March 1940. Discharge date: 18th October 1944. As I read eagerly through the weekly transcripts made on his file, his life unfolded before me.

He had enlisted in the army and was sent to Tobruk at the beginning of the Second World War as a 'Rat of Tobruk' where he became an orderly in the medical corps. My hand flew to my mouth when I read that his job was to collect the dead and injured on the front lines and bring them back for care, identification and burial. Two years later, he contracted tuberculosis and was dispatched home to have his left lung removed. One year later, he was transferred to New Guinea and six months later again, the day before he was due to sit for his final exam to become a registered nurse, he was sent home after a serious bout of Malaria. He was then discharged, totally and permanently incapacitated.

I dropped the paperwork on the table suddenly as I remembered standing in the file room of Greenslopes Hospital. His file had been right there, in my hand, and I hadn't opened it. The anger had been so intense; I couldn't find it in my heart to even open it. My chest ached now when I remembered how I'd shoved it back in, gritting my teeth in anger, mentally telling him to rot in hell.

I shut my eyes, feeling so ashamed of myself.

Through my tears, I picked up the next piece of paper. His death certificate. I ran my eyes down the sheet of paper, hungrily taking in his mother's name and pop's name.

Cause of death – emphysema of lungs, coronary artery occlusion, and pulmonary tuberculosis.

Died – 25th July 1968. Buried at Nudgee Cemetery.

Issue living – Paula 22, Terrance John 20, Sharon Therese 16.

Something was niggling at the back of my mind, but I didn't know what it was.

The cause of death was as I would have expected and I already knew of the other two children in Paula's family. So what was bothering me?

And then it suddenly hit me. It was the date!

25th July 1968!

I stared at it as my head spun. I blinked and reread the date. There was no mistake.

I had been thirteen years old in 1968. July was in the middle of winter and the beginning of the second semester in high school.

Flashes of sitting in the waiting room at Children's Services came to me as I watched the clock tick away the minutes and the hours. I saw the clipboard handed to me to sign and date – 25th July 1968 - and I saw myself in tears in the backseat of the car on the way home with Mr Anderson turning around and telling me my father had been drunk.

But he hadn't been drunk! He didn't turn up because he had died! All those years of pain and misjudging my father need never have been! All those years of wondering why he'd deserted me and left me to my own fate could have been avoided. How could Mr Anderson be so cruel? As if he hadn't hurt me enough!

I took deep shuddering breaths and threw my head back, trying to stem the tears and the ache in my heart. Finally, I blew breath out from my mouth as I collected myself. I wasn't finished yet. There was more to read.

The next page was two handwritten letters addressed to a caseworker and signed 'Ernie Gourgaud' in perfect handwriting.

I read the first one excitedly. The final words jumped out at me.

"There are two letters at Nazareth House for her, as I thought she was going back, so what exactly are the rules? You must realise I don't want her to forget me as she is all I have got in this world."

Those words finished me. Emotion so raw bubbled up and my heart felt like it was about to burst. I put my head on my hands and sobbed, feeling like I had done nothing else for the past week. I'd thought I'd finally put this part of my life behind me, especially after having found my sister, and now, here it was, all over again, only worse. It was like tearing a scab off a nearly healed wound and leaving it open and bleeding again. I'd come to terms with my childhood, rationalising that out of everything bad comes something good but nothing had prepared me for this new sorrow. First there had been the photo of Mum and me at Uncle Terry's house and now, here was Dad, writing letters that stated I was all he had left in this world.

I don't know how long I sat there but eventually the sobs subsided and I rose to grab a handful of tissues. I tossed the used ones away and grabbed a fresh handful then returned to the chair to finish what I'd started. There was more paperwork from Children's Services to go through.

I picked up the last letter in the package and scanned through it, sniffling loudly. And there, in the final paragraph, another shock awaited me.

"At the time Patricia's mother signed her adoption papers in 1969, she was accompanied by a two-year-old boy."

My mouth opened in shock as I realised what this meant.

I rushed to the phone and quickly dialled Sandra.

BILL BAILEY WAS HERE

"We've got a half-brother too?" Sandra asked, amazed. She couldn't quite believe what she'd started.

My letter had stated that when I was fourteen, one year after Dad's death, Mum had been living in Cairns and had signed my adoption papers in the Cairns department of Children's Services. Accompanying her was a two-year-old boy, who, it turned out, was our half-brother.

His name was William Bailey and he was now twenty-nine years old and living in Townsville. He had been adopted at four years old when our mother died. I hadn't known that Mum had died two years after signing my adoption papers but then, I didn't know a lot of things.

"Okay. Do you want to start looking for William?" I asked Sandra.

"Not me," she emphatically. "You go right ahead if you want to. I've got enough things to think about without adding to them."

It was up to me. I began looking half-heartedly in the phone book not expecting to find his name until I thought, *there has to be an easier way of doing this*.

The Salvation Army! The thought came to me like a bolt of lightning. They had people working for them who helped find lost family members every day. I needed to talk to someone who specialised in exactly this sort of situation that I found myself in.

I flicked the pages of a phone book over until I found the number and wrote it down.

The next morning at the coffee shop, Margaret walked in and tossed her bag in the back room and then turned to me.

I stood there smiling at her. She put her hands on her hips and said, "Okay. Out with it. What's happened now?"

"I got my papers in the mail." I grinned. "It says we have a brother, too."

She stared at me with her eyes wide open and her mouth in the shape of an 'O'. Then she bent over and laughed, shaking her head as she said, "I just love this job. There's always something happening with you. It certainly isn't boring around here. First Sandra, then Annette and now a brother. Okay. Where is he and what's his name?"

"His name is William Bailey. Bill Bailey," I said with a smile as I remembered a song from my childhood. *"Won't you come home Bill Bailey. Won't you come home,"* I sang and we both laughed.

"I'm going to ring the Salvation Army to see if they can help me, Margaret. Just call out to me if it gets busy," I said as I walked into the small office where the phone sat near the deep freezer. I had no idea where he lived but I was going to find out.

I dialled the number I'd written down and when a soft female voice answered I asked to be connected to a counsellor. After a few clicks and buzzes, then some elevator music, a deep, gravely male voice came on the line after nearly two minutes.

"Can I help you?"

"Yes, I hope so." I filled him in on the details of the past few weeks before asking my question. "My sisters and I have just found out that we have a half-brother and I'd like some advice on how to find him."

"Well, I can give you some ideas if that's what you're after. If you want us to find him for you, you'll have to come in with your birth certificate and the papers from Children's Services as proof of identity. What help would you like?" He sounded very sure of himself as if he did this every day of his life, which he probably did.

"All I really want is some sort of direction to start in. He's not in the phone book and probably lives in North Queensland. That's where he was born."

"Okay. There are four places to start looking," he said. "The best place to start is the Electoral Office. If he's on the rolls, you'll be able to find his last known address there. If he isn't, in that then you could try the armed forces. He could be in one of them. They don't have to register for voting. The next place to look would be the police force. Policemen don't have to enrol either, as a matter of security for their personal lives. The last thing I can suggest is he may be in jail. Obviously, they don't have to vote. Have you tried any of these yet?"

"No. You were my first phone call. This isn't going to be easy, is it?" I asked as I looked at the notes that I'd scribbled when he was talking. "Electoral Office, armed forces, police force or jail. That's it?"

"That's about it. You should find him in one of those. Just call back or come in if you still can't find him but I can't think of anything else that we would do."

"Thank you. I appreciate your help," I said.

I hung up and sat back in the chair. The closest Electoral Office was in West End about twenty minutes' drive away and probably only open between Monday and Friday. The only way that I would be able to get there would be to close the shop early one day and go straight from work. I hated doing that because I knew that at three in the afternoon I would be filthy and smell like the fish I'd been crumbing all day, but I could see no other way.

* * *

THE NEXT DAY, I shut the shop doors at 3.00pm sharp, sprayed perfume all over my clothes and myself, and set off for the Electoral Office. I was lucky enough to find a park between two cars directly outside the office and after three attempts at a reverse park; I finally managed to wedge my Nissan Pulsar between them. And with twenty-five minutes still left in the parking meter. Silently, I grinned to myself, *It's a meant to be.*

David often laughed at me when I said things were 'meant to be'. I remember one time we'd been looking through the paper trying to pick a horse for the Melbourne Cup. Almost every person in Australia stops for three minutes on the first Tuesday in November to watch the race after placing a bet. Even people who never place a bet on a horse the rest of the year do so on this day and we were no exception. I had already gone through the list of horses and one name jumped off the page at me.

"Concorde! That's the horse, Dave. That's the one that's going to win!" I yelled out to him as he stood in the kitchen making coffee.

"Why on earth would you pick Concorde?" he asked perplexed. "It hasn't even been tipped to place."

"The name, of course. Concorde is French!" I stated. "It's a sign!"

"Oh, a sign," he said with a broad smile on his face. "Let me see if I can guess the logic here. Concorde is French. You're part French. Napoleon is French too. Napoleon is also the name of a cake. People eat cakes in a coffee shop. You own a coffee shop. Oh, my God! It's a sign! It's meant to be!"

We had both been laughing by the time he'd finished, but I'd still put a bet on it. And lost.

As I walked into the small foyer of the Electoral Office, I noticed it was an historic building dating back to the turn of the century. I found the silence almost overpowering as I tiptoed over to the counter, my steps echoing loudly on the polished floors.

A sign said, 'PLEASE WRITE NAME AND ADDRESS CLEARLY IN REGISTER BOOK'. I pulled it over and did as I was told.

As I finished, a clerk came over and simply said, "Name?"

"Mine?" I replied in a like tone.

She eyed me over the top of her glasses. "Letter of the alphabet of the person you're looking for."

"B". I was getting used to staccato sentences.

She walked away and came back with a tray full of microfilm. She handed them to me and pointed over my shoulder to a desk in the corner where a machine sat waiting for the films.

Obediently, I walked over and sat down.

There were a few William Baileys but none of them had the correct birth date.

One down, three to go, I thought as I stood up and placed the tray back on the counter.

I waved and called out, "Thank you," as the clerk looked around the partition. Then I turned around and walked outside to my car.

As I sat down, I glanced at my watch and noticed I'd only been inside for fifteen minutes. It was too late to ring anybody else that day so I pulled out into the busy peak-hour traffic thinking of what I would do the next day.

* * *

"I'm not going back to school anymore," Tony informed me as he set the table that night.

"Here it comes, mum." Mark laughed.

"And why is that?" I asked as I turned the chicken pieces over in a pan.

"On parade today, over the loud speaker, Mr Davies told me to pull my pants up."

Mark roared with laughter at the memory of it. "It really was funny, mum. You're always telling Tony to pull his pants up and not wear them on his hips like a homey. Well, Mr Davies told him to do it in front of the whole school."

"Shut up, Mark!" yelled Tony, furious at his brother's laughter.

"Tony, there is no situation that can't be solved with a laugh," I almost laughed myself, although I stopped in time when I saw Tony watching me. "Don't take things so seriously, hon. Laugh about it. If you get upset everyone will make fun of you but if you laugh with them, everyone will just forget about it. Besides, I hope the two of you are going to be at school for a lot longer yet. Having an education makes you free because having a career gives you the freedom to do what you want with your lives. I wish I'd stayed at school for a while longer."

"Didn't you do what you wanted?" asked Mark between gulps of milk.

"Yes, I suppose I did. But I really didn't have much of a choice."

"Then why do you wish you'd stayed in school?"

"Because then you can do things you *really* want to do, not do them because there's nothing else to do."

"You didn't stay at school and you're all right. Why do *we* have to?" asked Tony petulantly.

"Because I don't want the both of you working as hard as I do to make a living." While I talked, I threw some parley in a dollop of cream and stirred it in with the chicken juices before spooning it over the chicken.

"Wouldn't it taste the same without the greenery, Mum?" asked Tony, obviously still in a mood.

"Probably. But let's have it looking nice anyway."

We all sat down and the mood lightened as it normally does when there is food in front of the boys. I poured myself a glass of wine and sat down at the table with them, all of us eating in contented silence.

Memories of Mum suddenly jumped into my mind as I looked at the glass. The last few weeks had been an eye-opener for me. My parents both drank too much. A slight understatement there. I'd never been a big drinker – I could never afford to be – but I had first-hand knowledge of the consequences of too much drinking. I'd heard it said that if a child has an alcoholic parent, there is a 50% chance that they would be one as well. What were my chances when both of my parents were heavy drinkers? Was it a genetic thing or was it the influence of your parents that turned you into one? I had no idea.

I decided not to take the chance and mentally limited myself to one glass of wine a night with a meal from then on.

***

BY MID-MORNING THE NEXT DAY, I'd called Directory Assistance for the numbers of the Navy, Army and Air Force in Canberra. I was passed from department to department in all three but eventually each had the same story. No William Bailey in any of the forces.

Only two choices left, I thought.

Images jumped into my mind of when I last worked at the restaurant chain. It was a night when two policemen had come in and ordered a pizza. They'd sat down in one of the booths and talked to each other while their pizza cooked and when it was ready, I took it over to their table and caught the end of their conversation.

"It costs $1000 a letter to have POLICE put on our cars. Did you know that? Now *that's* robbery," one said.

I'd smiled as I put the takeaway box on the table and said mischievously, "I could save the Police Force thousands of dollars by only putting three letters on the cars instead of six."

He raised his eyebrows and looked at me, "Oh, yeah? And what three letters would *you* use?"

"Cop!" I'd stated. "Goodness me. What did you think I meant?" I'd smiled a coy, little girl smile at him knowing full well what he thought I'd meant. We'd been friendly ever since that day.

I hadn't seen him since I left years ago but maybe he was the one who could help now. I was running out of options. The only choices left were on opposite sides of the law so I said a silent prayer, found the phone number in the phone book for Chandler Police Station, hoping he still worked there, and dialled the number.

As luck would have it, Damian answered the phone.

"Chandler Police Station. May I help you?"

"Hello, Damian. It's Trisha, here. Remember? Three letters on the police car?" I crossed my fingers as I asked. Surely that would jog his memory.

I could hear the smile in his voice. "Of course I do. I haven't seen you in ages. What are you doing these days?" he asked jovially.

"I've got my own coffee shop now."

"Can't stay away from the food business though, eh?"

"Ya gots to do what ya gots to do." I do very bad Jimmy Durante imitations.

He laughed and said, "What can I do for you?"

"I need your help. Just recently, I found I had this string of family members I never knew about. I've met all of them except for one. A brother. I've tried everywhere to find him. Electoral Roll, Armed Forces and there are only two other places to look. One is to see if maybe he's a policeman and the other is if he's in jail. Hopefully it's the former."

"I can give you a number to call to see if he's a policeman, that's the best I can do. I'm not supposed to give out any other information."

"Damian please, you're my last chance. His name is William Bailey and he could possibly be in Townsville. Can't you just see if he has a record?" I begged.

He hesitated and said, "I'm taking a big risk doing this. If I get caught, my butt will be on the line."

I could hear the clicking of keys on the other end of the line and then his voice saying, "Well, well, well."

"Have you found something?" I asked, not really wanting to know now.

"Oh, yeah. I found something. Four pages of something."

I groaned inwardly. "That doesn't sound good. Okay, you may as well tell me."

"The first offence was when he was eighteen; just drunk and disorderly. It says here that he was found wandering the streets and they brought him into the watch house. Apparently, he said that both his parents were dead and he got a letter in the mail from some government department telling him that he had been adopted. Bad timing if you ask me."

All I could see in my mind was the sad image of a forlorn young man feeling abandoned by the world. My heart immediately went out to him.

Damian continued. "After that, there are a few similar offences. A couple of D & D's. A couple of driving without a licence while under the influence of alcohol."

He kept clicking away as he continued. "Speeding. Nothing serious. Just community service and fines. Not really a criminal." Click, click, click. "Dropped out of sight for a while. No record of anything for a couple of years."

He suddenly laughed out loud. "The last offence was in Ingham six months ago. He must have hitched the 120 kilometres up from Townsville, because he sure doesn't have a licence. Anyway, he was brought in drunk after writing graffiti on a park bench. Guess what he wrote."

"Go ahead. Tell me", I said shaking my head.

"He wrote *'Bill Bailey was here'*. Can you believe that?" he laughed. "In a town of about 4,000 people, he wrote his name on a park bench. This guy is a classic."

"Okay, okay. You can stop with the chuckles, buster," I smiled. "That's my brother you're laughing at." I was laughing myself. "Do you have his last address?"

"Sure." He gave me the address and the name of an officer he knew in Ingham and wished me luck.

Damian was right. Our brother didn't sound like a criminal, just a guy who was handed a raw deal. Innocent and naive, probably. Set adrift at eighteen, lost but not a criminal.

I tried to imagine what it would have been like for him. Both his parents dead by the time he was eighteen and only then did he find out that he had been adopted. He would have felt totally alone. He must have had so many questions and been so confused. I could only feel sorry for him.

* * *

INGHAM IS a small town of several thousand people in Far North Queensland, Australia's equivalent of the Deep South in America. It sits part way between Cairns (tourism gateway to the Great Barrier Reef) and Townsville which is a predominantly industry and military based city surviving in its dust bowl by damming the Ross River and famous in Australia for its mosquito borne fever every summer. It survives as a local centre for the sugarcane industry, which is the mainstay of this area.

Directory Assistance had no listing for a William Bailey in Ingham so my next phone call had to be the local policeman who Damian had told me to ring. The chance of this policeman knowing Bill was my last shot, but it was all I had left.

To my surprise, or maybe it was dismay, he knew Bill instantly and he was able to lay his hands on Bill's address and phone number with no effort at all. I wasn't sure if that was a good sign or a bad sign. Bill was apparently living with some friends, he said, which was why I had been unable to find his phone listing anywhere.

With Bill now located, I rang Sandra and said, "We're wasting our talents here. With the way we've both been able to track down our family members, we should start up our own business. 'The Looney Mooney Detective Agency.' How does that sound to you?" I laughed.

"Catchy title." I could hear the smile in her voice, "but with a name like that, what sort of clients could we expect?"

"Gullible ones? Irish ones? The good part is we'd get to put on trench coats and 'Jackie O' shades. I've read enough spy novels to make a real go of this."

"Don't sell the shop just yet, will you," she replied, and we laughed in unison. This sort of banter between us was what I loved.

I said goodbye and dialled the number. A man answered, "Hello?"

I could hear noises in the background. Voices of children, men, women, loud music, laughter, clinking glasses. I looked at my watch and realised it was seven o'clock on a Friday night and probably not the best time to call. I'd been caught up in everything and had lost track of the hours.

"Hi." I said. "I'm looking for a Bill Bailey. Could you tell me if he lives there?"

"Yeah. Hang on," the male voice said as he dropped the phone with a clunk. Jimmy Barnes screamed out about cheap wine and a three-day growth, and just as I was thinking of hanging up and calling back the next day, a voice came on the line, slightly slurred but friendly.

"Yeah?"

"Hi. Is this Bill Bailey?" I asked.

"Yeah." I had a feeling this wasn't going to be easy.

"Bill, you don't know me and I'm not sure if this is the best time for you," I began. "Is it all right to talk right now?"

"Yeah."

I shouted over the music. "Bill, when I was young I was adopted and about six months ago, a woman contacted me who was also adopted. She found out that we were sisters and that we also have another sister in Cairns and a brother. I hope this is not going to be too big a shock, but it seems that you are our brother."

There was nothing but silence on the other end of the line except for music and laughter.

"Are you there, Bill?" I asked.

"I always wondered if I had a family somewhere," he started slowly. "I've been alone for years now, but I've always wondered." It sounded as if he had sobered up instantly.

"Your mother was Merle Rose Mooney, wasn't she?" I asked so that there could be no doubt we shared a mother.

"Yeah. That's what the letter from the government said. I didn't know I was adopted till I was eighteen. When I was sixteen, the woman I thought was my mother died and two years later, my father died too. It was a bad time for me. Then the letter arrived."

I had to strain to hear his voice as it gradually got quieter and quieter.

"You probably won't want to know me." With the music in the background, I could barely hear his soft voice. "I've been in a little trouble with the law. Don't get me wrong," he quickly added, "no robbery or murder or nothing like that," he laughed softly. "But I drink too much, I think. I'm going to stop soon."

"Bill," I started, "we already know about all of that and we still wanted to call you."

There was a silence for a few seconds before he continued.

"What are your names?"

"I'm Patricia. Trish. Then there's Annette and Sandra. Annette is the eldest and Sandra is the youngest. You're the youngest now, I guess." It had only just occurred to me.

"Do you remember Mum?" I asked.

"No. The letter said that I was four years old when she died and then I was adopted. I don't remember her at all."

He had started talking loudly again to be heard over the music and called out to someone in the background, "Hey! Keep it down!" The music volume went down a notch.

"I've got a couple of photos of her that I can make copies of, if you like," I said to him. "Would you like me to send them to you?"

"Yeah. That would be great." I could hear the wonderment in his voice and I smiled to myself. I knew that feeling well. My life of late was filled with it.

"I'll let you get back to your party. You'll probably get a call from Annette and Sandra sometime soon. They'll want to talk to you as well. Would you like my phone number just in case you want to call me?"

"Well," he began hesitantly, "we've got a sort of ban on the phone here. We can get calls but we can't dial out. Saves money, you know?"

"Sure," I said with a smile.

We said our goodbyes and hung up.

* * *

"He sounds really nice," I enthused to each of the girls on separate calls. "A little innocent but nice."

Sandra said she would ring him in a few days but Annette lived only about one and a half hours north of Ingham so she said she and her husband would go and meet him on the weekend.

Later, when she called to say she'd met him, I could hear a little something in her voice. A catch. Something I couldn't quite put my finger on. Something just out of reach. A hesitation.

He had light brown hair, hazel green eyes and a tattoo of a teardrop under one eye, she said. And a four-year-old daughter who lived with her mother. Thrown in like a 'by the way' was, "And he looks like Sandra." That was her only comment.

We must have all seemed like a dysfunctional, mismatched bunch to outsiders. Sandra and I with our hang-ups, Bill's wildness and recklessness, and then there was Annette, once confident and sure of herself, now a little lost and bewildered. And withdrawing from us.

She and Sandra barely spoke these days. Problems between them had begun soon after our first phone call. Sandra couldn't understand why Annette took on the role of the abandoned child, when in actual fact, Sandra and I were the abandoned ones and Annette had had a normal childhood with a loving family.

All Sandra had ever wanted was a mother and here was someone who had a mother but chose to focus on issues, important as they were to

Annette, did not seem so to Sandra. As soon as Annette found out she was adopted, she had begun to question her happy childhood with loving parents. She had everything that Sandra had always craved - a mother – which resulted in Sandra having little time for Annette's roller-coaster moods.

Even though I understood Sandra's reasoning, I knew it had been a shock to Annette to find she had been adopted at birth and I was prepared to try and to work through it all. Sandra, though, took her pain and began to withdraw from Annette and a little from me.

CHOOK LEGS

During the long weekend of Easter, two weeks after meeting Uncle Terry, Sandra and I flew the two hours north to Cairns to visit Annette.

Correspondence between the three of us had progressed with letters and recent photos but there was still tension in the air that morning as Sandra, Farouk and I boarded the plane. David had seen us off at the airport but was on duty over the weekend and so was unable to come with us.

Once on board, I stared out the window while attendants served food and drinks. I wondered if we'd done the right thing. I still wasn't sure.

Cairns, being in the tropics, is almost unbearable in summer and even though it was now autumn, the day we arrived was still hot enough to melt the tarmac.

Cairns airport was built low but spread out. As we walked toward the tunnel that led to the main arrival lounge, some people were collecting bags while others walked straight to the exit doors. This was the time of year when tourists came in their greatest numbers and the place was crowded with people meeting the new arrivals. Advertisements lined the walls and on the floor-to-ceiling glass partition, white dots had been painted at eye level to stop people from walking into the glass door on their way to the carpark. The screens high above our heads announced our flight's arrival.

Annette had given me a brief description of herself and I scanned the swarming faces, looking for a brunette that could be her. There were dozens of candidates. Tall ones, short ones.

Then, from behind me, I heard Sandra exclaiming, "There she is."

And she was. Smiling a big, wide smile and waving to us.

As we walked towards each other, I could feel the emotion swelling up inside me, growing with every step we took. While we all hugged, cried then laughed, I tried to take in every detail about her.

She was a little shorter than Sandra and me, probably about five-foot two, and small-boned, dark-haired with green eyes similar in colour to mine. She was so petite that even I, at 55 kilos, felt like a lumberjack beside her.

Looking at her heart-shaped face, her nose and eyes the same as our mother's, I had no trouble imagining that this was how Mum could have looked at the same age if life had been a little kinder to her.

She introduced us to her husband Don who, surprisingly, was an air traffic controller and had probably talked to David on numerous occasions, neither of them knowing whom the other one was. He led us to a van in the parking lot before driving us to their house and introducing us to their four daughters.

Their house was set in a garden with high palms in the front yard and a backdrop of nearby mountains. The humidity hung heavily on us like a wet blanket, making the glasses of chilled wine offered to us in a room adjoining the swimming pool very welcome.

I held up my camera to Don and said, "Would you take a photo of us, please?"

That started a flurry of activity as Sandra dug in her purse saying, "Yes! I nearly forgot. Could you take one for me too?" Annette ran to the kitchen and brought hers back to Don as well. We all smiled and held up our wine glasses in a toast to each other.

We had so much to talk about but no one knew where to start. Each of us was looking at the other two trying to see a resemblance between us all. Sandra looked at her hands and then leant over to see Annette's. She grabbed mine and we all placed our hands on the table.

"I hate my hands," I said self-consciously. I knew I didn't take enough care of them. They were always in hot sudsy water and detergent, so the skin was shiny and slightly red, and my nails were short and brittle. My knuckles seemed overlarge and veins could be seen close to the surface of the skin.

All of us looked from one set of hands to the other, comparing size and shape. They were all the same. Almost identical. Mine just looked more used.

I looked up at Sandra and Annette and noticed their heart-shaped faces looking back at me in surprise. Tears welled up in my eyes as I looked at them.

I could see a resemblance between all of us. I wasn't alone any more. I suppose sisters who grow up together and spend years looking at each other would take this for granted. I knew we never would.

I wondered what it would have been like growing up with them. I was the one in the middle so I would probably always have had one of them to play with. But would Sandra have been the one left out or would Annette, being the eldest, have been the outsider? Did one of them have to be an outsider?

I remembered not so long ago, before all this had happened, I'd been waiting in my doctor's surgery. In a corner sitting together, surrounded by the surgery's toys, were triplets. They were absolutely identical, to me anyway. Two sat together laughing and showing each other what they had built with their blocks while the other one sat by herself quietly reading, not in the least upset or disturbed about being left out. Was that the way of sisters? Was one invariably left out?

"Take another photo, Don," I said looking down again at my hands and placing them beside Sandra's and Annette's.

"Are you going to pay me by the hour or is it going to be a set fee for the weekend?" he laughed as he again shuffled from camera to camera.

I stood up and took my shoes off as I said, "What about our legs?"

We all stood in a tight circle and raised our skirts a little so that we could see, from above, our legs from the knees down.

"My God," was all I could say. "We've all got chook legs!"

We all laughed as we compared our skinny legs. Sandra looked at me and grinned, "I think yours are the skinniest and bandiest."

"Maybe so," I smiled as I looked down at all of our feet, "but I can tell you both this. I've got the prettiest feet out of all of us. Both of you have very ugly feet. Take another photo, Don," I laughed.

"Yes, massah," Don laughed as he bent forward in an exaggerated bow.

* * *

THE NEXT TWO days were spent trying to get to know each other and although the expected nervousness was always present, the weekend went quite well for three strangers thrown together so unexpectedly and from such diverse backgrounds.

We walked around the main tourist shopping centre simply talking and learning about each other. We had coffee in little tourist cafes and lunches in restaurants overlooking Cairns harbour. The weather was ideal: hot, sunny days with barely a cloud in the sky and warm nights with light breezes rustling through the palms.

Before we knew it, the weekend was over and we were on our way back to Brisbane.

I walked into my house and felt like I'd never been away.

Obviously, the boys had arrived back from their father's house because the television as on in the family room and Mark was playing Nintendo on the other television in the lounge room. I could hear music coming from Tony's room and I wondered if 'rap' was supposed to be called music.

"I hope you guys won money on Lotto last night," I called out as I turned the TV off. "Because the next electricity bill is all yours."

"I'm watching the TV, Mum," Tony called out as he poked his head out of his bedroom door. At the same time, there was a muffled hello from Mark.

"You're watching *Oprah*?" I asked him with raised eyebrows.

"Well, I was before *that* came on," he said half-heartedly.

"Mmm. Just turn it off when you're not watching it, hon."

I went through each room, collecting the dirty clothes and putting them into the washing machine after separating the whites from the colours. How could two boys wear so many clothes in just two days? Girls I could understand. I had seen Annette's girls change clothes three times a day when I'd been in Cairns. But my boys?

I walked into the kitchen and started taking vegetables out of the fridge to prepare a simple dinner of steak, scalloped potatoes and a green salad, as Tony threw himself into one of the swivel chairs at the kitchen bench.

"How did it go?" he asked.

"Great. Annette looks a little different from Sandra and me but the similarity is still there. Sort of like you and Mark. Mark is blonde and you've got dark hair but you're still clearly brothers," I explained.

"How could your mum give you up? Do you know why?"

"Nobody will ever know, hon. It's no use trying to find a solution. There isn't any."

"I'm never leaving you," he stated definitely.

"You will," I smiled. "It's the way of things."

"Nope. I'm going to stay with you always. What would you do with all of your spare time if I left?" he asked innocently.

I thought of the washing in the machine, dinner to prepare, lunches for school tomorrow, the ironing and the animals to feed and then I thought of all the things I'd rather be doing.

"Are you really sure you're never leaving?"

"You'd miss me if I left," he smiled at me confidently.

He was right.

* * *

THE NEXT WEEK, Annette's papers arrived in the mail but with hers came a bombshell.

We were indeed sisters, but only half-sisters.

The first shock was a comment at the bottom of her letter that read, "Your birth mother had two daughters born in 1955 and 1959 who were also adopted. Their details are attached. You and your sisters share the same mother but not the same father."

Her adoption papers stated her father's name as Michael Miller but her birth certificate said 'father unknown.'

"This has been the worst time of my life," she sobbed over the phone. "I've got no sense of myself any more. I feel so empty. Two months ago, I knew who I was and who my parents were. Now, everything's changed."

My mind flashed back to that night when I made the fateful decision to call her. If I had the time again, would I make that call knowing what I know now? I'd never meant to hurt anyone. I'd naively thought she would be as happy as I was.

"You're still my sister, Annette. This means nothing to me."

"Half-sister, Trish. Half-sister. That's all."

I heard the sound of a tissue being pulled out of a box and a sniffle. She continued, "I'm going to keep looking for my father, though. He'll probably be well into his seventies by now or dead but I have to know. It even comes down to a medical thing. If my doctor asks if there is heart disease or diabetes in my family, I just wouldn't know. I have to try and find him. You understand, don't you?"

"Of course I do." I had no idea how to comfort her. I always feel awkward around emotion. "This is something you have to do. I'm so sorry about all of this. I had no idea."

There was nothing more I could say. I couldn't get the sound of her tears out of my mind.

THE OTHER HALF

Six months passed, then another Christmas was upon us.

Don had accepted a job transfer to Brisbane and he and Annette were in the process of finding a school for Mary and a house for them all to live in. Annette complained that all the girls were protesting at the upheaval. The reasons given to them for the move were that Annette's parents, who lived in Brisbane, were old now and unwell. But we all knew that the main reason for it was so she could be near her sisters.

But things didn't turn out quite as she'd expected. On top of her and Sandra only speaking now and again, Annette's father died before she left Cairns. Everything, plus the move to Brisbane, almost unbalanced her completely. There was just too much for her to take in all at once.

Two weeks before Christmas, Bill and his little daughter, Josie, came down for a visit. They stayed with David and me during the Christmas break and Bill tried so hard to make a good impression by barely drinking at all.

We took them to see different parts of Brisbane when we could, but it wasn't easy with both David and me still at work for the first two of those three weeks. Qantas rostered all their pilots a month in advance so there had been no opportunity for David to ask for any extra time off. As for me, I only had one week a year off and that was between Christmas and New Year. Joining up all the public holidays during that time, gave me about nine days. It was better than nothing.

We drove Bill and Josie down to the beach at Burleigh Heads on the Gold Coast for one day and into the 'Coast Hinterland' another day. 'Natural Arch' has always been a favourite of mine and if it wasn't almost a two-hour drive away, I'm sure we would go more often. I love the coolness of the rainforest and the taste and smell of the fresh waterfalls that filled small swimming holes to the brim. Josie was amazed at the lizards, birds and bush fowl that came up to her for leftover food, eating right out of her hand.

That summer was hotter and stickier than previous years. Long drives to the coast were abandoned and South Bank became the alternative. We packed picnic lunches, swimsuits and towels and headed into South Brisbane. South Bank is a hugely successful development that once used to be an industrial area on the opposite side of the river from the city centre. It had always been an eye-sore until Brisbane hosted Expo '82 and it had been turned it into a huge complex with man-made beaches full of beautiful white sand, tourist shopping areas and scores of cafes, restaurants and little kiosks dotted over the three acres. A man-made rainforest with several rock pools overlook the river where a stage has been erected for evening concerts and New Year's Eve celebrations.

At the Christmas party, our last get-together for everyone, I could see reality setting in for Bill. He knew he had to go back.

A week after Christmas, they went home reluctantly. Bill was like a little boy being sent back to boarding school after a holiday. But he had his job, his girlfriend Daisy, and her small brood of two, to return to. His life, everything, was in Far North Queensland. I can see him always living there. Farming and fruit picking is the only life he knows. He's a simple man with simple tastes and the big cities would eat him alive.

Recently, he rang to tell me that he'd won third prize in a gardening competition in Bowen. My brother? Gardening?

"I didn't know you were a gardener, Bill."

"I'm not," he said. "I just do what Daisy tells me to do".

* * *

THINKING of my family at Christmas reminded me that I still hadn't ordered my own birth certificate. I'd seen Sandra's and Annette's and had copies of them tucked away in a special folder along with Dad's death certificate, my adoption papers, photos and the letter from the State Children's Department. All catalogued and at my fingertips when needed. But I still didn't have my own birth certificate.

David drove me to the Registry Office to order it and I paid the extra fee to have it ready in only two hours instead of the usual twenty-four hours. Once I set my mind to something, nothing short of an earthquake can budge me from doing it. I had to have my certificate and I had to have it now.

Back home, we sat at the breakfast bar while I smiled at the certificate with my parents' names below mine. I waver between being French and Irish depending on the situation but, in reality, I am immensely proud of my mixed heritage. I'm neither one nor the other. I'm both.

I glanced at the box marked 'Siblings.'

I knew I wouldn't find Annette's name there as she was born before me. I also understood that I was listed on Sandra's because I hadn't been adopted until much later and we were sisters until her adoption at almost four months old. But on mine, while the 'living' section was empty, the deceased section contained two words that jumped out at me. One female.

"Dave! What's this?" I asked as I pointed to the words.

He looked over my shoulder before saying, "Trish, it's probably just a typing mistake." He had been my rock over the past year, but I think he was hoping there weren't any more of us.

But this was an inconsistency. There were no deceased children as far as we all knew. We each had our relative paperwork and there had been no mention of a death in any of them.

I couldn't let this go. Somewhere on either side was a stubbornness gene and I had a full quota. I had to find out. The puzzle was not complete yet.

By 8.30am the next day, I was parking near the Registry Office. The

January sky was bright and blue, and the city rumbled with life. A heat haze was already rising from passing cars and the morning sun warmed my shoulders as I walked up to the office. In a few hours it would be has hot as nuclear heat.

I stepped through the door with gold lettering announcing, 'Registry Office' and let my eyes adjust to the dimness after the brightness of Brisbane's sun.

It had the glum atmosphere of a government department. I glanced around, looking for the clerk who had helped Sandra when she'd come in on previous occasions. *'A slight man. Short,'* she'd said.

There was only one man out of the four clerks. Through experience, I've learnt that *'you catch more flies with honey than with vinegar'*, so I walked over to him with a bright smile on my face and tried to look amiable and in need of help. It didn't take much effort – I had no idea what to expect. I asked him if he could help me with the problem I had and showed him the certificate.

"I remember your sister coming in here," he smiled. "So, she found you, heh? Good for her."

I smiled before plunging in. A few minutes later, I'd filled him in on the situation and I'd passed the certificate over for him to read.

"Can you help me?" I asked. "I'm not sure where to go from here."

He looked over his shoulder and whispered conspiratively. "Wait here a minute." It looked like I wouldn't have to go through the 'pay now come back tomorrow' routine that was normal for this department.

After five minutes he returned and said, "Yep, this is correct. There was a deceased female and she was one of a set of twin girls."

I almost cheered. *The twins! Paula was right!* Talking quickly, I said, "Okay. If there were twins, and one died, then there's one still alive. Right?"

He nodded, saying nothing. Spurred on with what could only be a positive response, I said, "So, my next question is, how do I find her?"

A smile slowly spread across his face and he shook his head slowly.

"No, you've misunderstood me. There were twins. And one did die." He hesitated as his eyes held mine. "But *you* were the other twin."

I must have stood with my mouth open for quite a while, not quite able to comprehend what he had said. Goosebumps popped out on my arms and the skin on my head prickled.

I stuttered, "But searches have been done and nothing about twins has turned up. Why is that?"

"Your twin was stillborn," he stated. "In those days, birth certificates were only issued to living children. If she had lived for even a minute," he went on to explain, "she would have been registered with a birth and death certificate, but as such, there were no certificates issued."

I thanked him and walked out in a daze. On that hot summer morning, people still walked to work, still shopped, and still stopped their cars at stoplights. Life continued around me. I saw none of it. I wandered for a couple of hours, oblivious before I came to a park bench and sat down. I must have sat there for an hour just staring at the ground.

I knew I had to call Blackall Hospital, where I was born, to make sure that everything the clerk had said was the truth.

* * *

BLACKALL IS in Central Queensland and being mainly a pastoral region, which is made up of fairly small properties that are passed on through generations of farming folk. Paula told me Dad took the opportunity to obtain casual work around these properties transporting stock and produce in the post-war years. Leaving the big city behind him and relocating to the fresh, clean country air seemed to help his ongoing chest troubles.

Knowing all about the delays that I could expect from hospital records sections, I expected a long wait for my records.

A bright, cheery female answered the phone at the hospital, and when I asked to be put through to the person who handled archived files, she said, "That's me. I also handle admissions, discharges, and a few other jobs. I just put a different hat on," she laughed. She told me that in the twelve years, she had been there; only a dozen babies had been born. Blackall was not a big town. My records would not be hard to find, apparently. The ease and speed of everything was astounding.

Barely five minutes later, she was back with my records.

"I've got them," she said. "Let me see." I could hear pages being turned and then, "Yep, that information is correct. It says here that your mother, Merle Rose Mooney, gave the father's name as Ernest Joseph Gourgaud. She gave birth to twin girls but only one survived. I'm sorry, but no cause of death has been written in the file. It just says that the surviving twin girl was 5 pounds 13 ounces and named Patricia Therese while the stillborn girl was only 4 pounds 12 ounces. No name."

I felt numb. Sad, with a heavy feeling of loss. How is it possible to miss something you've never had?

"There is one more piece of information that I'm not sure you're aware of," she continued. "It says that during routine tests, a small spot of tuberculosis was discovered on the lung of the surviving twin. Future and frequent X-rays was the recommendation by the attending medical staff."

Another piece of the puzzle had fallen into place. I'd never had any problems with my lungs in my youth, but I remembered the chest X-rays I'd had with Dad at Greenslopes Hospital.

Those many visits had been to keep an eye on any developments in my own lungs.

I thanked her and hung up, feeling somehow saddened at the news. A heaviness in my heart was beginning to overwhelm me again at the news of my dead twin. Somehow, I had to find the courage to let go of something I couldn't change.

A BLACK VELVET BAND

That's it. No more, I thought. I was sure I'd come to the end of my search. I'd reached saturation point and I resolutely decided to start concentrating on the future and not the past. I didn't want any more surprises.

It was now January, and a lot had happened since the previous February. So much in only eleven months.

Recently, I've wondered why things developed so fast after that first phone call from Sandra. At the risk of sounding whimsical, I can feel the presence of my father every day, guiding and helping me, and sometimes I truly believe he's here, standing behind me. The only way I can reconcile this with what I have been taught in Catholic institutions and what I believe now, is that my father has spent his time in 'Purgatory' doing his penance and is now actively redeeming his errors in life by enhancing mine. It's only wishful thinking on my part, I know, but it sits well with my Celtic origins. I believe he has given to me what I've always wished for and what he could never attain – a complete family. Maybe even Mum has been watching out for me.

There will always be doubts and unanswered questions about what happened those many years ago, but some things are best left as they are, since the people who could tell us their story have long since been buried themselves. All we can do is try to join the little pieces that we have together as best we can, be satisfied with what we do know, and then get on with our lives.

In my heart, I feel I shouldn't judge my parents without knowing the full circumstances. I should simply trust that they did the best they could and made their decisions in the hope that they were the right ones.

Friends and family would probably have influenced them a great deal and shame was probably uppermost in their minds. I have little comprehension of the times my parents lived in. They would have relied on their family for help, and if no offer came from them and with no government assistance available at the time, adoption or institutions were the only alternatives.

I do know that Mum had wanted both of the baby girls she had adopted out, Sandra and Annette. The hospital records show the comments, "This baby is not for adoption." But in both cases, within a few months, they had been given up with no explanation.

My heart swells with happiness now, knowing that I experienced my father's love, even my mother's in a strange sort of way, and I thank them every day for the choices they *did* make. I hate to think of where my sisters and I would be now if we had all been kept.

After Sandra, Paula, Annette, Bill, my twin, Uncle Terry, cousins, etc, etc, etc... I was just about to overdose on relatives, so with a silent prayer of thanks to Dad, I added a P.S.

"You can stop now."

* * *

THE FOUR OF us still struggle with all we have learnt. Phone calls between Sandra and Annette have become non-existent, something Annette could not understand. "After all, Sandra started this," she'd said. They never speak at all now and we speak on rare occasions. Annette finds it hard to recognise our pain when her own seems so overwhelming to her.

Also, she can't understand why Sandra held back part of herself in the early meetings when this was a time for each to be learning about the other.

I've tried explaining to Annette that time and patience were all Sandra needed. Just for Annette and me to be there whenever she needed us, with no reproaches on the length of time between calls.

"Call her and talk about everything and anything. That's what I do. Don't wait for Sandra to call you." I tried to make Annette see that establishing a sibling relationship was as big a step for Sandra as it was for her and that everyone reacts differently to situations.

This patience with Sandra has paid off for me. Sandra and I are as close as sisters could be. Closer. Not so with Annette.

I remember the exact day when Sandra's and my relationship became solid. It had been my forty-second birthday. David had refused to tell me where we were going. *"Dress up,"* was all he said. We drove towards the city but kept going alone Coronation Drive toward Mount Coot-tha. Every young couple in Brisbane has been to Mount Coot-tha at some time or other. The lookout from the top is spectacular especially on a clear night when the glittering lights of Brisbane twinkle below.

As we approached the turnoff, I exclaimed, "The Lookout Restaurant. How wonderful!" But as the summit came into view, David slowed down and did a U-turn. On the downgrade, where the city lights were brightest, we stopped. We stepped out of the car and leant back on the bonnet to admire the view. Then, while cars passed and horns honked, he knelt down, held an engagement ring up to me and proposed. It was the magical moment every woman dreams of and I took no time to accept.

We drove into the city, parked then started walking. I still had no idea where we were going, and I really didn't care. I was on cloud nine. I was with the man I loved and we would soon be married.

"How about a drink at Gilhooleys first," Dave said. "We've got time."

We'd been to Gilhooleys a couple of times before and it was turning into our favourite haunt. It was always busy, always noisy and very Irish. It was only 7.30pm but the place was packed with people and we had to push our way through the crowds. Every seat was taken and the air was so thick with smoke, you could cut it with a knife. *I'm already deaf in one ear, thanks to Michael. Now I'll probably be deaf in both after tonight,* was my first thought.

We passed booths filled with people eating and drinking and to my right I could see the band. One woman played a fiddle, one a penny whistle, while two men played mandolins.

"There's a band here tonight," I turned and yelled to Dave.

"That's not all that's here tonight," he yelled back over the din, smiling and pointing towards some tables.

The tables were set up around the dance floor and around one large table I saw Sandra, Farouk, Donna, Paula and Barry smiling at me.

Tears came easily as I hugged Dave then kissed and laughed with everyone else. I knew I would never forget this night as long as I lived. Donna said that Annette couldn't make it, and I knew the tension between Sandra and Annette had been a factor. But tonight, I wouldn't think about it.

After our meals, Paula, Barry and Donna said their goodbyes and left the rest of us to sit and listen to the band. They were in full swing by now and the noise level had risen even more. The lead singer started singing 'The Wild Colonial Boy' and everyone started clapping and singing along.

David and Farouk were trying to talk to each other, their words lost in the noise, as Sandra watched the band and I looked around. Old books lined the walls on picture rails and a map of Ireland hung on another wall showing the location of all the different clans. Every Irish pub I'd been in had a map like that hanging somewhere. I strained to see where 'Mooney' originated but couldn't see through the crowds and the smoke haze. On another far wall, pictures of people from the 1800's dressed in their best clothes, looking grim and uncomfortable, were scattered around.

I glanced back at the band. A few couples were dancing. The women were dancing jigs and the men were shuffling their feet and hopping from one foot to the other. Everyone was laughing and clapping.

The band started playing a song about a woman wearing a black velvet band, and simultaneously Sandra and I started singing along.

David and Farouk both stared at us. "How on earth do you both know the words?" David mouthed at me. I shrugged but kept singing.

Sandra leant over and yelled, "At the home... Sister Philomena..." I couldn't hear the rest of what she said because a roar of applause was followed by a fast tune that set our feet tapping. "Let's dance," I yelled to her.

She nodded and we fought our way through the mass of bodies.

There we were. Both jigging as we'd been taught so long ago – hands clenched by our sides and lifting our legs high, our backs ramrod straight. Identical steps. Identical moves. We'd learnt to do this so long ago, but everything came back so clearly. I could almost see Sister Philomena's smiling face in the crowd, spinning happing with her habit flapping and I understood the happiness she felt.

We fought our way back to the table, both laughing and puffing at the same time. Farouk held up a wine glass and two fingers to a waitress, and she disappeared into the crowd.

We both picked up our purses and made our way to a door marked 'Mna' and walked in. The sound was magically cut off as the door closed.

Sandra looked at me and I could see the emotion in her eyes.

"Please be patient with me. I look at you and I can't believe you're actually my sister. I've never felt like this before." She wiped the tears from her eyes.

"After forty-two years without you, I'd wait forever," I said. "I love you."

***

ANNETTE AND I, too, disagree about a lot of things. I think I disappoint her a little. She once said to me, "Why can't you just empathise with me? Why must you try to solve my problems? Why can't you be more like my friends and just show me sympathy? *They* know what to do."

I'd been very hurt by her outburst. Her way was not mine. I can see no use in sitting by and feeling sorry for her. My way is to find solutions. What about trying this? What about trying that?

I'd tried to explain my reasoning to her.

"It's like you're in quicksand, Annette, and all of your friends are standing around watching you sink but only saying, *'Poor Annette, I feel so sorry for you.'* What good is that? You'll still sink. I'm the only one with my hand out to you trying to pull you out. But you have to reach out to me, too. You have to come halfway to me as well."

But she feels that her life has been turned upside down and she is still trying to come to terms with the feeling that her life has been a complete lie. I've tried to convince her that she was the luckiest of us all and should be grateful to the Miners for all they've done for her but she is only now coming to terms with everything that has happened, and the fact that she is still the same person she was almost four years ago. A certain amount of acceptance has replaced her frantic search for a name to put on her birth certificate.

Sandra's pain comes from the rejection in her life.

As I had at fifteen, she left home as a rebellious sixteen-year-old to make a life of her own, having never really gotten over the hurt and rejection of her early years in Nazareth House. She made wrong decisions and jumped in at the deep end when choices had to be made.

For her, the experience of being rejected as a pre-schooler, in the choice between herself and her adopted sister, Jill, was devastating. To find that I had been brought back out of the home while she, as a baby, had been given away for adoption added to her feelings of rejection and was almost more than she could bear.

Like me, she finds it difficult to trust people, and is very wary. She has a quick sense of humour, a sparkling wit, but not wanting to be hurt again, will not let anyone close to her until she feels she can trust them. I can certainly understand and relate to this, since our early years are so very similar. From experience, I have learnt that trust is earned and only comes with time.

The misunderstandings and hurts are still raw, and these hurdles prevent reconciliation between Annette and us. Given time I hope this will change, but I'm not hopeful. We're just too different.

One thing I have learned is that my past has made me the person I am today. That's the process of life. I now feel strong in myself. I know it really wasn't *me* my mother was giving up. It was the life she had made for herself and the mistakes she'd made that she wanted to be rid of.

I am at peace with that.

Through all the hardships over the past few years, I've come to know just how much I love my sisters and how lonely my life once was before they changed it. I'm so proud to have them.

In a way, I've reached my own Nirvana.

SEIZE THE DAY

Through all of this, there were two things I felt that I still had to do. The first was to visit Dad's grave.

With explicit directions from Paula, I found it at the far end of a rather neglected part of Nudgee cemetery where some graves had clearly not been visited in many years and others had only a bare wooden cross to indicate there was even a gravesite present. Most of the headstones were concrete and sterile looking, while the grass that surrounded them had long since been mowed.

The afternoon sun cast long shadows around me as I sat cross-legged on the grass. Tears came easily as I touched his headstone, so hard, cold and barren. I so wished that things had been different: for Mum and Dad, for all of us. I wished that their dream of a happy future had been fulfilled. What would have started as a bright new life had soon turned into something else: a hopeless situation. The run-down flat would have soon lost its charm as the relationship deteriorated.

As I sat on the grass near Dad's grave, I still longed for that one last visit that he had asked for. I longed to hear his voice just one more time. I felt as vulnerable as the seven-year-old who held him tight, begging him not to leave me. The feeling was so intense I could almost smell the smoke that was always present on his clothes. His visits had given me hope, a feeling that I was worth something to somebody. Without those visits, I simply would have given up.

I've been back to Boundary Street, back to my roots, and like most things in life, everything has changed. Gone are the squalid flats and in their place are bright modern ones. Gone are the small shops, the electrical store, newsagent and bakery. All replaced with more flats. No trace of my childhood remains except for the Alliance Hotel.

David took me for a drink there one hot day when I was feeling melancholic. I sat in the same spot that I had when I was barely five with Dad and Larry, talking quietly together. Why did I have the urgent need to do this?

I took David to Rose Street to find Nana Mooney's old house. Gone were the fishbone-ferns outside the white picket fence where the hot sun beat down on a fresh coat of paint. I barely even recognised the tiny cottage.

As I looked around, it occurred to me that the past was gone. Replaced and forgotten. *Maybe I should do the same,* I thought. *Put the past behind me and look to the future, so full of hope and promise. Turn the page.*

But there was one more thing I needed to do. I needed to go back to Nazareth House.

* * *

"Trisha was like a little girl being told she had to go to the dentist," David told Sandra. "Even after she'd decided she had to go back, it took weeks for me to try and turn the plan into an event."

It seemed as though there was always an excuse as to why I didn't have time to drive the twenty minutes to Nazareth House. But David was insistent and wouldn't take no for an answer.

He continued. "I still remember as we finally rounded the corner and the beautiful old convent building appeared." Sandra pulled a face at the word 'beautiful' but let him continue.

"Trish started physically curling up in the car seat. I could see her hands clenched tight into fists and her knees pulling up towards her chest. As we turned into the long palm-lined driveway, she started looking around like a frightened animal. I must admit I was starting to worry, after telling her so confidently that it was just a building. She started talking softly as we slowly drove towards it. 'That gate was where we saw the black dog...we used to run amongst the cow pats over there... the gargoyles are gone...there's the statue of Mary...I hated that front door...that's the nun's quarters'."

"As we drove around the back of the building, her apprehensiveness lessened slightly as the renovated grounds became less familiar. There were car parks and new sections of the buildings that weren't there thirty years ago. While the unfamiliarity seemed to make her slightly more comfortable, as I went around to open her door, I heard her mumbling that she wasn't sure she could do this. My heart was starting to ache. I could see how much distress she was in, but I also knew that this had to be done, so I took her hand firmly and assured her I'd never let go and wouldn't leave her there. The main entrance is now at the rear of the building with modern automatic glass doors. From there on we had some great luck..."

***

IF I'D HAD to go back by myself, I would have turned around at the driveway and sped away without going in. I kid myself that I'm strong, but I couldn't have done it alone. With my hand firmly in his, David led me across the new car park and along the now carpeted corridor that had once been cold marble.

Two nuns were walking down the corridor and passed us with a smile and a nod. They still wore their traditional habits with only their faces showing and I almost smiled as I remembered the description from the movie *'The Blues Brothers'*. Penguins, they'd called the nuns. Nowadays, most orders wear normal clothes. Well, not really normal as such. They don't wear miniskirts, pumps and boob tubes, and you don't see nuns shopping at 'Dotti'. The severe habits showed how strict this order was. I could certainly vouch for that from experience.

It turned out that the room labelled 'Reception' was once the office where I sat like a street urchin, swinging my legs on my first day. A feeling of familiarity washed over me.

We walked into the office and behind the receptionist desk sat Michelle Dwyer, someone I'd played tennis with when my boys were little and lost touch with after my divorce from Rad.

"Michelle Dwyer?" I asked in shock. "Is that really you?"

"Trish? Wow, how long has it been?" She stood up and walked over to us.

"Too long," I replied. I hugged her then introduced her to David and explained to her why we were there. Some of the trepidation had disappeared with the sight of her. I had another ally.

"Is Sister Philomena still here?" I asked with apprehension in my voice. I expected to hear the clack of her beads at any moment, dreading the noise yet strangely wanting to hear it just the same. In my mind, she was still the robust nun who almost marched down the corridors. I had forgotten that thirty years had passed. I felt like that little girl again, waiting for her to turn the corner.

"No," Michelle replied. "Sister Philomena died about five years ago. She was sick for a long time. You'd probably remember Pat Kinnane though. I'd say she was here when you were. She works here now. I'll see if she's around."

Then in walked Pat Kinnane, or Pat Williamson as I knew her: the girl who 'confessed' to car stealing and smoking so many years ago. Life never ceases to amaze me.

She laughingly called herself the GDB (General Dogs Body) and with one arm draped casually over my shoulders, she explained to me that Nazareth House hadn't been an orphanage since 1982. It was now solely a home for the aged.

The changes were confusing after all those years. The dining room and all the dormitories were now sectioned off into separate units but my memory of up to fifty beds in my dormitory could not have been correct. Only a dozen units filled the entire space and the enormous bathroom that had seemed so cavernous was now only a storage room for the cleaners to use.

When we stepped into St Bernard's Hall, I looked around in amazement. I remembered it as being a huge room with what seemed like a hundred children either sitting or milling around. In actual fact, it could only hold forty people at a pinch. How had they all fitted in it? I had trouble believing it was the same room!

"It's been cut in half!" I mumbled.

Pat shook her head and smiled. "You were just little the last time you saw it."

As I looked around, I noticed that the windows were the original ones with the same brick border I remembered so well. The French doors that led out to the veranda overlooking the driveway and on to the ocean were still the same. The room that ran along the auditorium where the dentist had seen us was the same. But everything was so very much smaller.

Memories started flooding back.

.... Sister Philomena directing us to have all the chairs lined up in perfectly straight lines for when families and relatives came to sit and watch us singing and dancing at Christmas,

.... the children performing our own version of 'Swan Lake' as we tried to stand on our toes while pirouetting clumsily in our ballet outfits, our arms above our heads with fingertips touching in the classic 'Swan Dance', and every bit as graceful as baby elephants,

............the monthly Sunday movies when we were packed so tight you could feel the other kids around us breathing as we all sat watching the screen and eating the sweets we had bought down at the shopping centre.

The tour continued to the classroom, now a bright cheery sunroom, not the gloomy room cluttered with desks that I could still see in my mind. Backtracking down the corridor and passing through what was now the cleaner's room, we walked on through my old locker room, now another bright, sunroom overlooking a courtyard.

This courtyard was once the concrete playground where I had spent so many hours. I'd sat there on my first day and once a month I'd waited there for Dad to arrive. I'd skipped rope there and danced jigs there. As I stared at it, it was unrecognisable. It was now a compact garden with seats scattered around and flowers swaying in the breeze. Everything was so peaceful.

I remembered walking the interminable distance every morning from my dormitory to the dormitory assigned to the little ones. Incredibly, they were each on opposite sides of this small garden, only a short walk across from one to the other. Barely a one-minute walk!

The chapel where I had stood shivering from the cold those many mornings in winter, now had carpeting and padding for the knees and smelt of incense and candle wax. Light filtered through the stained glass behind the altar giving it softness that I hadn't noticed when I was a child.

The corridor that led to the chapel from my dormitory had seemed to go on for miles to my tiny young legs but was only a matter of about fifty metres from one end to the other.

I must have looked like an imbecile as I gaped at everything in disbelief. The doorways weren't as big and the windows weren't as dark and as I stood staring, I felt like I had come to the wrong orphanage. Everything was familiar but not quite the same. As I looked around, it suddenly occurred to me that the problems and hurts, so huge at the time, had grown as I grew until they were all out of proportion. There were no demons in the rafters or devils in the hallways. It *was* just a building!

According to Pat, over the years other girls I remembered have also returned, with much the same result. Monica. Christine. Freda. It had even taken Pat's husband three attempts before he convinced her to step back through those doors again and face her past.

It's said that we all have our own private demons that torment us. We all have to fight them and even though we may not come out unscathed, we hope to come out stronger for the battle and with a certain degree of confidence.

I still have days when I try to think of a memory that doesn't hurt. But mostly now, I look back without the fear and bitterness that once consumed me. I've come to realise that no one can change what happened because the past is just that – past.

Because of that, I'm not the frightened child I was, filled with a need to please and to be accepted. I have lost most of my shyness and timidity and I am very different from the child who saw her life spread before her in hopelessness and pain. These days, people too readily discount human resilience believing they are compelled to react to external forces that are beyond their control.

I've tried filling the gaps in my life, reliving the uncertainty and pain, and I've discovered that filling in all those gaps doesn't necessarily make everything right. What it does do is help me to cope with what I *do* know. The picture may not be whole but at least it's recognisable.

As a fanciful child, I had always dreamt of a perfect world but now, as an adult, I know there is no such thing. And neither are the people in it. All of us are simply striving to do the best we can with the hand we've been dealt. I've come to realise that it's not only the choosing of the right path that counts, it's the journey as well – what we learn and how we use that knowledge.

There were times in my life when I felt the darkness I was experiencing start to overtake me. Times when I thought the loneliness would be too much to bear as I drew away from everyone and everything. It is only when I remember those days that shadows form and darkness sets in. But I've heard it said that people are lonely because they build walls not bridges, and I guess I believe that. Those same walls keep everyone out, sure, but they also keep us inside.

I've been able to clarify everything and put it all into perspective. I've been able to rid myself of the anger and bitterness that I kept within me for so long and I've come to realise that there is no point in being angry anymore.

The most important thing of all is the learning process in recognising the cowpats when they appear again. As hard as it is, what you have to understand is that you're in a mess and make the decision to get yourself out of it, wash yourself down and clean yourself off. Accept the fact you may wear the smell for a while and learn to recognise that smell again when it comes. You have to have commitment and direction. What happens too often is people take themselves out of bad situations and put themselves back into the same situations again. Just like an alcoholic we see lying in the street. It doesn't make you feel like a drink, it makes you more committed to NOT have another drink. Use that first whiff of something foul as reinforcement, NOT as something that drags you down.

Thank God that period of my life is well behind me now. I've come through the 'broken' part of my jigsaw puzzle and I've managed to re-sculpt my life. These days, I feel fulfilled and whole, rejoicing in the things that most people take for granted. I have more assorted relatives than I could ever have imagined, and a future filled with people I have come to love and who love me. I've written this memoir and I've gone on to write a trilogy on British Monarchy throughout the ages. And just recently, a mystery/crime novel. I try to spend more time with my family and friends and less time worrying about non-essential things. Whenever possible, life should be savoured, not endured. I'm trying to recognise these moments as they happen now and cherish them. *'Some day'* and *'one of these days'* have gone from my vocabulary. I try to keep in touch with family members and close friends as much as possible. It's those little things left undone that annoy me now. Angry if I put off seeing good friends I've been meaning to get in touch with – someday. Or if I don't tell my husband and my children how much I truly love them.

I'm trying not to put off, hold back or save anything anymore. When I open my eyes every morning, I tell myself that this day is special. I'm living every day now as if it were my last, enjoying what I have missed all my life up till now.

It's times like these that I remember my parents the most. Many people imagine lost parents as hovering close by. For me the jury is still out on that one. I *do* sometimes feel they're here with me, watching and protecting me in their own way. But what I truly hope is that they're free of all their earthly worries. They never have to look down on me and witness the pain that was once my life. I'd like them to know that I am strong now, strengthened by my experiences, and able to face my battles with courage and a stoic belief in both my abilities and myself. I have taken the time to cradle my heart and I've been able to heal. For that I am so very grateful. I am the epitome of the saying, *'what doesn't kill me makes me stronger'*.

It seems like such a long journey in such a short time from the loneliness that was my world.

Carpe Diem! (Sister St. Jude would be proud of me.)

www.ingramcontent.com/pod-product-compliance
Lightning Source LLC
Chambersburg PA
CBHW072150070526
44585CB00015B/1080